Words and Contents

CSLI
Lecture Notes
No. 222

Words and Contents

Richard Vallée

foreword by
John Perry

CSLI
PUBLICATIONS

Center for the Study of
Language and Information
Stanford, California

Copyright © 2018
CSLI Publications
Center for the Study of Language and Information
Leland Stanford Junior University
Printed in the United States
22 21 20 19 18   1 2 3 4 5

Library of Congress Cataloging-in-Publication Data

Names: Vallee, Richard, 1957- author. | Perry, John, 1943- writer of foreword.

Title: Words and contents / Richard Vallee ; foreword by John Perry.

Description: Stanford : CSLI Publications, 2018. | Series: CSLI lecture notes ; no. 222 | Includes bibliographical references and index.

Identifiers: LCCN 2018005815 | ISBN 9781684000388 (paperback : alk. paper) | ISBN 1684000386 (paperback : alk. paper) | ISBN 9781684000401 (Electronic) | ISBN 1684000408 (Electronic)

Subjects: LCSH: Semantics. | Indexicals (Semantics) | Connotation (Linguistics) | Context (Linguistics) | Proposition (Logic) | Semantics (Philosophy)

Classification: LCC P325 .V26 2018 | DDC 401–dc23

LC record available at https://lccn.loc.gov/2018005815

CIP

∞ The acid-free paper used in this book meets the minimum requirements of the American National Standard for Information Sciences—Permanence of Paper for Printed Library Materials, ANSI Z39.48-1984.

CSLI Publications was founded in 1988.
CSLI headquarters and CSLI Publications are located in Cordura Hall at Stanford University.

Visit our web site at
http://cslipublications.stanford.edu/
for comments on this and other titles, as well as for changes
and corrections by the author and publisher.

To Suzanne

Contents

Foreword

In the early 1990s, Richard Vallée came to the Center for the Study of Language and Information to join me in my sandbox. "Sandbox" is Richard's apt term for what philosophers have instead of labs. He was in my sandbox because he was interested in the things I was interested in and pretty much accepted some of my central ideas. You don't need to have a special equipment, a grant, or beg for space from the dean to have a sandbox. My mathematician friends claim philosophy is the least expensive discipline to work in because we don't even need wastebaskets, but that's a bit of an exaggeration.

I borrowed a lot of sand for my sandbox from David Kapan's. I was interested in the word "I", and he was the man when it came to indexicals. But my interest in personal identity led me to work in indexicals and in the philosophy of language. If you want to understand personal identity, you've got to understand "I". So in the center of my sandbox are words like "I" and "now" that play big roles in traditional philosophical problems. Any other words you find in it are just there because I need to think about them to make sure I have things straight.

Richard didn't stay in the center of my sandbox for long. He went to the edge. Richard loves philosophy of all sorts, but his passion is words. Geoff Nunberg once got me thinking about "we". For about a day. What a mysterious word! And what a pain to think about! Kaplan's approach to the singular "I" didn't solve the problems with the plural "we". Frege didn't have anything to say about it. I left it at the edge of the sandbox and returned to the center. Richard went right to the edge and started thinking about "we". It wasn't that he was interested in the Philosophy of Constitutional Law and wanted to understand "We the people..." I suppose, even as a Quebecois, he could work up an interest in that sentence, but not more than "We need to have some lunch." (see Chapter 7) Richard performed magic with "we". He made it fascinating. He used a couple of tools from my sandbox, but he has had to build a sandbox of his own to deal with "we" and "us" and "but" and the mysterious way that when we say "that so-and-so" the "so-and-so" phrase does and doesn't contribute to the semantics of the sentence it finds itself in, and in general how words that aren't there sometimes seem to contribute more than the ones that are there. And slurs! Slurs have become a big topic in philosophy, even Kaplan has written about them, but no one, in my honest opinion, approaches it with all the tools Richard has at his disposal.

Linguists and AI researchers working on machine translation sometimes drop by my sandbox, but don't stay for long. "Good point about 'I'," they will say, "But what about 'we' and anaphora and..." They gravitate to Richard's, and then stay there. But he has plenty of room, and plenty of ideas to keep everyone interested. And he still likes "pluripropositionalism," his phrase for my approach, for which I invent a new term every couple of years. So maybe a few who go to Richard's sandbox will spend a little time in mine, where there is also plenty of room.

More likely though, Richard's interest in, and worries about, words, all sorts of words, big words, small words, words that aren't there and words that are, will infect them, as they have me. Philosophers have a gift for becoming puzzled by ordinary things. The few that have this gift have also the ideas to enjoy the puzzles they find. Richard Vallée is one of those rare ones. Enjoy the book, and learn from it!

John Perry
Center for the Study of Language and Information
Stanford University.

Introduction

The papers included in this book cover a twenty-one-year stretch. They mark the discovery and exploration of different expressions of language as well as a different perspective on them. At some point, for various reasons, good and bad, I thought that, with the exception of indexicals, philosophers were not paying sufficient attention to *prima facie* philosophically interesting categories of linguistic expressions, like plural pronouns and certain context sensitive adjectives. The situation is different today as slurs, for example, are the object of much investigation. In those days however, I was prompted to look at the semantics of certain lexical items. The book thus contains papers addressing specific philosophical issues connected to words, beginning with referring expressions, namely plural pronouns, and complex demonstratives, and then moving away to context sensitive common nouns and adjectives, I call these contextuals, comparatives, ethnic slurs, color terms, and conjunctions such as but. The first papers date from my stay at CSLI as a postdoc in the early 1990s and show my interest for reference problems. Later papers address different issues that are not so much connected to reference as they are to the context sensitivity of nonreferring expressions. The notion of proposition is central in semantics, as is monopropositionalism or the idea that each sentence or utterance of a sentence determines one proposition only. John Perry proposed a new framework in the philosophy of language, pluripropositionalism[1], in *Reference and Reflexivity* (Perry, 2012). From that point of view, utterances are true or false. Each linguistic expression has linguistic meaning as type, and each utterance of a sentence determines many truth conditions, or contents, depending on what is taken into account, starting with semantically determined content. For example, the linguistic meaning of I

---

[1] Also called multipropositionalism.

determines *the speaker of the utterance*. For my utterance **u** of I am a philosopher we obtain, when considering meaning only, the content *the speaker of* **u** *is a philosopher*. Once facts about the utterance are considered, we obtain the content **RV** *is a philosopher,* where **RV** is the speaker himself. Things look very different once such a perspective is adopted. This is especially true since the focus is put on utterances of sentences, rather than sentences, and on the linguistic meaning of specific lexical items with their contribution to contents, rather than complex linguistic entities like sentences. The framework, as I understand it and exploit it at different periods, gives a different angle on language and, I must add, on linguistic intuitions. Pluri-propositionalism has actually proven to be a great tool for throwing a different light on certain lexical items whose semantic contribution to truth conditions is hard to account for in traditional monopropositionalism. In addition, it puts together in a single framework various ideas on lexical items, providing unity when dealing with words which, needless to say, do not have much in common.

The first two papers, "Who Are We?" and "Talking About Us," articulate a picture of plural pronouns. The first paper mainly motivates and states my underlying view. The second one goes into details and examines examples. At the time, I did not unfortunately give enough consideration to the important literature on collective and distributive readings of plural sentences and utterances.

"Complex Demonstratives, Articulation, and Overarticulation" is my take on complex demonstratives and a first use of pluri-propositionalism. I introduced the idea that a semantically articulated constituent, for example man in an utterance of the complex demonstrative this man, has no echo in official content and plays no role as far as the truth of the utterance considering facts is concerned. "Unarticulated Comparison Classes" came into being at CSLI when I was trying to understand the place of comparison classes in semantics. In this case, a constituent of the intuitively truth relevant content of an utterance is simply not to be found in the sentence and, as a consequence, it is not semantically determined. Comparison classes are also very utterance specific. Pluri-propositionalism is exploited and comparison classes are found not to be semantically determined even if they are truth relevant for the utterance. Such classes finally prove not to be as threatening as they first appeared to be in semantics.

I was always puzzled by the idea that but" can, for purposes of simplification, be treated like "and." That is fine in logic. It is a bad idea in semantics. What Grice writes about "but" in "Logic and Conversation" is fascinating, even if it does not give a complete picture of this preposition. I wanted to capture the intuition that there is a difference between an utterance of "He is rich, but he is honest" and an utterance of "He is honest, but he is rich". Such a difference is not to be found if "but" is replaced by "and". In "Conventional

Implicature Revisited," I use the idea of cognitive significance and contrast it with the official content of an utterance in my proposal concerning "but" and similar expressions. "But" is shown to be a much more complex and interesting, cognitively important expression than expected. "On Local Bars and Imported Beer" emerged from a problem about the context sensitivity of some adjectives and common nouns discussed in a seminar by John Perry. We examined this issue from different angles and, as is common in seminars, we did not arrive at a "definitive solution." Years later, I came up with an idea found in that paper. Basically, I contend that some adjectives have a rather rich linguistic meaning and should be parsed when examining their contribution to truth conditions or contents of utterances. My suggestion needs development, but it takes care of basic linguistic intuitions.

I went to Barcelona for a workshop, where both Chris Hom and Tim Williamson were giving papers on slurs. The topic was fascinating. There is a clear difference between "Hans is German" and "Hans is a boche". The problem is to capture it in semantics. With the help of pluri-propositionalism and Grice's idea of generalized conversational implicature, I came up with "Slurring and Common Knowledge of Ordinary Language." The paper offers an analysis of slurs fitting semantics and takes into consideration their nonsemantically conveying very-context-bound insulting contents.

Finally, a paper by Lahav (1989, 264-279) on the principle of compositionality puzzled me for years. Charles Travis wrote several papers following the same trail. Though the two authors identified many problems worthy of being addressed, the issues raised by one of these topics, color terms, finally stood out as being manageable in pluri-propositionalism. In addition, the two authors called into question the principle of compositionality. This being a good occasion to bring compositionality and pluri-propositionalism together, I wrote "Color Adjectives, Compositionality, and True Utterances." It was a fun paper that dealt with serious issues and that preserved the principle of compositionality from approaches to language that reject this central principle.

All these papers examine how specific words contribute, each in their own way, to contents of utterances. Pluri-propositionalism is a framework that can be used to give a second look at words, like fictional names, which resist monopropositionalism, or to have a new perspective on words like epistemic modals, which challenge semantics. It makes room for a detailed and unified view on words and utterances.

References

Lahav, R. 1989. "Against Compositionality. The Case of Adjectives." *Philosophical Studies* 57: 264-279.

Perry, J. 2012. *Reference and Reflexivity*, second edition. Stanford: CSLI Publications.

1

Who Are We?[1]

1 Introduction

Personal and demonstrative pronouns ("I," "you," "s/he," "we," the plural "you," "they," "this" and "these") are notorious for challenging any theory of natural language. Singular pronouns have received much attention from linguists and philosophers alike during the last three decades. Plural pronouns, on the other hand, have been neglected, especially by philosophers. I want to fill this gap and suggest accounts of "we," the plural "you," and "they."

Intuitively, singular and plural personal pronouns are "counterparts." Any account of personal pronouns should make sense of this intuition. However, the latter is not very sophisticated and, as we move along, it will be reexamined and relativized. As we shall see, plural pronouns are much more than mere counterparts of the familiar singular ones. It is well known that third person singular pronouns have puzzling behaviors, acting as coreferential terms, bound variables, or unbound anaphora. But coreference, binding, and unbound anaphora are not confined to the usual examples and extend, in a way, to plural pronouns. My discussion of the latter is partly motivated by this particular behavior. Shedding light on these linguistic phenomena will show in what sense plural pronouns differ

---

[1] I wrote this paper while I was a visiting scholar at CSLI (Stanford University) supported by a postdoctoral fellowship from the Social Sciences and Humanities Research Council of Canada. I want to express my gratitude to both institutions. I would like to thank Jane Aronson, Renée Bilodeau, Eros Corazza, Adèle Mercier, Michael O'Rourke, and John Perry for helpful comments.

from singular ones: some are combinations thereof, and this gives them unique features. Let me first set the stage.

2   Indexicals, Demonstratives, CoReferences, and Anaphora

Philosophers (Castaneda 1996, 130-57; Perry 1977, 474-97; Perry 1979, 3-12; Kaplan 1989, 481-536) have recently paid considerable attention to "I," "you," "this," and "s/he". Here is a brief and standard summary of their findings. These expressions are directly referential: their referent is not given by a Fregean sense, and the subject/predicate sentences in which they occur express singular propositions of the form $<\,,\,F>$ containing that referent and a property F as components. If they had a Fregean sense, all utterances of "I am tall" would express the same thought or proposition and have the same truth-value. However, using this sentence, I (not being tall) would be expressing something false, while Magic Johnson would be expressing something true. So we cannot both be expressing the same proposition. If "I" had a Fregean sense, using this term, Magic and I would be referring to the same thing. Fregean senses determine a referent with no regard to the context of utterance. But these terms are context-sensitive expressions: their referent changes from context to context. Using "I," I would be referring to myself, while Magic Johnson would be referring to himself. Of course, one could invoke private senses to explain the relevant differences. But I am reluctant to make this metaphysical claim.

Now, we can draw a distinction between indexicals ("I," "you") and demonstratives: "this" and the demonstrative use of "s/he." The difference is that the semantic rules or characters of the former fix their referent in a context-sensitive way, while the latter require supplementation by a demonstration or an intention to reach an object (Kaplan 1989).[2] Both Kaplan and Perry ("Frege on Demonstratives") introduced the object referred to by an indexical expression in the proposition expressed by the utterance of a sentence containing that expression, making it express a singular proposition. Hence, two uses of "I am tall" by two different speakers may express different (singular) propositions. This sketches, with respect to indexicals, the basic points of what is now known as the Direct Reference Theory.

---

[2] For recent discussions of demonstratives, see M. Reimer, "Do Demonstratives Have Semantic Relevance?" *Analysis* 51(1991) 177-83, and K. Bach, "Intentions and Demonstratives," *Analysis* 52 (1992) 140-6. I will not take sides in the debate concerning the question whether intentions or demonstrations are relevant to fix the referent of demonstratives.

Third person singular pronouns are also famous for exhibiting an impressive flexibility. In addition to being demonstratives, "s/he" can also be *coreferential* (as in "Mary will be late. She missed the bus") or a *bound variable* (as in "Every man believes that he is mortal"). Other uses of "s/he" are more controversial. Consider the sentences "A woman called today. She will call back tomorrow." The quantified term most likely to bind "she," namely "a woman," cannot do so since it occurs in a different sentence and binding does not cross sentences (Neale 1990). On the other hand, "she" has none of the features of directly referring terms. If it were a directly referring term, "a woman" would be irrelevant to understanding its semantic value. However, most of us feel that the semantic value of "she" depends upon the semantic value of "a woman." These are cases of *unbound anaphora* (Evans 1977, 467-536; Neale 1990).

Donkey sentences also raise problems for third person pronouns. In "Every man who owns a donkey beats it" or "If a man owns a donkey, he beats it," the third person pronoun "it" is semantically linked to "a donkey," but cannot be bound by the indefinite description. Needless to say, it can hardly be considered as a referring term (Evans 1977, 467-536; Heim 1988; Neale, 1990). This occurrence of "it" is also a case of unbound anaphora. But a new twist is added here. The singular "it" has what some called a universal force since the sentence "Every man who owns a donkey beats it" should be interpreted as conveying that every man who owns a donkey *beats all the donkeys owns*. Direct Reference theorists have no contribution to make concerning our understanding of these uses of third person pronouns. My views on plural pronouns will force us to have a new look at coreference, binding, and unbound anaphora. If I am right, these phenomena are not confined to the standard examples and are much more widely spread than commonly thought. Let us first look at plural pronouns.

We all learned in school that "I," "you," and "s/he" have their plural counterparts in "we," "yous" (I add an "s" as a convenient means to indicate the plural), and "they." Direct Reference theorists focused on the singular form and never really considered plural pronouns. I suspect most of us thought it would be easy to analyze the semantic behavior of the plural indexicals and demonstratives on the basis of their singular counterparts. We were partly right: "they" is easy to account for. But "yous" and "we" present new problems I want to examine. The main part of this paper is devoted to "we." I am interested in plural indexicals and demonstratives in the framework of the Direct Reference Theory and will neither argue for the latter, nor consider alternatives. Finally, I will not dive into the details of the various linguistic theories of the plural.[3] Only a weak involvement in that domain is required to make my point. I want to fit plural pronouns into Direct Reference Theory. Once this is done, I suspect that different theories of the plural will compete to accommodate them, but I will leave the discussion of this second step for another occasion.

3   The Idea of the Plural Counterpart

It is easy to make sense of the idea of plural counterparts of "I," "you," and "s/he." Such counterparts will also be directly referential and context-sensitive. I take for granted that these expressions are plural.[4] In virtue of the fact that they are plural, their referents will be at least two objects. Singular referring terms require individuals in the universe of discourse. Plural referring terms require at least groups of two individuals as referents (Massey 1976, 89-107; Hoeksema 1981, 63-83; Link 1983; Lascrosohn 1990). Take a group to be an *n*-uple of two or more individuals. Some (e.g., Link) may want to distinguish what I call a group from plural objects or individual sums. The latter are groups considered as a special kind of individual referred to as one single object by a singular referring term. For example, "the cards" is sometimes said to refer to a group of playing cards (containing each card of a deck), while "the deck" is said to refer to the group of cards as an individual. Some (e.g. Massey) understand these sums in mereological terms and consider them as full-fledged individuals. Insofar as the terms we are concerned with are all plural terms, there is no need for this distinction between groups and plural objects. Others may want groups to be constructed out of groups as well as individuals—and also treat groups as individuals of a sort. For present purposes only groups understood as *n*-uples of two or more objects are needed. In this picture, subject/predicate sentences in which "we," "yous," and "they" occur express propositions containing more than one object—because each plural pronoun refers to more than one object[5]—and a property.[6] I represent these

---

[3] See J. Hoeksema, "Plurality and Conjunction," in A. Ter Meulen, ed., *Studies in Model-Theoretic Semantics. Groningen Amsterdam Studies in Semantics 1* (Dordrecht: Foris 1981) 63-83; G. Link, "The Logical Analysis of Plurals and Mass Terms: A Lattice-Theoretical Approach," in Bauerle, Schwarze, and von Stechow, eds., Meaning, Use, and the Interpretation of Language (Berlin: De Gruyter 1983); F. Feldman, "Groups, 1," *Linguistics and Philosophy* 12 (1989) 559-605; P. Lascrsohn, *A Semantics for Groups and Events* (New York and London: Garland 1990).

[4] The fact that in sentences in which they are subjects the predicate is plural, as in "We are philosophers," is good evidence.

[5] Can a plural pronoun refer to a group of objects as an individual? This is an interesting question I will not discuss here.

propositions by $< [,], F >$, where $[,]$ leaves room for the relevant objects and can be expanded to have as many places as necessary, while F is the relevant property. For example, an utterance of "They are sick" would express the Russellian proposition $<[,],$ the property of being sick$>$, where the empty places in $[,]$ should be filled in by the relevant objects. Two or more objects can fill the places. The order of the objects is irrelevant, so $[a, b]$ is identical with $[b, a]$. In case there is no group of objects—only one object or no object at all—there is reference failure because the places the referring term should fill, in $[,]$, are not all filled. When the plural pronoun has no referent at all, no proposition is expressed because no complete Russellian proposition of the relevant form is expressed. I want to develop this aspect of the counterpart picture and say how plural pronouns introduce these objects in these propositions.

Let me introduce one more point before going any further. We are all familiar with the collective/distributive distinction, the latter being the background of any discussion of the plural. In a nutshell, the idea is the following. Take for example "They are rich," said pointing to a group of persons. This utterance expresses a true proposition read *distributively* if and only if each member of the party referred to is rich. It expresses a true proposition in the *collective* reading if and only if that party as a group, that is, as a single unit, is rich. This difference in interpretation could be easily echoed in the proposition by adding an indicating device, say by putting a '$_d$' after $[,]$ in $< [,], F >$, to indicate a distributive reading, and a '$_c$' in the same way to indicate a collective reading. Should this difference in interpretation of the plural be reflected in the *proposition expressed*? This is a complex question, and my policy here will be very conservative. As a matter of principle, I will not introduce additional information, that is information relative to the proposition I introduced earlier, in the structure of the proposition unless strong justifications are offered. The requirement that such information should be part of either the syntax of the sentence, or the semantics of the terms occurring in that sentence, seems natural. But neither the syntax of "They are rich" nor the semantics of "they" or "are rich" carries the relevant information, that is, information that would force a specific reading of that sentence. So, following my policy, the plural proposition will not reflect the distributive/collective distinction. Note also that, were we to read a collective or distributive interpretation in the semantics of "They are rich," the sentences "Each of them is rich" or "Together, they are rich" would be semantically redundant. And they are not. I

---

[6] I will not address problems raised by plural identity sentences like "We are The Beatles."

will come back to this issue in Section 6. From now on, I will focus on direct-referentiality and context-sensitivity.

As far as the plural pronouns we are concerned with are directly referential terms, their referent is not fixed by a Fregean sense or something similar. The main problem is to specify how this is achieved. Finally, since these terms are context-sensitive, the objects they refer to may vary from utterance to utterance.

Another point that highlights the "counterpart" aspect should be emphasized: "we" would be the plural of "I," "yous" the plural of "you," and "they" the plural of "s/he." That does not sound very controversial, and this paper is written under this assumption, understood at a very intuitive level. But this is nothing more than a crude correlation and it is hard to make sense of this claim in a philosophically interesting way. In what sense is "we" the counterpart of "I"? What semantic relationships do these two expressions have? I will come back to this question at the end of the paper.

4 "S/he" and "They"

Let us first look at "s/he" and "they." The first expression should be used with a demonstration (or a proper intention),[7] the demonstratum of which is the referent (Kaplan). In case there is no demonstratum, no proposition has been expressed. Like "s/he," "they" does not have a rich descriptive semantic content and cannot, by itself, fix a referent. A demonstration (or intention) is needed, and the demonstratum is just two or more objects. A speaker uttering "they" should refer to two or more objects. Suppose it is thirty degrees below zero and, looking through the window, you see two persons walking outside. You tell your friend, "They are crazy." You referred to those two persons and expressed a proposition containing them and their property of being crazy. But a speaker can refer to different objects on different occasions. Two days later, it is still freezing. Looking out the window, you now see three persons outside and say, "They are crazy." The proposition you expressed using this sentence is true if and only if the objects you referred to are crazy. While "S/He is crazy" expresses a proposition containing one object demonstratively referred to by the speaker and the property of being crazy, "They are crazy" expresses a proposition containing the objects demonstratively referred to by the speaker and the property of being crazy. In case there is only one or no demonstratum, the utter-

---

[7] That is, the "correct" referring intention or intentions.

er of the plural sentence does not express a proposition because the relevant places in the proposition are not filled. In addition, "s/he" and "they" exhibit a similar behavior relative to binding and coreference. Both can be bound, as in "The man in the bar believes that he is home" and "Some men in the bar believe that they are home." Both can also be coreferential, as in "Mary will be late. She missed the bus," and "Mary and Sue play violin. They sometimes play duets," where "she" is coreferential with "Mary," and "they" is coreferential with "Mary" and "Sue." "They" also raises problems in sentences like "Some men entered the bar. They then started shouting." Here, "they" is not a bound variable and it is not a directly referring expression. It is an unbound pronoun. The third person plural pronoun can also occur in donkey sentences like "Every farmer who bought donkeys vaccinated them." "S/he" and "they" exhibit a very similar behavior: they can play the same roles in sentences. Let us say that they are perfect counterparts.

5 "You"

Let us now consider "you." It is a term referring to the addressee of the speaker in its singular version. It is easy to formulate a semantic rule fixing the referent of "you" in a context-sensitive way, what Kaplan would call its character:

singular: the addressee of the speaker.

But how does the plural version work? A very closely related character like "the addressees of the speaker" seems fine at first sight. The use of "Yous" better win tonight" by a coach facing his team fits that picture. Call it the pure plural use of "you." However, it hardly accounts for all linguistic facts. Take, for example, a woman saying to her oldest daughter: "Mary is coming. Yous will help me paint the fence," or saying: "Mary believes that yous will win the game," where her oldest daughter is the only addressee. Still, the speaker used the plural, "yous," and can be presumed to refer to more than one object. In both examples, it makes sense to assume that she referred to the addressee and to Mary. The referent of "yous" can be partly fixed by a previously occurring term, like "Mary" in our examples.

Unfortunately, the *characters* "the addressees of the speaker," "the addressee and a group containing it," or "a group containing the addressee" do not let "Mary" partly fix the referent. In that respect, they fail to account for some strong linguistic intuitions. Each of them has other shortcomings. As we saw, the character "the addressees of the speaker" would not fit "Mary believes that yous will win the game," said by a mother to her daughter, since there is only one addressee. "The addressee and a group containing it" will not determine a specific group. The indefinite description occurring in the second part of the character does not go to a specific group since the addressee can be a member of many groups—for example, the Californians, the fans of Elvis Presley and the Republican party—at the same time. The character would then be too broad to determine one specific group. In case we have an indefinite description, like "a group containing the addressee," as a character, the description would be far too unspecific to do the job for the same reasons.

Note also that "yous" can be, so to speak, "bound" by a quantified term. You can tell a friend, "The police officer in charge believes that yous should discuss that point," where "yous should discuss that point" can be used to mean that you and he—the police officer—should discuss that point. Finally, unbound anaphora also enters the picture. During a police interrogation, a police officer saying "A man called that day. Yous met later" refers (partly) to the addressee by his use of "yous." But his utterance of "yous" is understood also as sensitive to the quantified term "a man"—the police officer using "yous" is understood as saying that the addressee and the man who called that day met later—and as having a semantic value partly fixed by the quantified term "a man" occurring in the first sentence. A phenomenon similar to the one characteristic of donkey sentences also occurs. In "If a linguist were here, yous would have a hard time understanding each other," the semantic value of "yous" is understood as sensitive to "a linguist." The speaker is saying that the addressee and the linguist would have a hard time understanding each other. So things are not so easy and the counterpart idea does not run smoothly.

These examples can be approached from a different point of view. Remember that "yous" introduces at least two objects in a singular proposition. But why should they all be addressees? In a sense, what matters is not really that they are all addressees, but that at least one of them is, as in "Mary is coming. Yous will help me to paint the fence." So, besides the pure plural use of "yous," which I will denote with "youse," there are other plural uses of "yous," that are sensitive to the linguistic context and to features of the extralinguistic context other than the addressee. The most natural way to account for this sensitivity is to introduce context-sensitive expressions, like "s/he" and "them," in the interpretation of the utterances of these sentences. These uses of "yous" can be given by:

"you and s/he,"
"you and them,"
"youse and s/he,"
"youse and them,"

where "s/he" and "them" can be demonstratives, coreferential pronouns, bound variables, or unbound variables. Even if these are used to express a determined proposition in a context, one needs to look for the proper interpretation of "yous" to get that proposition. When you hear a "yous"-sentence, you understand it by finding the interpretation of the use of "yous," maximizing the relevance of the utterance.

Sentences containing "yous" are ambiguous in a context like the second sentence in "Mr. Evans is coming. Yous will paint the fence," uttered by a father in front of his two boys. The last sentence can be interpreted as conveying the proposition the use of "youse" would convey—with the two boys as referents—or the use of "youse and he" would convey—with the boys and Mr. Evans as referents. One of the two boys could even understand the last sentence as conveying what "you and he will paint the fence" conveys, where "he" is coreferential with "Mr. Evans," and argue that his brother should also give a hand. I emphasize that the speaker expressed a determinate proposition. The hearer's job is to find the right interpretation of the plural pronoun used. This approach can also account for the apparent presence of an unbound variable in some cases, like "A man called that day. Yous met later," where "yous" can be read as "you and he" and "he" used as an unbound variable. Finally, donkey sentences are also easy to handle. In "If a linguist were here, yous would have a hard time understanding each other," "yous" can be read as "you and s/he," and "s/he" used as an unbound variable.[8] "You" and "yous" are not perfect counterparts because of the sensitivity of the latter to the linguistic context.

6 "I" and "We"

It is time now to put "yous" aside and look more closely at "we." "I" and "we" share certain properties.[9] I assume that both are directly referential, in the sense that they refer to objects without the mediation of a Fregean sense expressible by a description, and are used to express singular propositions—containing objects and not Fregean senses. Remember that "I am

---

[8] Notice, however, that it docs not have the universal force "it" has in a typical donkey sentence.

[9] I disregard some aspects of "we," such as the use of "we" to refer to himself by a King, or the use of "we" by a nurse to refer to a patient ("We are going to have surgery today").

a philosopher" does not express a Fregean proposition. The reason is that "I" does not have a Fregean sense (see Perry). If "I" had a Fregean sense, because Fregean senses are not context-sensitive, this expression would not be sensitive to contexts and would refer to the same object in different contexts. "I" does not work that way. If I use it, "I" refers to me; if you use it, it refers to you. It is widely agreed that the referent of "I" is fixed by a character, "the speaker of this utterance." What about "we"? The reasons put forward by both Perry and Kaplan to claim that "I" is context-sensitive and not used in utterances expressing general propositions easily extend to "we." Even if the extension is natural enough, the arguments backing an interpretation of "we" as context-sensitive and used to express singular propositions deserves a full discussion because of its importance to my main point.

One could argue that a "we"-sentence expresses a general proposition expressible by the use of a description instead of "we." For example, a hockey player uttering "We won the game" could be said to express or mean that the players of the Los Angeles Kings hockey team won the game. Of course, different utterers of "we" in different contexts could express different propositions. A player of the Boston Bruins uttering "We won the game" would mean that the players of the Boston hockey team won the game. In this case, contrary to our initial assumption, "we" is not a referring expression. It is used to express what a definite description expresses and, as far as definite descriptions are quantified terms used to express general propositions, "we" is just a placeholder for a quantified term in a sentence that should be used to express a general proposition. Let us accept this consequence for a moment. If the speaker tries to communicate a general proposition expressible by a sentence containing a definite description instead of "we," he runs the risk of using a description he does not satisfy. Suppose a player of the Boston Bruins says, "We will win the game tonight," meaning "The players of the Boston hockey team will win the game tonight." But he does not know that he has been fired two minutes ago. So he is no longer on the team and he is not talking about himself. This consequence goes against a deep intuition: when I use "we," I cannot fail to talk about myself. This assumption is quite natural.

Suppose I say, "We went to the beach yesterday." I refer to myself and some other persons, and attribute to that party the property of having gone to the beach yesterday. I am also presumed by my audience to be a member of that party. And any theory of "we" should account for this intuition. If, as it happens, I did not go to the beach that day, I misled my audience, even if my closest friends went there. In that case, "They went to the beach yesterday" would have been more appropriate. Some could reply that John Smith, a San Franciscan, said in 1990, "We won the Super Bowl," even if he was not on the payroll of the 49ers. I do not think that, strictly speaking, John Smith said something true. His utterance is a tribute to the team's marketing executives. But he probably meant something different, which he would express by "Our home team won the Super Bowl." Note that our fan would not say "I do not want to go to Fresno" or "We do not want to go to Fresno" if the owners decided to move the team to Fresno. "I do not want them to go to Fresno" or "We do not want them to go to Fresno" would be more appropriate. I take for granted that an utterer of "we" cannot but talk about himself.

This argument also goes against the use of "we" as a placeholder for a definite description understood as a referential term: if "The players of the Boston hockey team will win the game tonight" expresses a singular proposition containing the objects referred to by the description, it could express one not containing the speaker, contrary to our intuitions. This approach is not plausible. So "we," like "I," does not express, and is not normally used to express, what a description would express. In some cases, however, "we" seems to express what a description would express. For example, if a Canadian says "We eat a lot of meat," he apparently means that Canadians eat a lot of meat. I will come back to this point later on.

"I" and "we" share three more important properties. They are both context-sensitive. If I say "I am sick," "I" refers to me, the speaker, while if you use the same sentence, "I" refers to you. "We went to Paris last year" can be used to refer to my wife and me; used by you, it can be used to refer to your husband and you. I can even use this sentence in a different context to refer to my child and me. Our problem in this paper is to determine how "we" achieves that role. Second, neither "I" nor "we" can be coreferential. In an interpretation of the utterance "Mary and Sue play violin. We sometimes make up a trio," in which "we" refers to Mary, Sue, and the speaker, "Mary and Sue" does not fix the referent of this utterance of "we." Otherwise, "we" would not have the speaker in its referent. Of course, this is not to say that "Mary and Sue" do not contribute, one way or another, to the referent. (More on this later.) Finally, neither "I" nor "we" can be a bound variable.[10] In "The police officer believed that we were having a nice discussion," "we" is not a variable bound by the quan-

---

[10] See G. Nunberg, "Indexicality and Deixis," *Linguistics and Philosophy* 16 (1993) 1-43 for a different view on "we" concerning this feature.

tified term. But, strangely enough, in one interpretation of the last example, "we" is not totally insensitive to the quantified term "the police officer." "We" could be used to say something about the speaker and the police officer. In the same vein, in the donkey sentence "When a customer enters my office, we usually spend one hour together," "we" is usually understood as referring to the speaker and the customer. Finally, "we" is sometimes tied to a quantified term occurring in a different sentence. Remember the police interrogation. The suspect may well reply, "Yes. A man called that day. We met later in a bar" meaning that he and that man met later in a bar.

Nevertheless, "I" and "we" are quite different. A character, "the speaker of this utterance," fixes the referent of "I." But it would be wrong to think that something like "the speakers of the utterance" is the character of "we"; each utterance has one and only one speaker. Partee notes that the *referent* of "we" is a class of objects containing the speaker of the utterance (Partee 1989). She is quite right. Another candidate as a *character* could then be "a group of people including the speaker." This will not do. If I say, "We went to Paris last year," I am not merely asserting that I and at least one other person in the world went there last year. When I say that, I mean something with much more specific truth-conditions. Not any other person will do. I do not mean, for example, that I and a busload of Germans went there. When people use "we," they refer to themselves and a specific class of objects. It is also amazing that a quantified term like an indefinite description can fix a referent: quantified terms are not referring expressions. But even a definite description like "the group of people including the speaker"[11] will not do because it is not a complete definite description: there is more than one group that includes the speaker.[12]

Why not try another character? A child of Paul and Mary uttering "We went to Paris last year" could be said to let "we" have the character "the children of Paul and Mary" would express. However, this character is not context-sensitive. It does not determine different referents in different contexts. If one wants to follow this line and take "we"-sentences to be context-sensitive, one has to argue that the character changes with each utterance. But since the character is the linguistic meaning of an expression, one is committed to the thesis that a speaker can change the meaning of an expression. This is not an acceptable result. And again, note that such a character may determine a group of objects that does not contain

---

[11] Nunberg, in "Indexicality and Deixis" discusses at length this character and provides interesting details.

[12] A feature Nunberg emphasizes in "Indexicality and Deixis."

the utterer, contrary to the basic idea that an utterer of "we" cannot fail to refer to himself. There is something worse: if a character fixes the referent of "we" as a character fixes the referent of "I," it is difficult to account for cases in which one of the persons referred to by an utterance of "we" has been previously referred to, and in which the reference of "we" is, hence, partly fixed by an antecedent expression. In one interpretation of an utterance of "Mary plays violin. We sometimes play duets" the referent of "we" is Mary and the speaker, and is then *only partly* fixed by "Mary." But our tentative characters do not let an antecedent fix part of the referent of "we." I want to emphasize that the use of the notion of coreference to argue against the idea that the referent of "we" is only partly fixed by "Mary," and in favor of the view that "we" refers to what "Mary" refers to, is simply wrong. "We" does not refer to Mary but to Mary *and* the speaker. Finally, we saw that, like "yous," "we" is also sometimes closely related to a quantified term as in one interpretation of "The police officer believed that we were having a nice discussion," "A man called that day. We met later in a bar," and "When a customer enters my office, we usually spend one hour together." Unfortunately, the proposed characters will not account for this relation.

There is another contrast between "I" and "we." The former is intentionproof. Try as hard as you will, no intention can make "I" refer to anything other than what the character fixes as its referent in the context. Things are different with "we." Part of the referent of an utterance of this expression is bound to be the speaker. But *intentions* may play a major role in the determination of *part* of the referent. By saying that we went to Paris, I may mean that my wife and I went there. By using "we," I referred to myself and another object I intended to refer to, namely my wife.

In order to account for the role of intentions in the determination of the referent of "we," one could suggest that the character of "we" is something like "the speaker and some individuals the speaker focuses his intention on," or "the speaker and some individual having the relation R to the speaker," (where the relation R is contextually /intentionally defined).[13] Nevertheless, these characters fail to account for coreference, binding, and unbound anaphora. Consequently, they should be rejected.

In addition, both characters raise specific problems. Consider first "the speaker and some individuals the speaker focuses his intention on." Such a character invokes intentions even when none are required. Suppose that Peter and I form a tennis team. Using "Peter believes that we will win the game," I would *refer* to myself, the speaker, thanks to the first part of the

---

[13] I owe the first suggestion to a referee, and the second one to David Martens.

character, and would have to *intend to refer* to Peter, because the second part of the character requires such an intention. But we are losing something. There is an intuitive semantic relationship between "Peter" and "we," and the notion of coreference can account for it, while the notion of an intention would prevent us from grasping it. Introducing a coreferring term would permit us to dispense with intentions at this step; not introducing a coreferring term would require intentions that we should avoid in order to keep track of the semantic relation. Using a coreferring term is, then, the best move at this stage.

The second suggested character, "The speaker and some individual having the relation R to the speaker," raises a slightly different challenge since the relation R plays a major role. The proposal is twofold. What about a "contextually defined relation"? Unless the notion of a context is clarified, and unless the way it defines the relation is specified, the proposal remains rather vague. I prefer to let a would-be advocate of this position articulate the view before I discuss it. Consider the proposal invoking intentions. Here, the character can restrict the individuals to the intended subgroup through the relation R. But the relation R introduces a new element interfering with the "immediacy" of "we." We saw earlier that a definite description cannot take the place of "we" because it could fail to comprehend the speaker. "R," even intentionally defined, allows that "we" could fail to comprehend the party other than the speaker. Suppose a speaker using "we" intends to refer to a woman he thinks to be his sister. So, the other party is given by the relation "being the sister of" the speaker has in mind. He would fail to refer to her if he is wrong in thinking that they are brother and sister. But he could be wrong in taking her to be his sister. Still, using "we," he would be referring to her. Note also that, in the proposal under examination, we have to introduce intentions. And it is easy to apply to that character the objections raised against the one invoking what the utterer focuses his intentions on.

There is another difference between "I" and "we," with respect to what Castaneda called ontological priority. Using "I," I cannot fail to refer to the relevant object. "We" is not that infallible. Remember that its referent is a group of at least two objects. If "we" were like "I," an utterance could not miss these objects. But as we know, it can. A drunk man can say: "We are enjoying the breeze" referring to himself and what he thinks is a person besides himself, when there is no one there. I would say, then, that there is no referent here, and that the person failed to say anything true.[14]

"I" and "we" differ in one more respect. The character of "I" fixes a referent univocally in each context, while "we" does not refer univocally or unambiguously to a certain group of objects. I am, with you, in the middle of a group of persons and I utter: "Mary will enter. We will then start talking." My utterance is ambiguous in at least eight ways; depending on the setting, the sentence I utter may express eight different propositions. "We" can be used to refer to (1) Mary and "I"; or (2) you the addressee and "I"; or (3) you the addressees and "I"; or (4) s/he (a person I designate) and "I"; or (5) they (some persons I designate) and "I"; or (6) me, a person I designate, and you; or (7) me, some persons I designate, and you; or (8) me, some persons I designate, and you (a small group), depending on our interpretation of the component of "we" other than "I." In each case, the interpretation of "we" makes the second sentence of our example express a different proposition. Note that this is not a case of indeterminacy of the proposition expressed. Uttering the "we"-sentence, I intended to express a specific proposition. The hearer's task is to find the relevant interpretation of "we" in the context—the one fitting the expressed proposition. How can we account for these ambiguities?

I think the best way is to argue that "we" is not an irreducible indexical: it is not an irreducible expression with a specific character or linguistic meaning. The objects "we" refers to are given by "I" and at least one and at most two other indexicals or demonstratives terms, among "s/he," "they," "you," and "yous." The distinctive feature of "we" is that it refers to objects among which one finds the speaker. This idea is supported by linguistic facts. A speaker using "we" cannot fail to refer to himself, as if he had used "I." So I suppose "I" or a semantic device achieving the same effect is present in "we." In opposition to "I," the referent of "we" can be partly fixed by terms that previously occurred. In one interpretation of "Sue stayed after class. We talked about Kant," "we" refers to me and Sue. These sentences can be rendered by "Sue stayed after class. She and I talked about Kant." Note that "We talked about Kant" and "She and I talked about Kant" express the same proposition, containing Sue, me, and the property of talking about Kant. Generally, when "we" does not have a referent partly fixed by previously occurring expressions, it should be read

---

[14] Did the speaker express a proposition containing himself and the property of enjoying the party? I am inclined to say yes. But this proposition is not enough to make it the case that he expressed something true.

"I and s/he (or they)," where "s/he" and "they" are demonstratives, or "I" and "you." The reduction thus enables us to account for multiple ambiguities in the use of "we." "We" has a sensitivity to the linguistic and extralinguistic contexts that sets it apart from "I," which is sensitive to the extralinguistic context only. In addition, we can make sense of the fact that "we" behaves like "I" in some respects — it is never a bound variable and never completely or fully coreferential — by invoking the presence of an "I" in the analysis of "we."

At the same time, this approach easily accounts for the sensitivity of "we" to quantified terms since "s/he" and "they" in the analysis of "we" can be bound variables or instances of unbound anaphora. For example, in "The police officer believed that we were having an interesting discussion," "we" is tied to "the police officer," and if "we" is read as "he and 1," "he" can be understood as a bound variable. In "A man called that day. We met later in a bar," the second sentence can be read as "He and I met later in a bar," where "he" is an unbound pronoun. Finally, in "If a customer enters, we usually talk for one hour," "we" can be read as "she and I," where "she"[15] is an unbound pronoun linked to "a customer." We then have the following:

> "we" = "I and you,"
> "I and you and yous,"
> "I and you and s/he,"
> "I and you and they,"
> "I and s/he,"
> "I and s/he and they,"
> "I and yous,"
> "I and yous and s/he,"
> "I and yous and they,"
> "I and they."

The choice between one interpretation or another of "we" depends on maximization of the relevance of the utterance of the speaker. It is plausible to argue that "I and you and yous" and "I and yous" as well as "I, s/he, and they" and "I and they" are merely stylistic variants with no semantically relevant difference. "You and yous" just puts emphasis on one addressee while the use of "yous" does not. This is immaterial to the means by which the object is referred to and to the proposition expressed. A similar remark applies to "s/he and they."

---

[15] See note 8.

What happens to this list if we take our analysis of "yous" into account? Remember that we had five interpretations of "yous." If we accept the idea of stylistic variation mentioned in the previous paragraph, we can substitute the pure plural use of "you," "youse," everywhere in the list. "I" and "we," just like "you" and "yous," are not perfect counterparts because of the sensitivity to linguistic, as well as the extralinguistic, features of the plural version.

Nunberg recently proposed a different account of "we." According to Nunberg, the character of "we" is something like "the group of people instantiated by the speaker or speakers of the utterance" ("Indexicality and Deixis," 7) or, alternatively, "the group of people including the speaker" (Ibid., 8). He uses such a character to ground a two stages account. Here is how it goes. A semantically competent agent hearing a "we"-sentence would first go to the speaker and second, using clues (speaker's intentions, context, and so on), identify a property, one the speaker need not have in mind, having the referent in its extension. The property provides an interpretation of "we." Suppose a police officer says to a suspect: "We have been watching you for days." According to Nunberg, the hearer would first go to the speaker, then identify a plausible property having the speaker and other persons as extension, and finally interpret this utterance properly. The utterance could be interpreted as expressing the (general) proposition expressed by "The police officers of the Section 21 of the San Francisco Police Department have been watching you for days." Notice that Nunberg also allows the proposition expressed to be a singular proposition in some circumstances, but he does not explore this possibility. This view strikes me as not very plausible.

On the one hand, it is descriptively inadequate. Nunberg's use of the notion of character raises problems I already discussed. If the utterance of a "we"-sentence is understood as conveying a general proposition in the way Nunberg describes, the hearer risks identifying a property not countenancing the speaker in its extension and, thus, risks interpreting the uttered sentence as expressing a proposition not fitting our intuition that a speaker using a "we"-sentence is talking about himself. I think such a situation never occurs.

On the other hand, its explanatory power is weak. The approach is rather insensitive to the fact that "we"-sentences exhibit a very systematic behavior with respect to proper names and quantified terms. For example, in one interpretation of "The police officer believed we were having a nice discussion," "the police officer" and "we" have close ties. I think the latter should be reflected in a proper interpretation of "we." Nunberg's strategy, invoking intentions and contextual features, misses these regularities. He would be right in arguing that "the police officer" can act as a contextual feature. However, an approach relying on contextual features sheds no light on the tight relationship my view highlights. Furthermore, such a procedure is rather ad hoc. It works on a case-by-case basis and leaves much room for the interpreter's imagination. According to my suggestion, "we"-sentences express determined propositions and their interpretation is strongly constrained.

7 Two Puzzles

Nunberg isolates a use of pronouns that is still unexplored, and unaccounted for. In some cases, plural pronouns apparently behave like placeholders for general terms. Consider an Angeleno saying to a San Franciscan, "Yous will never understand why we love our city." What does "yous" refer to? What does "we" refer to? Similarly, suppose that a Canadian visiting the United States goes to a party and is told by someone, "We will never invade Canada." What does "we" refer to? On one reading, these pronouns conform to the theory I just sketched. The speaker may be referring to himself and some friends. On another, though, these pronouns are *not* used as referring terms. The Angeleno may well be expressing what "San Franciscans will never understand why we love our city" expresses, while the guest is expressing what "Americans will never invade Canada" expresses. This is a very particular use of pronouns. Here, the pronoun is not used as a referring term and can be neither bound nor anaphoric. As Nunberg emphasizes, singular pronouns can also be used this way. A condemned prisoner saying, "I am traditionally allowed to order whatever I like for my last meal" may well mean, "The condemned prisoner is traditionally allowed to order whatever he likes for his last meal." My theory does not apply to these cases, and they call for a different analysis, one I will not provide. This is certainly unfortunate, but I share this misfortune with all Direct Reference theorists. I do not think they threaten my views more than they threaten the standard view on indexicals.

The second puzzle is familiar to philosophers. As we have already noticed, plural sentences are famous for having a collective and a distributive reading. Consider "The men lifted the piano." One can draw the distinction between these two readings in terms of truth conditions:

> Collective: "The men lifted the piano" is true if and only if the men lifted the piano together.

Distributive: "The men lifted the piano" is true if and only if each man lifted the piano.

My view on plural pronouns is neutral concerning these readings. It neither solves problems raised by these readings, nor adds new puzzles. The distributive/collective readings of plural sentences is a major problem as far as these sentences provide no clue in favor of one interpretation or another in a context. The idea of togetherness is no more part of the meaning of "the men" than it is of the meaning of "we." On the other hand, the predicate here does not appear to be semantically ambiguous. The distinction itself is not really satisfying. Consider the following. Suppose there are three men, John, Jim, and Mike. Take the sentence "The men lifted the piano." According to the standard distinction, this sentence has two possible truth conditions, collective and distributive. But what if John and Jim lifted it together for a while, and Mike, a really strong guy, lifted it alone for a while? This possibility fits neither with the collective nor with the distributive reading (Gillon 1987, 199-219; 1990, 477-85). One could take "We lifted the piano" and face a similar problem.

Do plural sentences semantically indicate a reading (collective or distributive)? Is the predicate responsible for different readings? Are some predicates semantically ambiguous? Are predicates neutral with regard to these readings? Are these readings echoed at the level of the term in the subject position? For example, does "we" sometimes refer to each member of a group, and sometimes refer to the group as one single individual? These are vexing questions I cannot engage here. The problems connected to these readings of plural sentences should be dealt with on the basis of the phenomenon of plural sentences. Plural pronouns are just special cases.[16]

8 Conclusion

Now, in what respects are the singular and the plural counterparts? "S/he" and "they" are clear cases. The same means—a demonstration—is used to refer to one or many objects when these expressions are demonstratives, and they can both be coreferential, bound variables or unbound anaphora. "You" and "yous," just like "I" and "we," have more complex relationships because the plural leaves room for anaphora and binding. But "you" and "yous" have a common feature: their referent should contain at least one addressee. In the case of the singular, the addressee is the only referent, while the plural accepts an addressee or some addressees and other

---

[16] See Link, Hoeksema, Gillon, and Feldman on these issues.

persons as referent. "I" and "we" also have such a feature in common: their referent should contain at least the speaker of the utterance. The referent of "I" is only the speaker, while the referent of "we" is the speaker and some other person or persons. This is not the end of the story on plural pronouns. But it is certainly a beginning.

Let me conclude on a more general note. The preceding discussion forces a new perspective on old issues. Russell's Principle, according to which one can refer only to individuals one is acquainted with (Evans 1982) is widely shared even if controversial. Proper names already threaten its credibility. Once we take plural into account, the principle faces more serious challenges. Consider a rock star facing a crowd of twenty thousand fans after a concert, barely seeing the first rows because of the lights' intensity, and saying, "You are great." Obviously, he means that each of them is great. However, I doubt he could be said to be acquainted with his fans—each of them. Still, his utterance is fine.

Plural pronouns should, more broadly, make us think twice about the relationships among language, mind, and the world. Philosophers too often work with a simple view of these relations, a view based on an oversimplified picture of language. The complex syntactic relations that emerged during our discussion of plural pronouns suggest a quite complex picture.

References

Castaneda, Hector-Neri. 1966. "He: A Study in the Logic of Self-Consciousness." *Ratio* 8:130-57.

Evans, Gareth. 1977. "Pronouns, Quantifiers, and Relative Clauses (1)." *The Canadian Journal of Philosophy* 7: 467-536.

Evans, Gareth. 1982. *The Varieties of Reference*. Oxford: Clarendon.

Gillon, Brendan. 1987 "The Readings of Plural Noun Phrases in English." *Linguistics and Philosophy* 10: 199-219.

Gillon, Brenden. 1990. "Plural Noun Phrases and Their Readings: A Reply to Lasersohn." *Linguistics and Philosophy* 13: 477-85.

Heim, Irene. 1988. *The Semantics of Definite and Indefinite Norm Phrases*. New York and London: Garland.

Hoeksema, Jack. 1981. "Plurality and Conjunction." In *Studies in Model-Theoretic Semantics. Groningen Amsterdam Studies in Semantics 1*, edited by A. Ter Meulen, 63-83. Dordrecht: Foris.

Kaplan, David. 1989. "Demonstratives." In *Themes from* Kaplan, edited by Joseph Almog, John Perry, and Howard Wettstein, 481-563. Oxford: Oxford University Press.

Lascrsohn, Peter. 1990. *A Semantics for Groups and Events*. New York and London: Garland.

Link, Godehard. 1983. "The Logical Analysis of Plurals and Mass Terms: A Lattice-Theoretical Approach." In *Meaning, Use, and the Interpretation of Language* edited by Bauerle, Schwarze, and von Stechow. Berlin: De Gruyter.

Massey, G. 1976. "Tom, Dick, and Harry, and All the King's Men." *American Philosophical Quarterly* 13: 89-107.

Neale, Stephen. 1990. *Descriptions*. Cambridge: The MIT Press.

Partee, Barbara. 1989. "Binding Implicit Variables in Quanified Contexts." In *Papers From the Twenty-Fifth Meeting Chicago Linguistics Society: Parasession on Language and Context*. Chicago: Chicago Linguistics Society.

Perry, John. 1977. "Frege on Demonstratives." *Philosophical Review* 86: 474-97.

Perry, John. 1979. "The Problem of the Essential Indexical." *Noûs* 13: 3-21.

2

Talking About Us

1   Introduction

I am about to leave my office and my daughter calls me with a request:

(A)   We want pizza.

I did not know that she was hungry for a pizza. I would like to know who is with her. Is her utterance about my wife and herself, or about her best friends and herself? Should I bring a small pizza or two large pizzas? "We" is a directly referential expression; it does not introduce descriptive conditions but objects into the truth-conditions of an utterance. It is also, arguably, a context-sensitive referring term.[1] Suppose that I tell you "We are going to the movie tonight." My daughter's utterance of "we" and my utterance of "we" can be referring the same people or to different people. A colleague tells you "We want pizza." My daughter's utterance and his utterance of "we" refer to different people. However, any utterance of "we" refers to the speaker of the utterance. Uttering "we", my daughter is talking about herself, and your colleague is talking about himself.

Two ways of approaching the so-called context-sensitivity of lexical items divide the sandbox. Kaplan's focuses on sentences as types in context. A context is an abstract, finite list of elements, containing the speaker, the hearer, time, place, and any other objects referred to by a demonstrative. Perry started off playing in Kaplan's sandbox, but his part of the sandbox now looks somewhat different. First, he focuses on utterances. An

---

[1] Plural sentences have distributive and collective readings (See Yi, 2002, and MacKay, 2006). Suppose that I say "We lifted the piano". Did we do it collectively, or did each of us lifted the piano? This issue is independent of the referring nature of "we" and I will not address it in the actual paper.

utterance is a concrete event with many properties, not only those that inspired the contextual items that Kaplan recognizes, such as being located in a certain place, and occurring at a certain time, but also such properties as being produced with certain intentions, and related to certain beliefs, and, like any concrete entity, indefinitely many others. Second, Perry recognizes many contents for an utterance, in addition to that which captures our concept of "what is said". In particular, he recognizes various "reflexive" contents. These correspond to the conditions required for truth with various combinations of referential and contextual factors quantified over, rather than taken as fixed.

It is widely assumed that all context-sensitive terms determine a constituent into the truth-conditions of sentences in context (Kaplan) or utterances (Perry), either via their lexical meaning, for pure indexicals, or through a directing intention (see Kaplan b) for pure demonstratives or some combination. Call the truth-conditions of a sentence in context, or the truth-conditions of an utterance, its 'content'. Perry (2001) recently argued that some expressions, like "here" and "now" require both lexical meaning and intentions to contribute to the content of utterances. "Here" means something like *the place of the utterance* and semantically designates a location. However, intentions are required to delimit the specific area designated by an utterance of "here." A student says "It is boring here." He is talking about a place, but is it the classroom or the university? What does he intend to refer to?

I want to argue that "we" as a type, in contrast with "I", does not have a *content-determining linguistic meaning* in the sense that it does not semantically express a context-sensitive condition fit for determining the referents of any utterance of "we". Moreover, its contribution to content does not come from a simple directing intention. Finally, a combination of both linguistic meaning and intentions cannot account for the semantic behavior of "we". I suggest that the semantic contribution of an utterance of "we" to the truth-conditions of an utterance is given by the semantic contribution of a combination of "I" and "you", and/or the plural "you", and/or "he"/ "she" and /or "they" to that utterance.

Kaplan's model requires lexical meaning to *determine* a constituent of the content of a pure indexical in a sentence in context. That is, the contextual feature itself determines the reference, with no role for the speaker's intentions. If I am right, "we" lacks such reference-determining meaning, and so the context-sensitivity of "we" is not captured by Kaplan's approach to pure indexicals. I propose an account of "we" following Perry's Reflexive Referential framework, with its recognition of different levels of content. However, the semantic behavior of "we" has an unexpected impact on what Perry calls reflexive content of the utterance.

2 Determining

Pure indexicals have a content-determining meaning. In Perry's vocabulary, the context-sensitive linguistic meaning of "I" as type, the *speaker of the utterance*, as well as the linguistic meaning of "you", *the addressee of the utterance*, goes straight to a single object, the speaker of the utterance and the addressee of the utterance, and introduces it into the content of the utterance or the sentence in context.

> The conventional meaning of a pure indexical determines a constituent into the content of a sentence in context or an utterance if and only if given the meaning of the term and the contextual parameters, the meaning unequivocally selects a specific constituent for the content of the sentence in context, or utterance, and systematically select different specific constituents for the sentence in different context or different utterances.

I call "parameter" any relevant feature of an utterance: speaker, time, place, addressee. For example, given the meaning of "I", the latter unequivocally selects a specific parameter, the speaker of the utterance, and systematically selects different speakers for different utterances. Intentions have no grip on how the referent of an "I" utterance is determined. More generally, intentions have no grip on the truth-conditional constituent determined by the conventional meaning of pure indexicals. Pure demonstratives do not determine constituents into contents. The determination relation holds between linguistic meaning and content constituents. The relationship between an utterance of a pure demonstrative and a content constituent holds between an intention and an object. It is not a determination relation. I will say that the directing intention backing the use of a pure demonstrative fixes the contribution of the latter to the content of an utterance of a sentence containing that pure demonstrative.

3 Varieties of Context Sensitivity

Perry calls context-sensitive referring terms that have a meaning that determine an object in a context, with no need of additional intentions and no intention playing a role in reference, "automatic" (Perry, 2001, p.60). "I" and "today" are automatic context-sensitive terms. I set aside the problems, mentioned by Perry, raised by conversations across time zones which can affect the reference of "today" and apparently depend on intentions. Suppose that I call a Chinese friend and tell him that today is a holiday. I intend to be talking about today in my time zone, not about today in his time zone. Such problem has no impact on the issues I want to examine, and I will not explore it further. "We", as a plural referring term, refers to objects. My daughter's utterance is referring to herself and at least another person. However, "we" does not have a context-sensitive descriptive linguistic meaning that determines specific objects, in a context, and different one in different contexts.[2] An utterance of "we" always refer to the speaker, and any candidate context-sensitive descriptive linguistic meaning for "we" must refer to the speaker of the utterance and another person. It must also leave room for binding. For example, in an utterance **u** of "A student believes that we have a meeting at two," "we" designates the speaker of the utterance, and contains a variable bound by "a student." An utterance **u** of that sentence is true if and only if a student believes that the speaker of the utterance **u** and himself have a meeting at two or, if and only if there is an x such that x is a student and x believes that the speaker of the utterance **u** and x have a meeting at two. In the same way, Nunberg (1993) gives as an example "Whenever a pianist comes to visit, we play a duet." Reference-determining context-sensitive conventional meaning does not contain free variables and does not leave room for binding. For example, the meaning of "you" or the meaning of "I" does not leave room for binding. Were "we" to have a context-sensitive meaning containing a variable, it would not refer to objects. Consider now an utterance of "Whenever Paul comes to visit, we play a duet." That utterance of "we" refers to the speaker of the utterance and Paul. An utterance of "we" can also be anaphorically linked with a name. Were "we" not leaving room for an anaphoric pronoun, that reading would be unaccountable for. Finally, context-sensitive descriptive meaning can hardly explain the facts. Remember the context-sensitivity of "we" and its flexibility. Using "we" in (A), my daughter may be talking about her addressee and herself, friends and herself, or the addressee, some friends and herself. "We" does not express any plausible reference-determining descriptive condition, but it requires the truth-conditions of the utterance of a sentence containing that pronoun to include the speaker of the utterance and at least another individual. "We" is not an automatic context-sensitive referring term. Perry calls context-sensitive referring terms requiring speaker's intentions to fix a component into the truth-conditions of utterances "discretionary" (Perry, 2001, 59; 2006). Pure demonstratives are discretionary. "We" is not a pure demonstrative, since, for example, it does not require the speaker to intend to refer to him/herself.

Perry (2001; 2006) further draws attention to the fact that the linguistic meaning of some indexicals, discretionary indexicals like "here", does not determine a referent for an utterance of that indexical. The speaker's intentions are also required to introduce a constituent into the content expressed by an utterance of "here." Discretionary indexicals do not fit the

---

[2] See Vallee, 1996.

strong linguistic meaning/intention opposition I invoked to distinguish pure indexicals and pure demonstratives. They share features with indexicals in that they have a descriptive linguistic meaning introducing conditions, for example, *the place of the utterance*; they also have a feature in common with pure demonstratives, requiring a directing intention to reach a content component. However, in contrast with pure demonstratives, they have a referent-constraining descriptive meaning. For example, "here" requires the relevant intention to be an intention to refer to a place. Thus, meaning and intentions work as a team to determine a truth-conditional constituent of discretionary indexical utterances. Discretionary indexicals are midway between pure indexicals like "I"—because of the existence of context-sensitive meaning—and pure demonstratives like "this"—because directing intentions are required to reach an object. "We" is not a discretionary indexical like "here."[3] Remember that the *descriptive meaning* of a discretionary indexical like "here" is *the place of the utterance*, and that the speaker's intention must be an intention to designate a specific place. The intention is constrained by the descriptive condition given by the linguistic meaning of the discretionary indexical.

"We" is different. As a plural referring term, it lacks referent-determining or intention-constraining descriptive linguistic meaning and the intentions, if any, backing the use of that term do not have to conform to a condition provided by the descriptive linguistic meaning of "we."

4 "We"

Listening to my daughter's utterance of (A), I know that she wants pizza. However, "we" is not specific enough to determine specific constituents other than the speaker of the utterance in the content (Kaplan), or in the official truth-conditions (Perry), even when a context is provided. I do not know who is with her. "We" is also silent on how many people are part of the truth-conditions of the utterance or the sentence in a context. How many people want pizza? Semantic competence and context are not enough to pick him or them out. Remember also my interrogations concerning my daughter's utterance. How can we account for them?

---

[3] See Kepa Korta, 2008, unpublished, for that idea. He articulates it by saying that "we" includes the meaning of "I"—and is hence partly automatic—and the meaning of other intended expressions—and is hence partly discretionary. There is a disanalogy between discretionary indexicals, like "here", and "we". The first expressions have descriptive meaning and the second one lacks descriptive meaning. In the latter case, and not in the former, the speaker must also select between different expressions.

1 Reflexive Semantics

Perry (2001; 2006) focuses on utterances and grounds his view on the token reflexive nature of the meaning of pure indexicals. The meaning of a pure indexical is a property of the indexical as type, and is given by a reflexive condition on reference. It is called reflexive because it is a condition on the utterance itself. For example, the linguistic meaning of "I" is *the speaker of the utterance*. The linguistic meaning of a lexical item or a sentence is not a truth-valuable entity. A proposition is a truth-valuable abstract entity. A proposition can be extracted from the linguistic meaning of indexical sentences. When information is provided on the relevant utterance, one can obtain the object part of the content of the utterance, the speaker in the actual case. Perry also adds semantic values, including different contents which are propositions.

role or linguistic meaning	property of a sentence type
content M of utterance	proposition extracted from linguistic meaning
content C of utterance	official truth conditions of the utterance

The Content M is the reflexive content of an utterance. It is a truth-valuable proposition, and it is reflexive because it contains a reference to the utterance itself. Suppose that we know the linguistic meaning of "I" as a type, *the speaker of the utterance*, and the meaning of "I am sick" as a type. The Content M my utterance **u** of "I am sick" carries is

The speaker of **u** is sick

Content M can be reached thanks to knowledge of linguistic meaning only, with no extralinguistic information other than the identity of the utterance. The reflexive content is however not the content conveyed by the speaker. From Content M and further facts about the utterance, in this case the speaker of the utterance, one can identify the Content C, or official truth-conditions, of the utterance:

¤¤, being sick

¤¤ stands for the speaker. The official truth-conditions of the utterance are what ordinary speakers want to conveyed by an utterance. In the actual case, these truth-conditions contain the speaker of the utterance himself. The meaning of "I" as type is a rule determining a content constituent for the reflexive content of the utterance and, in a context, the official truth-conditions of the utterance. In contrast with most semantic frameworks according to which an utterance expresses one unique proposition, the Reflexive Referential framework is multipropositionalist. A single utterance can express many different propositions in addition to Content M and

Content C, depending on how many features of the context are taken into consideration[4]. I will come back to this.

5 "We" in Reflexive Semantics

Hearing my daughter asking for pizza, I know that she is hungry and that she is not alone. I do not know who she is talking about. How many people want pizza? One option is to argue that an utterance of "we" designates the speaker of the utterance and the person(s) s/he has in mind. That makes "we" partly automatic and partly discretionary (see Korta, unpublished). A more specific suggestion, accounting for our understanding and reasoning about "we" utterances, can be offered. I contend that "we" is a placeholder for a combination of "I", "you" (singular and plural), and/or "he"/"she" or "they". My view captures very fine-grained intuitions concerning "we" utterances.

> "We": "I and you"
> "I and you and he/she"
> "I and you and they"
> "I and you (plural)"
> "I and you (plural) and he/she"
> "I and you (plural) and they"
> "I and he/she"
> "I and they"

Table 1

Call these options the available readings of a "we" utterance[5]. "He"/"she" and "they" are either referring terms, bound variables, or anaphoric expressions. The plural "you" and the plural demonstrative "they" designate, respectively, the addressees of the utterances, and the persons the speaker has in mind. I take "he"/"she" and "him"/"her" as well as "they" and "them" to be lexical variations. I propose an account of "we" utterances exploiting the available readings of "we." In the present paper, I do not consider anaphoric pronouns or quantified terms and binding, mentioned earlier in the paper.

If "we" is both a directly referential expression and a plural term, then mastering "we" one plausibly knows what I call the available readings of "we." I exploited these readings when I heard (A): my daughter wants pizza. But who else is she talking about? Now, "we" as a type does not conventionally means the context-sensitive "I and you" in some utteranc-

---

[4] See Perry, 2001.

[5] See also Vallee, 1996.

es, and conventionally means, as a type, the context-sensitive "I and them" in other utterances. "We" would then be a semantically ambiguous expression, but it is not. Semantically ambiguous terms are lexical items having at least two descriptive linguistic meaning, and the same lexical item paired to different meanings can be seen as different words. For example, "crane" has at least two descriptive meaning. It is a word for a kind of bird and a kind of machinery. It can also be taken as two different words: one for a type of bird and another for a type of machinery. Learning and mastering an ambiguous term is like learning and mastering different words, and just like learning different words, learning and mastering one meaning of an ambiguous term does not imply learning and mastering the other. "We" as a type is not assigned different context-sensitive conventional descriptive meanings registered in a dictionary, as is the case for the context-insensitive "crane." In addition, one can be semantically competent with the semantically ambiguous "crane," know that it is a type of machinery, and ignore that it is also the name of a type of bird, or vice versa. One can hardly be semantically competent with "we" and ignore the available readings of "we." Finally, there is *prima facie* only one single word "we." We do not learn many "we"s. The relationship between the linguistic meanings of semantically ambiguous terms and the readings of "we" differ. The available readings do not give the conventional meaning, or meanings, of "we" as type. "We" as a type lacks context-sensitive descriptive conventional linguistic meaning and it is not a semantically ambiguous expression. Speakers do not learn that "we" conventionally means any of the available readings, and do not learn "we" as they learn semantically ambiguous terms.

"I" has a context-sensitive descriptive conventional linguistic meaning as type, *the speaker of the utterance*, and the latter determines a content component to the reflexive content of an utterance. To have "I" in one's linguistic repertoire is to know the descriptive content it contributes to the reflexive content of "I" utterances. "We" as type lacks context-sensitive descriptive conventional meaning. However, "we" sentence utterances are true or false. I suggest that to have "we" in one's linguistic repertoire is not to master a content-determining rule, but to know the contribution of "we" to the reflexive contents of "we" utterances, that is, to know the semantic contribution of any of the available readings of "we" to the reflexive content of the utterances. The range of readings are not assigned to "we" as a type. Readings are assigned to utterances and to the reflexive contents of "we" utterances. Each specific "we" utterance has one single reading and one single relevant reflexive content. Speakers mastering "we" deploy the available readings and zoom in on that one single reflexive content. Let us see how it works.

Suppose that I have a discussion on past vacations with my wife. I tell her

(B)   We went to Spain in 2005.

That utterance of "we" refers to individuals. "We" has the readings mentioned in Table 1. These readings are echoed in available reflexive contents. My utterance is true if and only if

Reflexive Contents 1

(1)   the speaker of **u** and the addressee of **u** went to Spain in 2005, or

(2)   the speaker of **u**, the addressee of **u** and the male/female the speaker of **u** is thinking about went to Spain in 2005, or

(3)   the speaker of **u**, the addressee of **u**, and the persons the speaker **u** is thinking about went to Spain in 2005, or

(4)   the speaker of **u**, the addressee of **u**, and the persons the speaker of **u** is thinking about went to Spain in 2005, or

(5)   the speaker of **u**, the addressee of **u**, and the male/female the speaker of **u** is thinking about went to Spain in 2005, or

(6)   the speaker of **u**, the addressees of **u**, and the persons the speaker of **u** is thinking about went to Spain in 2005, or

(7)   the speaker of **u**, and the male/female the speaker of **u** is thinking about went to Spain in 2005, or

(8)   the speaker of **u** and the persons the speaker of **u** is thinking about went to Spain in 2005.

I am talking about my wife and myself, and what I said is true. Under what conditions is my utterance, **u**, true? What is the reflexive content of my utterance? I am the speaker, and she is the unique addressee of the utterance. My utterance of "we" is a placeholder for an utterance of "I and you" and what these terms introduce in reflexive contents[6]. That gives the relevant reading of that specific utterance. We have the reflexive content of my utterance:

Content M: the speaker of **u** and the addressee of **u** went to Spain in 2005.

I will be mainly interested in the reflexive content of "we" utterances in the actual paper. Content M does not give the official truth-conditions of the utterance. Given Content M and more facts about the context, including the speaker's intentions, the official truth-conditions of the utterance are reached.

Content C: <¤¤, ¤¤¤>, went to Spain in 2005.

---

6 See also Korta, "Borges and I", Perry and "us", 1998, unpublished

"¤¤, ¤¤¤" represents my wife and myself. Using extralinguistic information, my wife correctly identified the reflexive content of my utterance, the speaker of **u** and the addressee of **u**, and its truth-conditions, containing myself and herself. I can use my name and her name rather that "we" and (B) to express the same content C. The effect of my utterance on my wife would have been very different. I can use "you and I" and make an utterance of "you and I went to Spain in 2005". The effect would not have been much different, but my utterance would have been easier to understand and its truth-conditions easier to reach. The semantic problem with "we" is not about the official content of a "we" utterance. It it about how the official content is reached via a reflexive content. "We" is very flexible and "we" utterances are open to different assignments of truth-conditions. My view reflects "we"'s flexibility.

Suppose that when uttering (B) I was talking with my wife and also had our daughter in mind. That utterance of "we" is a placeholder for "I and you and her." That gives the relevant reading of my utterance; my utterance **u** is true if, and only if, the speaker of **u,** the addressee of **u** and the female the speaker of **u** is thinking about went to Spain in 2005.

Content M: the speaker of **u,** the addressee of **u** and the female the speaker of **u** is thinking about went to Spain in 2005.

My wife used contextual information to identify the relevant reflexive content. One could argue that Content M and contextual facts, including directing intentions, give the official truth-conditions of the utterance.

Content C: <¤¤ , ¤¤¤, ¤¤¤¤>, went to Spain in 2005

"¤¤ , ¤¤¤, ¤¤¤¤" represents my wife, my daughter and myself. Relying on more extralinguistic knowledge, my wife identified the official truth-condition of my utterance. Not distinguishing the addressee of **u** and the female the speaker of **u** is thinking about, and lumping them together under "The persons the speaker is thinking about" would oversimplify our intuitions concerning "we" utterances, and fail to make relevant distinctions.

What if a hearer does not know who the speaker is talking about? An utterance of "we" offers many points to zoom in and get to the official truth-conditions of the utterance. The zooming in process is an important feature of linguistic communication, a process depending heavily on extralinguistic information. Suppose that at a party you hear an utterance of

(C)   We will go to Spain in 2009.

The speaker is out of your sight. Being semantically competent, you know how expressions contribute to the reflexive content of an utterance. You deploy the available readings of "we" and grasp the possible reflexive contents of the utterance. The utterance **u** of "We will go to Spain in 2009" is true if and only if

Reflexive Contents 2

(1) the speaker of **u** and the addressee of **u** will go to Spain in 2009, or

(2) the speaker of **u**, the addressee of **u** and the male/female the speaker of **u** is thinking about will go to Spain in 2009, or

(3) the speaker of **u**, the addressee of **u**, and the persons the speaker **u** is thinking about will go to Spain in 2009, or

(4) the speaker of **u**, the addressee of **u**, and the persons the speaker of **u** is thinking about will go to Spain in 2009, or

(5) the speaker of **u**, the addressee of **u**, and the male/female the speaker of **u** is thinking about will go to Spain in 2005, or

(6) the speaker of **u**, the addressees of **u**, and the persons the speaker of **u** is thinking about will go to Spain in 2009, or

(7) the speaker of **u**, and the male/female the speaker of **u** is thinking about will go to Spain in 2009, or

(8) the speaker of **u** and the persons the speaker of **u** is thinking about will go to Spain in 2009.

The problem is not to disambiguate "we" or that utterance of "we," or to identify one of the conventional linguistic meaning of "we," but to eliminate irrelevant reflexive contents, and to identify the actual reflexive content and the official truth-conditions of the utterance. A plausible interpretation of the utterance is that the speaker of **u** and the person he is addressing in uttering **u** will go to Spain in 2009. But you can be wrong. Maybe the speaker was talking about himself and some friends. More extralinguistic knowledge would make you assign a different reflexive content to the actual utterance. Knowledge of the conversation and the speaker's intentions would make clear what the speaker had in mind in making the utterance. Extralinguistic information is needed to exclude irrelevant options and to zoom in on the actual reflexive content of the specific utterance. In contrast with singular indexical utterances, like "I" sentence utterances, identifying the relevant reflexive content of a specific "we" utterance **u** does not depend on identifying the linguistic meaning of the sentence uttered only.

 Suppose that you take a look and recognize the speaker, Paul. You get closer to the official truth-conditions of the utterance. Let PAUL stand for Paul himself. You know that the utterance is true if and only if

Mixed Contents 1

(1)   PAUL and the addressee of **u** will go to Spain 2009, or

(2)   PAUL, the addressee of **u** and the male/female PAUL is thinking about will go to Spain in 2009, or

(3)   PAUL, the addressee of **u**, and the persons PAUL is thinking about will go to Spain in 2009, or

(4)   PAUL, the addressee of **u**, and the persons PAUL is thinking about will go to Spain in 2009, or

(5)   PAUL, the addressee of **u**, and the male/female PAUL is thinking about will go to Spain in 2005, or

(6)   PAUL, the addressees of **u**, and the persons PAUL is thinking about will go to Spain in 2009, or

(7)   PAUL, and the male/female PAUL is thinking about will go to Spain in 2009, or

(8)   PAUL and the persons PAUL is thinking about will go to Spain in 2009.

Some conditions are purely qualitative in that they do not contain objects. "The persons PAUL is thinking about" is a condition on a referent containing an object, Paul. Perry (2001) calls it a lumpy condition.

Who does Paul have in mind? Who is Paul talking about? You are curious and look again. Paul is talking to his wife, Mary. She is the addressee of the utterance. You focus on plausible options, eliminate possibilities, and get closer to the relevant reflexive content of the utterance. You have plausible official truth-conditions of the utterance. I also put them under Mixed Contents for convenience. MARY stands for Mary.

Mixed Contents 2

(1)   PAUL and MARY will go to Spain 2009, or

(2)   PAUL, MARY and the male/female PAUL is thinking about will go to Spain in 2009, or

(3)   PAUL, MARY, and the persons PAUL is thinking about will go to Spain in 2009, or

(4)   PAUL, the addressee of **u**, and the persons PAUL is thinking about will go to Spain in 2009, or

(5)   PAUL, the addressee of **u**, and the male/female PAUL is thinking about will go to Spain in 2005, or

(6)   PAUL, the addressees of **u**, and the persons PAUL is thinking about will go to Spain in 2009, or

Some lumpy conditions are eliminated. Listening to the conversation, you realize that the utterance is about the addressee, and that (7) and (8) are not plausible reflexive contents.

(7)   PAUL, and the male/female PAUL is thinking about will go to Spain in 2009, or

(8)   PAUL and the persons PAUL is thinking about will go to Spain in 2009.

Overhearing more of the conversation, it becomes clear that any third party should be excluded. Paul had himself and the addressee of the utterance, his wife, in mind when making the utterance. **Reflexive Content 2** (1) remains the only plausible relevant reflexive content of the utterance. You know that they are not going with the kids. **Mixed Content 2** (1)**,** a singular proposition containing the objects referred to, gives the official truth-conditions of the utterance. A lot of information on the utterance is required to zoom in on the relevant reflexive content and even more to identify the official content of the utterance. Using reflexive contents as steps toward the relevant reflexive content and the official truth-conditions of specific "we" utterances is fairly common. Suppose that I tell you "We are going to a restaurant." Am I talking about you, the addressee, and myself? Or about some friends and myself? I add "Are you coming?" I was not talking about you. You are interested, realize that you are asked to join a group, and ask me who is coming.

The fact that the speaker uttering a "we" sentence to refer to himself/herself and people he/she is thinking about does not mean that the speaker does not have a context-insensitive descriptive modes of presentation of these individuals. Paul makes an utterance of (C). Suppose that Paul is teaching in an archaeology department and has graduate students in mind. The description "the graduate students from the XXX University Archaeology Department" provides a decent mode of presentation of the people he had in mind and a plausible candidate mode of presentation. If asked for more details about who he was talking about, Paul would probably say "myself and the graduate students from the XXX University Archaeology Department" or something similar. However, the use of "we" precludes any context-insensitive descriptive mode of presentation from being semantically conveyed and from surfacing in any proposition expressed by the utterance.

Suppose now that while you are talking to David at a party a person out of your sight say "we will go to Spain in 2009." David mumbles "sure." What is going on? David is the addressee. You rely on the available readings of "we" given in Table 1, and you know who the addressee is, David. Let DAVID stand for David himself:

Mixed Contents 3

(1)   the speaker of **u** and DAVID will go to Spain 2009, or
(2)   the speaker of **u**, DAVID and the male/female the speaker of **u** is thinking about will go to Spain in 2009, or
(3)   the speaker of **u**, DAVID, and the persons the speaker of **u** is thinking about will go to Spain in 2009, or
(4)   the speaker of **u**, the addressee of **u**, and the persons the speaker of **u** is thinking about will go to Spain in 2009, or
(5)   the speaker of **u**, the addressee of **u**, and the male/female the speaker of **u** is thinking about will go to Spain in 2005, or
(6)   the speaker of **u**, the addressees of **u**, and the persons the speaker of **u** is thinking about will go to Spain in 2009, or
(7)   the speaker of **u**, and the male/female the speaker of **u** is thinking about will go to Spain in 2009, or
(8)   the speaker of **u** and the persons the speaker of **u** is thinking about will go to Spain in 2009.

Since the speaker was addressing David, **Mixed Contents 3** (7) and (8) are excluded as plausible options. You look behind you. There is no one. David was the unique plausible addressee, and **Mixed Contents 3** (4), (5) and (6) are also eliminated. You ask David who talked to him. It is Ralf. RALF stands for Ralf. You register that information in contents.

Mixed Contents 4

(1)   RALF and DAVID will go to Spain 2009, or
(2)   RALF, DAVID and the male/female RALF is thinking about will go to Spain in 2009, or
(3)   RALF, DAVID, and the persons RALF is thinking about will go to Spain in 2009.

You then ask if both of them are going alone. He says no. Mixed Contents 4 (1) is eliminated as an option. Mixed Contents 4 (2) and (3) are left. You wonder who else is invited.

Note that we are prone to be misled. Suppose that the speaker was not addressing David who was just mumbling. You ask David who talked to him. He said no one. The speaker was talking to a different person. If you are curious enough, you will try to identify the speaker and who he was talking about, i.e., the relevant reflexive content and the official truth-conditions of the utterance.

Very often, we cannot reach the official truth-conditions of the utterance and must stop at reading-fixed reflexive content. Suppose that your friend Bill is talking to a woman over the phone and makes an utterance of

(C). You have "we" in your repertoire and can use Table 1. Bill is the speaker of the utterance, and BILL stands for Bill. What are the options?

Mixed Contents 5

(1)   BILL and the addressee of **u** will go to Spain 2009, or
(2)   BILL, the addressee of **u** and the male/female BILL is thinking about will go to Spain in 2009, or
(3)   BILL, the addressee of **u**, and the persons BILL is thinking about will go to Spain in 2009, or
(4)   BILL, the addressee of **u**, and the persons BILL is thinking about will go to Spain in 2009, or
(5)   BILL, the addressee of **u**, and the male/female BILL is thinking about will go to Spain in 2005, or
(6)   BILL, the addressees of **u**, and the persons BILL is thinking about will go to Spain in 2009, or
(7)   BILL, and the male/female BILL is thinking about will go to Spain in 2009, or
(8)   BILL and the persons BILL is thinking about will go to Spain in 2009.

Mixed Contents 5 (4)—(8) should be excluded: he is talking to one single person and the utterance is clearly addressed to her. By the way he is talking to her, and the rest of the conversation, it is obvious that they are not planning to invite anyone. **Mixed Contents 5** (2) and (3) should also be excluded. He is planning a trip for himself and the woman he is talking to. **Mixed Contents 5** (1) remains the only plausible reflexive content of the utterance.

(1)   BILL and the addressee of **u** will go to Spain in 2009.

However, you really cannot identify her and cannot get the official truth-conditions of the utterance. Reflexive contents are sometimes the best we can get. What you have is not merely that the speaker and a person he has in mind will go to Spain, but the more specific (1). Not introducing that option would miss a specific reflexive content and specific information we can get from overhearing conversations. For example, arguing that "we" is sometimes a placeholder for "the speaker of the utterance and individuals the speaker has in mind would fail to capture the information you get when hearing Bill's utterance. You look at a friend, and ask "Who is Bill talking to?"

I am drawing attention to the fact that assigning "we" as type a context-insensitive or context-sensitive descriptive meaning cannot account for the data. These approaches cannot make sense of why different "we" utterances can designate a diversity of people, of why reflexive contents are relied on to ask specific questions to Paul and David, and used as steps toward official truth-conditions of utterances. Invoking only directing intentions to account for utterances of "we" masks the detailed intuitions we have concerning such utterances, for example that the speaker of the utterance is always a referent, that there is more than one single object referred to, and that whatever the other referents are, they are not given by descriptive meaning. Assigning "we" as type the available readings and making it semantically ambiguous is not plausible.

A speaker making a "we" utterance exploits the available readings of "we" and selects one relevant reading. A hearer trying to identify the reflexive content and official truth-conditions of a "we" utterance deploys the available readings of "we", and needs much detailed information on the utterance to zoom in on the relevant reflexive content of the utterance, and more to get to the official truth-conditions of the latter.

6   The Determining Aspect of Character

Kaplan's project focuses on singular indexicals and assumes that meaning of pure indexicals determine the object referred to in a context. Kaplan (1989a) articulates his view around sentences in a context and he introduces two semantic values:

Character determines	a property of sentence types
Content	a property of sentences in context

The character of the sentence type is the linguistic meaning of the sentence type, and the content is identified with the proposition expressed by the sentence in context. Kaplan's framework is monopropositionalist. Kaplan assumes that "what is common to the words or usages in which [he is] interested is that the referent is dependent on context of use and that the meaning of the word provides a rule which determines the referent in terms of certain aspects of the context" (Kaplan, 1989a, p. 490; see also p. 505). The character of "I" is a function from context to content determining the agent in that context. Change the context, and you will get a different agent. Kaplan adds that the linguistic rules governing indexicals "*fully determine* the referent for each context." (Kaplan, 1989a, p. 491). Pure demonstratives are difficult to deal with, and Kaplan's view on pure demonstratives has changed. He acknowledges some difficulties with pure demonstratives.

Character is a content-determining function, and "we" does not have a content-determining character. In addition, if "we" has a reference-determining linguistic meaning, it cannot account for natural readings captured by binding for "whenever a pianist comes to visit, we play duet", and anaphora for "whenever Paul comes to visit, we play duet." Kaplan's framework with no modification cannot assign objects to "we" in the content of a "we" sentence in context: The linguistic meaning of "we", whatever it is, neither determines specific objects in a context nor determines the number of specific objects to be selected in a context. Now, one can argue that the available readings of "we" are just different characters of "we." If the character of a referring term is its linguistic meaning, then that view turns "we" into a semantically ambiguous expression. The arguments I invoked against the semantic ambiguity of "we" apply here. In addition, Kaplan's framework is monopropositionalist, the content being the only proposition that we have available to characterize what a listener has grasped. Monopropositionalism does not account for the reasoning we do when hearing a "we" utterance in order to zoom in from available reflexive contents to the relevant reflexive content and official truthconditions of the utterance. Finally, one can contend that a sentence in a context comes with what I called a reading. "We went to Spain in 2005" is assigned a reading in a context, say "You and I went to Spain in 2005" and then assigned a content in that context. Now, that picture dispenses with reflexive contents, and misses facts about communication. For example, it cannot provide

(1)   BILL and the addressee of **u** will go to Spain in 2009.

as what is finally grasped when hearing Bill talking over the telephone. Moreover, it does not make sense of the chain of reasonings made about Paul's or David's utterance, leading to specific questions about utterances. Kaplan's monopropositionalist framework has difficulties accounting for common facts about linguistic communication.

7 Puzzling Thought Contents

Two principles are common, if controversial, in semantics. The Thought Content Principle

> Thought Content Principle
> Complete sentences express complete thought contents.

and the Attitude Report Principle

> Attitude Report Principle:
> If S is a sentence, then the sentence X Vs that S reports the thought content S expresses.

These principles fit the sentence

(D)   The sky is blue.

(D) expresses a thought; every utterance of that sentence express the same thought, and "Peter believes that the sky is blue" reports that thought. Supposé now that Roger utters

(E)   I went to Spain in 2005

What is the thought expressed? It is not plausible to argue that every utterance of that sentence express the same thought (Perry, 1977). The idea that a concept or mode of presentation of oneself is semantically expressed by a first person sentence utterance is controversial (Perry, 1979). First person thoughts raise serious and well known difficulties (Castaneda, Perry). The Thought Content Principle is not fit for utterances of context sensitive sentences, and it does not clearly apply to them. The Attitude Report Principle is also difficult in application. Reporting what was expressed by Roger's utterance of (E) by uttering

(F)   Roger believes that I went to Spain in 2005.

will not do. Castaneda (1967) suggests that "Roger believes that he* went to Spain in 2005" reports a first person thought. However, quasi-indicators like "he*" hardly explain intuitions (See Perry, 1982; Corazza, 2004). I do not want to insist on these well known issues. I prefer to address the problem of thoughts expressed by "we" utterances. Let us go back to my daughter's utterance of (A).

What is the thought content expressed by her utterance **u** of (A)? Thoughts expressed by utterances of "we" sentences are puzzling. To argue that when uttering "we" a speaker has a concept or mode of presentation of the individuals he is referring to, an "ourselves" concept, and a different one for different utterances lacks plausibility. The various reflexive contents of utterances are not candidate thought contents (Perry, 2001). Suppose that uttering (A), my daughter was talking about my wife, myself and herself

> The speaker of **u**, the addressee of **u** and the person the speaker of **u** is thinking about want pizza

is a plausible thought content. However, following that picture, making an utterance **u'** of the same sentence a few seconds later, she is expressing a different thought content because the utterance is different.

> The speaker of **u'**, the addressee of **u'** and the person the speaker of **u'** is thinking about want pizza

She is apparently conveying the same thought. Suppose that I make an utterance **u"** of (A) with the same people in mind

> The speaker of **u"**, the addressee of **u"** and the person the speaker of **u"** is thinking about want pizza

I am also expressing a different thought because the utterance is different. I am, however, *prima facie* expressing the thought she was expressing, or a similar thought. I uttered (A) to inform a friend about what I am going to have for dinner. He thinks:

> The speaker of **u"**, the addressee of **u"** and the person the speaker of **u"** is thinking about want pizza

This is the reflexive content of my utterance. But he does not want pizza. He would not make an utterance of (A) or call for a pizza. The reflexive content is too narrow as a candidate for thought content—because two persons making two different utterances of (A) and talking about the same people plausibly have the same thought—and too wide—because I have an attitude toward pizza my colleague does not have. We do not have the same thought. Reflexive contents of "we" utterances are poor "we" thought content candidates. However, the reflexive content of my daughter's utterance and the reflexive content of my utterance capture the fact that my daughter and I said the same thing when making the utterance: we were talking about the same people and saying that they want pizza; the reflexive content of my utterance and my colleague's thought capture what both my colleague and myself have in common. He is thinking about the people I was talking about. However, my colleague would not be thinking and talking about the same people by making an utterance of "we want pizza." Thanks to the reflexive content of his utterance, he would not be thinking and talking about us but about himself and other people. What motivates my utterance of (A) differ from what motivates his utterance of (A).

If reflexive contents of "we" utterances are good guides to "we" thought contents, then making an utterance of

(G)   You and her and I want pizza

rather than an utterance of (A), my daughter would express the same thought. Suppose that we both utter (A). We are plausibly having the same thought or a similar thought, and the latter does not have the first person aspect "I" utterances exhibit. Uttering (A) she is not thinking about herself in a first person way, while she does in uttering (G); uttering (A) I am not thinking about myself in a first person way, while I am in uttering

(G). Uttering (A) and (G), we believe the same content, but in different ways. *Prima facie*, the thought expressed by a "we" utterance is not as fine grained as the thought an utterance of (G) expresses. I see no semantic argument motivating the view that "we" thoughts echo the fine grainedness of the readings of "we" utterances.

The Attitude Report Principle also raises perplexity. An utterance of

(H)   Paul believes that we want pizza.

does not report the expressed thought content. *Prima facie*, "we" does not have a counterpart quasi-indicator. What is the belief sentence fit to report the thought content expressed by my daughter's utterance? Remove that sentence. Unfortunately, there is no available candidate thought content to be reported. Introducing a "we" notion or mode of presentation of the group referred to and a different one for different utterances is not plausible. Trying to fit a term reporting such a notion in a belief report also lacks plausibility.

Traditionally, thought contents and belief reports echo the context insensitive descriptive meaning of lexical items and sentences. If I am right, because "we" as type lacks context insensitive or context-sensitive descriptive meaning, there is no descriptive content semantically expressed by a "we" sentence utterance, and none to report. The reflexive content of a "we" utterance is the best guide to content of mind we can have. That does not mean that my daughter had no modes of presentation of the persons she had in mind when uttering (A). It means that whatever these modes, they are not semantically conveyed in a "we" sentence utterance. "We" utterances resist the two principles introduced at the beginning of this section, and suggest that the latters are not fully general. Sentences are famous for being tools fit for thought expression. On that picture "we" utterances express thoughts. The apparatus I introduced can focus on sameness and differences in reflexive content expressed and what people say when uttering "we" sentences. It is plausibly the best that can be offered when trying to identify and to report a "we" thought.

8   Conclusion

Speakers learn how to use "we", know that it does not express a descriptive condition, and know that an utterance of it replaces a combination of "I" and "you", and/or the plural "you", and/or "he"/ "she" and /or "they" in an utterance. Davidson advocates the idea that to know the meaning of a sentence is to know its truth conditions. That principle can accommodate pure indexicals; to know the meaning of a pure indexical sentence and the context of utterance is to know the truth conditions of this sentence in that context. However, if an expression is analyzed away, like "we," the strict truth conditional program cannot be followed. For some expressions, to know how it contributes to the truth conditions of utterances—here, the available readings and reflexive contents—and the context of utterance does not imply knowledge of the truth conditions of the utterance. One needs much extralinguistic information on the utterance to know the specific reflexive content of the utterance. Fortunately, this is of no consequence for semantics. Truth conditional semantics is interested in sentences as types and semantic competence, not utterances. Semantics has done its job after having explained what it is to have "we" in one's repertoire and giving the available readings clipped to "we."

References

Castaneda, H.N. 1967. "Indicators and Quasi-Indicators", *American Philosophical Quarterly* 4. 85-100.

Corazza, E. 2004. *Reflecting the Mind*, Oxford University Press.

Kaplan, D. 1989a. "Demonstratives", in Almog, J., Perry, J. and H. Wettstein (eds.) *Themes from Kaplan,* Oxford, 481-563.

Kaplan, D. 1989b. "Afterthoughts", in Almog, J., Perry, J. and H. Wettstein (eds.) *Themes from Kaplan,* Oxford, 1989, 565-614.

Korta, K. 2008. "'Borges and I", Perry and "Us"'", unpublished.

MacKay, T. 2006. *Plural Predication*, Oxford University Press.

Nunberg, G. 1993. "Indexicality and Deixis", *Linguistics and Philosophy* 16, 1-43.

Perry, J. 1979. "The Problem of the Essential Indexical", *Noûs*, 13, 3-21.

Perry, J. 1983. "Castaneda on *he* and *I*", in Tomberlin, J. (ed.) *Agent, Language and the Structure of the World*, Hackett, 15-42.

Perry, J. 2001. *Reference and Reflexivity*, CSLI publications.

Perry, J. 2001. "Using Indexicals", in Devitt, M. and R. Hanley (eds.) *The Blackwell Guide to the Philosophy of Language*, Oxford, Blackwell, 314-334.

Vallée, R. 1996. "Who are We?", *Canadian Journal of Philosophy*, 211-230.

Yi, Byeong-uk. 2002. *Understanding the Many*, Routledge, 2002.

3

Complex Demonstratives, Articulation, and Overarticulation

1 Referring Terms and Singular Propositions

Indexicals ("I," "you"), bare demonstratives ("he," "this"), and proper names ("Peter") are referring terms. Utterances of referring terms designate specific objects. For example, an utterance of "I" designates the speaker of the utterance and an utterance of "Steven Seagal" designates the person bearing that name. Two arguable assumptions concerning referring terms are widely shared in the field. First,

Lexical Simplicity Assumption: Referring terms are lexically simple, unstructured linguistic expressions.

The Lexical Simplicity Assumption is concerned with the syntactic structure, or the lack of it, of referring terms; they are primitive, unstructured, noncompositional, lexical items. Second, according to a fairly common point of view, referring terms introduce the objects they designate, and nothing else, into the truth-conditions of utterances. For example, an utterance of "I" introduces the speaker, and nothing else, into the truth-conditions of an utterance of

(1)   I am sick,

and an utterance of (1) is true if and only if the speaker of the utterance is sick; an utterance of the bare demonstrative "that" introduces the designated object and nothing else into the truth-conditions of an utterance of a "that" sentence, and an utterance of

(2)   That is yellow

is true if and only if the designated object is yellow. This view is encapsulated in the idea that referring terms have a singular reference.

Singular Reference Assumption: The only semantic contribution of utterances of referring terms to the truth-conditions of utterances of sentences is an object.

The Singular Reference Assumption is concerned with the semantics of referring terms. Referring terms are semantically defined by their introducing objects, and nothing else, into the truth-conditions of utterances (Kripke, Kaplan, Perry). Let us say that utterances of sentences of the form

Referring term + predicate

express singular propositions of the form

$$< \quad , \quad >$$

where the first gap is filled in by the object referred to by the utterance of the referring term, and the second gap is filled in by the condition expressed by the predicate.

2   Enter Complex Demonstratives

Indexicals and bare demonstratives are context-sensitive referring expressions. The objects they introduce into the truth-conditions of utterances may vary from utterance to utterance. Another category of *prima facie* referring terms exhibits context sensitivity. Complex demonstratives (CDs) are *prima facie* referring terms of the form "that F,"[1] where "that" is a bare demonstrative and F is a common noun or a noun phrase.[2] For example, "that man talking to Mary" is a complex demonstrative containing the bare demonstrative "that" and the nominal "man talking to Mary." If CDs are referring terms, they contribute an object to the truth-conditions of an utterance. CDs are context sensitive because they can be used to designate different objects in different contexts. An utterance of "that man talking to Mary" can be used to designate Paul, and another utterance of the same CD can be used to designate Peter. Complex demonstratives threaten both the Lexical Simplicity Assumption and the Singular Reference Assumption. On the one hand, CDs are syntactically structured, complex terms containing a bare demonstrative and a nominal. The latter can be simple ("car") or complex ("man

---

[1] Some (for instance, King 2001) contend that complex demonstratives are not referring terms. I do not want to address that issue.

[2] I assume that bare demonstratives and the "that" occurring in a CD are tokens of the same type (see Johnson and Lepore 2002 for evidence).

talking to Mary"). If CDs are referring terms and also are lexically complex, structured terms, then the Lexical Simplicity Assumption is false. On the other hand, according to the Singular Reference Assumption, if "that car" is a referring term, then it introduces an object into the truth-conditions of the utterance, and an utterance of

(3)   That car is yellow

is true if and only if the object referred to by the CD is yellow. Following the Singular Reference Assumption, an utterance of (3) expresses a singular proposition containing the object referred to and the condition *being yellow*.

    <CAR , being yellow>

where CAR is the object itself. As a rule, the nominal "car" semantically expresses a condition, *being car*. The latter is also truth-conditionally relevant in an utterance of a sentence containing that term. For example, in "A car is yellow," "car" introduces the condition of being car, and the sentence is true if and only if there is an x, such that x is a car and x is yellow. I call the condition "car" expresses its standard semantic contribution. Let us say that

Semantic Stability Assumption: In virtue of its linguistic meaning, a nominal contributes a condition and the semantic contribution of a nominal does not change from sentence to sentence.

If the Singular Reference Assumption is true, and if CDs are referring terms, we lose semantic stability. If the standard semantic contribution of "car" is a condition, and if the condition "car" expresses is excluded from any proposition which an utterance of a CD sentence expresses, then the nominal's standard semantic contribution drops out as being irrelevant in utterances of CD sentences. The CD semantically contributes an object, not a condition, to the semantic value of an utterance. However, the standard semantic contribution of the nominal cannot be discarded without an explanation. Notice that if a quantifier is substituted to the bare demonstrative in (4), to obtain as in these examples, "Some car is yellow" or "A car is yellow," the Singular Reference Assumption does not apply and the problem under consideration does not surface.

3   Misdemonstrations

Let me add a twist and consider what I will call a misdemonstration. Suppose that in designating a person, Mary, I say

(4) That student is smart.

You correct me: the person I am designating is not a student but a faculty member. Still, you agree, she is smart. I will say that if the nominal does not fit the designated object, then we have a misdemonstration. There are conflicting intuitions concerning the truth-conditions of my utterance of (4). Kaplan (1989a) contends that my utterance of "that F" designates nothing if the designated object is not an F. It is nonetheless widely agreed that my utterance of (4) expresses a true proposition even if the designated object is not an F (Larson and Segal 1995, p. 213; Lepore and Ludwig 2000, p. 211), or that I express a true proposition even if the designated object is not an F (Braun 1995). We are willing, in some circumstances, to drop the nominal semantic contribution as semantically irrelevant with respect to the utterance. Some (Larson and Segal 1995) argue that the nominal always plays a merely pragmatic role—helping the hearer to focus on the relevant object— and no semantic role at all. My utterance of (4) is then true since the bare demonstrative picks out the relevant object and the nominal is not semantically relevant and does not alter the truth-conditions of the utterance. This view is not acceptable for anyone thinking that the nominal plays a semantic role. If the nominal has only a pragmatic role and does not bring its standard semantic contribution to a CD, and if the cognitive value of an utterance is determined by the meaning and the standard semantic contribution of the terms occurring in it, then the nominal does not contribute to the cognitive value of the utterance of a CD sentence. This is not acceptable. Intuitively, it does contribute to the cognitive value of the utterance. My utterance of "that lemon is yellow" and "that fruit is yellow" may share the same truth-conditions, but they differ in cognitive value, and the linguistic meaning of the nominal is responsible for this difference. If we ignore the linguistic meaning of the nominal, then we fail to capture this difference.

One can also argue that a hearer does not even have to understand the linguistic meaning of the nominal or know its standard semantic contribution to know the truth-condition of an utterance of a CD sentence. Suppose that in designating a mushroom you utter, "that *Claraveriadelphus truncatus* is great." I do not know the meaning of "*Claraveriadelphus truncatus*," but I think that the mushroom you designated is great and that the singular proposition you expressed containing that mushroom and the condition of being great is true.[3] You are not, but you might be, designating either the form or the color of that object. I will not consider these options here, since they are irrelevant to my main point. I simply assume that you intended to designate an object. I will come back to misdemonstrations and the semantic relevance of the nominal.

---

[3] I want to thank Arthur Sullivan for bringing this type of example to my attention.

4 Framework for a New Suggestion

Most philosophers of language accept the Semantic Stability Assumption and want the nominal to preserve its standard semantic contribution, a condition, or at least to play a decent semantic role in a CD sentence (Borg 2000; Braun 1995; Corazza 2002; Dever 2001; Richard 1993). Two options have been explored. Some preserve both the Semantic Stability Assumption and the Singular Reference Assumption, but they reject the idea that CDs are syntactically complex referring terms. On that picture, the burden of reference is carried by the bare demonstrative and the condition introduced by the nominal is part of a proposition which is expressed by an utterance of CD sentence (Corazza; Dever; Lepore and Ludwig; Richard). Corazza goes on to argue, however, that the nominal is irrelevant to the truth-conditions of the utterance. Others preserve both the Singular Reference Assumption and the idea that CDs are syntactically complex referring terms, but they reject the Semantic Stability Assumption. On that picture, the nominal does not carry its standard semantic contribution into a proposition expressed by the utterance of a CD sentence (Borg; Braun; Kaplan). On that view, the bare demonstrative and the nominal are put together to jointly contribute to the complex linguistic meaning of the CD, and the latter introduces only an object into the truth-conditions of an utterance. The semantic complexity of CDs, their being composed of a bare demonstrative and a nominal, then finds no echo in a proposition expressed by an utterance of a CD sentence. I want to suggest a third option. I offer a picture of CDs preserving both the Singular Reference Assumption and the idea that CDs are complex referring terms. I also contend that the nominal introduces a semantically relevant condition. However, the Lexical Simplicity Assumption has to be abandoned.

My suggestion focuses on the syntax and semantics of CDs. Syntax concerns the structure of linguistic expressions. Semantics is trickier. Frege left us with the notion of sense as the semantic value of linguistic expressions (I will not pay attention to the denotation of a term as its semantic value). David Kaplan and John Perry transformed the semantic landscape in the 1970s.

The linguistic meaning of a term is a property of an expression as type and a rule assigning the truth-conditional contribution of that term to the truth-conditions of a sentence in a context or to an utterance. Kaplan (1989a, 1989b) focuses on sentences in a context and places the notion of character, a function from context to content, at the center of the stage. In Kaplan's view, the character of a term is the linguistic meaning of that term. It goes without saying that rules, and hence characters, are not part of a proposition expressed by a sentence in a context, and not part of the truth-conditions of a sentence in a context. According to Kaplan, characters *determine* the truth-conditions or proposition expressed by a sentence in a context. He calls the truth-conditions of a sentence in a context its content, and from that point of view, content is the only truth-valuable entity. The content of a sentence containing a referring term in a context is a singular proposition.

Perry (1996, 2000, 2001) makes a different suggestion. He places utterances, rather than sentences in context, at the center of the stage. He also unfolds and clearly distinguishes the functions of senses found in Frege's semantics and extract propositions (that is, truth-valuable entities) out of the meaning of the sentence. He makes a distinction between the linguistic meaning of a sentence type, the Content M, or the proposition given by the linguistic meaning of the sentence, the Content C of an utterance, or the proposition given by the meaning plus facts about the context of utterance, and the Content D, or the proposition obtained once the referents or designata are determined. The Content D gives the official truth-conditions of an utterance. I rely on this unfolding and the distinctions introduced. The linguistic meaning and all three propositions—Content M, Content C, and Content D—belong to semantics. In Frege, these functions are satisfied by one single entity, a sense. The sense of a sentence is a proposition. Let us say that Frege's semantics relies on one semantic value (sense) and that Kaplan's semantic relies on two semantic values (character and content). Perry assigns to each function a different semantic value, and relies on many semantic values. Perry uses the notion of a role to replace the function of linguistic meaning. The role of a context-sensitive referring term is a reference rule mentioning the utterance itself. For example, the role of "I" is "The speaker of the utterance." The role is complex. It provides a property, being speaker of, and an argument, the utterance. In that sense, the role is reflexive since it refers to the utterance itself. It must be emphasized that this picture does not use Kaplan's notion of character, and that the reflexivity of the role is crucial to Perry's picture. Kaplanian characters are not reflexive. Perry distinguishes himself from Kaplan, who does not introduce any semantic entity fit to assume the role of cognitive significance beyond content, by doing just that. Now, "cognitive significance" is terse and deserves an explanation.

In Frege's semantics, the cognitive value is a property of a sentence and it is a proposition identical with the proposition giving the truth-conditions of the sentence. I assume that the cognitive value is a truth-valuable entity or proposition. However, being at the center of the stage on our picture, utterances will have cognitive values. Perry identifies a useful condition on the cognitive significance or cognitive value of an utterance, a condition tied to the cognitive notion of acceptance:

> If there is some aspect of meaning, by which an utterance u of S and an utterance u' of S' differ, so that a rational person who understood both S and

S' might accept u but not u', then a fully adequate theory of linguistic meaning should say what it is. (2000, p. 194)

One can accept or reject propositions. Accepting is a cognitive attitude, and acceptance or rejection is acceptance that p or rejection that p, where p is a proposition which is the cognitive significance of an utterance. On that picture, the cognitive significance of an utterance is not a linguistic rule. Note that a speaker must understand the linguistic meaning of a sentence type to grasp the cognitive value or cognitive significance of an utterance of that sentence, and that cognitive value might differ from linguistic meaning. For example, two utterances of "that car is yellow" differ in cognitive value even if the sentence has the same meaning in both utterances, the referring term designates the same object in both cases and the utterances have the same truth-conditions: a hearer can accept an utterance of the first sentence and reject an utterance of the second sentence. Suppose that I am designating a car in full daylight and make an utterance of "that car is yellow." You accept my utterance. Suppose now that I make an utterance of the same sentence at night and designate the same car. You do not recognize the car, and do not accept my utterance even if the latter has the same truth-conditions. On Kaplan's view, the only available proposition is the content of a sentence in a context and the content is hence the only candidate to play the role of cognitive value. Perry's framework makes available a proposition fit for the role of cognitive value of the utterance. I will come back to this.

Finally, the truth-conditions of an utterance of a sentence are fully determined by the meaning of this utterance. It is also a proposition. Perry calls the truth-conditions of an utterance its official content. The truth-conditions of an utterance containing a referring term is a singular proposition containing the object referred to by the referring term.

From the linguistic meaning of a sentence one can extract the Content M which is just the proposition one obtains when one understands the linguistic meaning of the sentence; adding contextual features to Content M, one obtains Content C, which is just the proposition one obtains once the utterance is fixed; and, finally, once the referents are determined, one obtains Content D, or the official content of the utterance. Let us see how the whole machinery works for indexical sentences. Consider an utterance of (1), and suppose that you understand the meaning of the sentence type but know nothing about the utterance. Following Perry's picture, given the meaning of "I," you know that

Content M <The speaker of the utterance of "I" in the context c is
        sick>, u

where c is the context and u is an utterance. The Content M, i.e., the content in angle brackets, is general and echoes the linguistic meaning of the sentence, including the role or meaning of the indexical, with no extra element, and it does not contain any object. Note that the lexical item "I" is simple and lacks structure, but that its linguistic meaning is complex, mentioning the speaker and the utterance. Content M is utterance sensitive. I introduce Content M because it is part of the Reflexive-Referential Theory. However, it plays no major role in my view on CD. Content C will. Suppose that you focus on a specific utterance *u*. You know that this specific utterance is true if and only if the speaker of this utterance is sick. You can now drop generality from the role of "I" and focus on *u*.

Content C <the speaker of the utterance u of "I" is sick>

Content C mentions the utterance u itself. It is the reflexive content of the utterance. Content C is reached from Content M plus facts about a specific utterance. One can recognize this content without knowing the specific truth-maker of the utterance, that is, the object referred to by the utterance of the indexical. One can also accept or reject the Content C while ignoring which object is referred to by the utterance of the indexical. Content C is the cognitive value of the utterance. Notice that the Content C is fully explicit and is a property of a specific utterance. There is no reason to see it as an implicit speaker's background assumption.

Suppose now that you know enough about the context of the utterance to identify the object referred to, i.e., the speaker of this utterance. You can focus on the world, identify the referent of the indexical, and get the Content D of the utterance or the official, nonreflexive, language-independent, truth-conditions of the utterance.

Content D <ME, being sick>

The Content D is what we usually take to be the truth-conditions of the utterance. It lacks generality and contains the object determined by the meaning of the indexical in that context rather than a condition. My utterance of (1) is true if and only if I am sick. The sentence (1) has the form

referring term + predicate

and its utterance expresses the singular proposition mentioned in the Singular Reference Assumption.

The overall picture can be summarized in the following diagram:

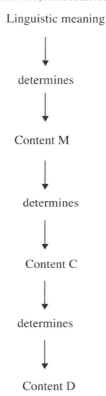

Linguistic meaning

determines

Content M

determines

Content C

determines

Content D

A different picture of semantics emerges once many semantic values are made available, a picture suggesting a different way to deal with CDs.

When only one semantic value—a Fregean sense—is available, things are rather straightforward. Now that there are at least two, several options show up. For instance, both the cognitive value and the truth-conditions of an utterance of a sentence are propositions, and they need not be identical.

5 One Word of Caution

From a standard viewpoint, pragmatics concerns the nontruth-conditional aspects of utterances. Pragmatics, understood as concerning the nontruth-conditional aspects of a sentence or an utterance is not involved in my picture. All we need is the linguistic meaning of the utterance and facts about the context of the utterance, because we are interested in terms whose contribution to the truth-conditions of an utterance depend on the context of utterance. Recently, it has been argued that sometimes the linguistic meaning of an utterance does not determine its truth-conditions and that it is then necessary to complete the proposition one way or another with extra material to obtain truth-conditions (see Recanati 1992, 2004). If so, one can argue that pragmatics also concerns the truth-conditions of utterances. Pragmatics understood either in its standard sense or in truth-conditional terms, plays no role in this article. I am interested in the Singular Reference Assumption, a principle concerned with how linguistic meaning determines truth-conditions—cases where more than linguistic meaning is required are irrelevant to my point.

First, I would like to examine the two previously mentioned views on CDs with the Singular Reference Assumption and misdemonstrations in mind. I will then introduce difficulties these views face. I do not think that these difficulties are insurmountable, and my arguments are not intended as providing knock-down reasons to reject them. Second, I want to suggest an option that preserves both the Singular Reference Assumption and the idea that CDs are referring expressions, which fits the condition contributed by the nominal at the right place and which semantically accounts for our intuitions concerning misdemonstrations. My suggestion is an account of CDs fitting them in the complex picture of referring terms found in the Reflexive-Referential Theory (Perry 2001).

6   Suggestions on the Market

Corazza (2002), Dever (2001), and Richard (1993) reject the Singular Reference Assumption. Alternatively, one can argue that they preserve the Singular Reference Assumption but do not take CDs to be referring terms. I call their view the Articulated View on CDs. Corazza, Dever, and Richard offer different versions of the Articulated View. I will neglect the divergences here and will focus instead on the basics of the Articulated View. Advocates of that approach to CDs contend that "that" in a CD behaves like a bare demonstrative and that the nominal expresses a condition part of the truth-conditions or part of the proposition expressed by a CD utterance—"that" in "That student" is the referential device, and the nominal is referentially irrelevant. In that respect, the expressions have their standard semantic values and the Semantic Stability Assumption is preserved. According to Dever's Multiple Proposition View (Dever 2001), the syntax of CD sentences is misleading, and a CD sentence "That F is G" contains in fact two independent sentences. For instance, (3) has the following structure:

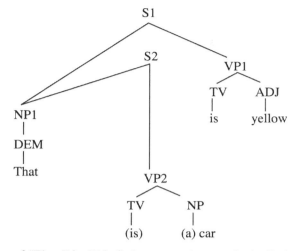

An utterance of "That F is G" is fit for expressing two logically independent singular propositions, < , F > and < , G>, both containing the object referred to by "that." For example, an utterance of (3) expresses <CAR , being car> and <CAR , being yellow>. CDs are then not referring terms. They are *prima facie* syntactically complex referring expressions. However, sentences containing these expressions have a logical form such that the bare demonstrative and the nominal are syntactically separated. Hence, CDs are eliminated from the class of referring term. The bare demonstrative carries the referential weight, and the nominal plays no referring role, not even constraining the sort of object referred to. In that respect, this view also preserves the Lexical Simplicity Assumption. According to Dever, we have no clear intuitions concerning the truth-value of an utterance of "That F is G" when the object referred to in not an F. Corazza (2002) advocates a version of Dever's Multiple Proposition View. He distinguishes, among the propositions expressed by an utterance of "That F is G," the background proposition, < , F>, and the principal proposition, < , G>, and argues that when the object referred to is not an F, the utterance is still true because the principal proposition is true. According to Richard (1993), the utterance of a CD sentence of the form "That F is G" expresses a unique complex singular proposition, < , F . , G>, containing twice the object referred to by "that", whether or not that object is an F. An utterance of "That is F and that is G," where "that" refers to what "that" in the initial example refers to, would express the same complex singular proposition. If the designated object is not an F, then the first singular proposition expressed is false and the complex proposition expressed by the utterance is also false.

If CDs are referring terms introducing objects rather than conditions into the truth-conditions of an utterance, then one expects the nominal not to introduce any condition into the truth-conditions of utterances of CD sentences. In the Articulated View, the demonstrative in the CD refers to an object and the nominal contributes a condition to the truth-conditions of the utterance. In that respect, the Articulated View preserves the Lexical Simplicity Assumption and the Singular Reference Assumption. However, it drops the idea that CDs, *qua* complex expressions, are referring terms because the nominal plays no referring role. All versions of the Articulated View take "that," not "That F," to be the referring term and to introduce an object into a singular proposition.

If that view is correct, the explicit syntax of a CD like "that car" would be given by

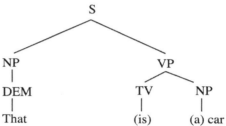

CDs are thus not referring terms designating objects but sentences expressing propositions. Such a view makes the false prediction that "that F" and "that is an F" have the same meaning and are semantically equivalent.[4]

On the Articulated view, given the predicative role assigned to the nominal, the latter cannot help the hearer to identify the object referred to. The descriptive material introduced by the nominal is true or false of that object, and in no way does it help to identify the relevant object. Finally, in Corazza's, Dever's, and Richard's view the two simple singular propositions expressed by an utterance of a CD sentence are semantically independent. However, CD sentences exhibit a very strong syntactic unity, and one expects them to also exhibit a strong semantic cohesion not found in the Articulated View. It is widely assumed that the utterance of a simple sentence, like (3), expresses one single, simple proposition giving the truth-conditions of the utterance. In the actual case, the utterance of a simple sentence like (3) expresses two propositions, or one complex proposition (Richard), identified with the truth-conditions of the utterance. The logical independence of the two expressed propositions, or the complex proposition (Richard), is an undesirable aspect,

---

[4] I want to thank Rob Stainton for suggesting this argument.

one introducing a crack in the semantic cohesion expected from these sentences. The syntactic complexity and sophistication of CDs as referring expressions should be accounted for rather than analyzed away.

How does the Articulated View deal with misdemonstrations? According to Richard's picture, my utterance of

(4)   That student is smart

literally expresses a complex singular proposition,

<MARY, being student . MARY, being smart>.

We have two independent propositions connected by a conjunction. Because one of the conjuncts is false, the complex singular proposition is also false. According to Dever's picture, the utterance of (4) literally expresses one false proposition, <MARY, being student>, and one true proposition, <MARY, being smart>, and the truth-value of such an utterance is not clearly assessible. As we saw, according to Corazza, it is true because what he calls the principal proposition is true.

Braun's (1995) and Borg's (2000) Kaplanian view on CDs rejects the Lexical Simplicity Assumption and preserves both the Singular Reference Assumption and the idea that CDs are referring terms. However, it loses semantic stability. Call it the Character View on CDs. According to that picture, a CD is a lexically complex referring term having a complex structured character or linguistic meaning. Here "that" in a CD does not behave like a bare demonstrative designating an object—the CD, *not the bare demonstrative*, designates an object—and the linguistic meaning of the nominal is introduced into the character or meaning of the CD. However, the condition determined by the nominal is not echoed in the content of CD sentences in context. According to the Character View, the content of a CD sentence in context is a singular proposition containing the referent of the CD and the condition determined by the predicate occurring in that sentence. For example, an utterance of (3) expresses a proposition containing the unique designated car and the condition of being yellow. This fits the Singular Reference Assumption. However, there is a price to be paid. Intuitively, "that" is a bare demonstrative referring to the designated object, and normally the nominal semantically contributes a condition to the semantic value of a sentence containing it. According to the Character View, "that" in "that student" does not refer—"that student" does—and the nominal does not semantically introduce a condition into the content or truth-conditions of the sentence in context. The demonstrative "that" and the nominal do not have their standard semantic-behavior and do not play their standard semantic role (i.e., referring to an object and introducing a condition) when they occur in a complex demonstrative (see also Dever 2001 and Predelli 2001 on that). Semantic Stability is lost because the nominal does not introduce a condition. This picture raises some difficulties. On the one hand, one does not want the concatenation of these two terms to alter their semantic behavior and to go against our basic intuitions concerning the semantics of "that" and the semantics of the nominal. On the other hand, as a rule the components and structure of a complex term are echoed in both the character and the content of that term. In the case under examination here, the components and structure of the CD are echoed in its character but not in its content: the nominal does not introduce a condition into the content.[5] I find these aspects of the Character View objectionable. They go against some very simple, widely shared semantic principles.

Finally, we want utterances to have both truth-conditions and cognitive values. In a Fregean understanding, the cognitive value of an utterance is a proposition one can recognize, thanks to one's linguistic competence, and accept or reject. In that respect, the cognitive value of an utterance cannot be a singular proposition making true the sentence or the utterance. Otherwise, my utterance of "I am sick" and your utterance of "you are sick," where I am the referent of the utterance of "you," would have the same cognitive value, and this is not plausible.

If, on the Character View, the nominal does not introduce any condition in the content, if the content, a singular proposition, is the only available proposition, and if the cognitive value of an utterance is a proposition-like entity, then the nominal does not contribute to the cognitive value of the utterance. My utterance of "That is yellow" and "That BMW is yellow" would have the same cognitive value, and that is not plausible. A natural reaction is to rely on the character of a CD to discriminate between cognitive values (see Braun 1995 and Kaplan 1989a). Since on that view the bare demonstrative and the nominal jointly contribute to the character of a CD, two CDs containing different nominals will differ in meaning. Intuitively, the meaning or character of a CD makes a difference to its cognitive value, and explains difference in cognitive value. This is not controversial. However, the linguistic meaning of an expression as a type is its character, not the content or proposition expressed by an utterance. The character of a sentence determines a proposition, but it is not a proposition. Neither is it a truth-valuable entity or something one accepts or rejects. Now, one does not want an utterance of

(5)   That faculty member is smart

and an utterance of

---

[5] Predelli (2001) raises serious objections to the Character View picture of CDs.

(6)   That philosopher is smart

to have the same cognitive value even if they both express the same singular proposition. *Prima facie*, the nominal makes a cognitive difference, one that should be echoed in a proposition. In the Character View, utterances of (5) and (6) differ in cognitive value and have the same truth-conditions. However, this difference in cognitive value cannot be cashed out in propositional terms.[6] The challenge here is to extract from the linguistic meaning or character of the CD a truth-conditional item, an element fit to be introduced in a proposition. Unfortunately, a two-value semantics like Kaplan's does not leave room for that item. The Reflexive-Referential Theory does, or so I shall argue. One might reject the idea that the cognitive value of a sentence or an utterance is a proposition and thus suggest a different, non-Fregean, nonpropositional notion of cognitive value. The suggestion is that the cognitive value of a sentence is identical with its linguistic meaning. However, that suggestion implies that, as distinct from Perry's view, all utterances of "that car is yellow" have the same cognitive value insofar as all tokens have the same linguistic meaning. This does not seem to be right. Now I am not saying that a non-Fregean position cannot be developed and I do not offer my criticism as a knock-down argument against the Character View. I will let the advocates of that view flesh out their point. I just assume a specific notion of cognitive value and suggest a more appealing alternative.

How does the Character View deal with misdemonstrations like (4)?

(4)   That student is smart.

According to Braun, it literally expresses a false proposition. Braun (1995) explains away our intuitions concerning the truth-conditions of my utterance of (4) by invoking Kripke's speaker's reference/semantic reference distinction: *I* expresses a true proposition even if the sentence I uttered does not. Braun proposes a pragmatic account for our intuitions concerning misdemonstrations.

7   Reflexive-Referential Suggestion

The views on the market face well known difficulties, but I do not want to focus on them. Neither do I contend that these problems cannot be solved one way or another. I want to explore a different option. The Articulated View has two desirable features: it preserves (i) semantic stability and (ii) the idea that the nominal is cognitively significant, in a Fregean understanding of this notion, since it is part of an expressed proposition. But it rejects the idea that CDs are referring terms. In contrast, the Character View has one desirable

---

[6] This problem with the Kaplanian account of indexicals is well known (see Perry 2001).

feature: it preserves the idea that CDs are referring terms. But it does not fare very well with respect to (i) or (ii). As I mentioned, on that view misdemonstrations are not semantically accounted for but pragmatically explained. A semantic analysis would have much in its favor. As a rule, semantic accounts should be preferred over pragmatic explanations. I cannot argue for that principle here, but it is widely shared by philosophers of language. I contend that the Singular Reference Assumption, the Semantic Stability Assumption, and the idea that CDs are referring terms are compatible. I offer a suggestion following from an independently motivated view on the semantics of context-sensitive referring terms. The suggestion also accounts for our intuitions concerning misdemonstrations in semantic terms.

Richard's, as well as Dever's and Corazza's, Multiple Proposition View is a syntactic approach to CDs. It assigns CD sentences a logical form breaking apart CDs, distinguishes different sentences, and then gives the truth-conditions of these sentences in context. CD sentences express many propositions for syntactic reasons. As a consequence, CDs are excluded from the list of referring terms. Perry introduces a suggestion according to which an utterance of a sentence expresses many propositions for semantic, rather than syntactic, reasons. It is also a "Multiple Proposition View." Now, on the Reflexive-Referential Theory, expressing many propositions is a general semantic feature of utterances, and it is not introduced to deal with the specific problems raised by complex demonstratives and CD sentences. In that respect, the framework is available to account for the many propositions an utterance, like an utterance of a CD sentence, expresses and no new analysis is needed. In addition, from that point of view the propositions expressed by an utterance are semantically related and exhibit a strong cohesion not found in the Articulated View.

The Reflexive-Referential picture is not introduced to deal with complex demonstratives, but it nicely accounts for complex demonstratives. It also accounts for the role of the nominal and makes sense of our intuitions concerning misdemonstrations. Let us consider an utterance of (3) and examine the contents expressed. Now, I want to add one detail not found in Perry's view. In order to preserve the structure of a complex demonstrative in the contents expressed by a CD utterance, I will introduce structure-indicating devices into the propositions expressed by a CD utterance. A comma distinguishes what belongs to the semantic contribution of the referring term from what belongs to the semantic contribution of the predicate. This device is standard and is not very controversial, distinguishing the semantic contribution of the referring term from that of the predicate. Indexicals have a complex meaning. Still, indexicals lack syntactic structure. Because indexicals lack syntactic structure, no structure is exhibited by what indexicals express in propositions. Things are different with complex demonstratives. A CD is a complex referring term having both a structure and a complex meaning. That structure and semantic complexity are reflected in the propositions expressed. We also want to capture the difference between structured and unstructured referring terms. If we do not do so, then our picture will fail to take into account the semantic differences between unstructured referring terms like "I" and structured referring terms like "that man talking to Mary." A set of angle brackets distinguishes what is semantically contributed by "that" from what is semantically contributed by the nominal in a complex demonstrative—a condition. We end up with propositions reflecting the logical form of the sentence. I utter (3). Suppose that you understand the language and grasp the Content M of (3), but set aside what is specific about the utterance. You understand that

Content M< [One object x most salient to the speaker of "that" in c]
[x is a car], x is yellow>, u

In plain English, it means that an object is salient to the speaker of "that" in the context, that that object is a car, and that it is yellow. U is just any utterance. Focusing on the specific utterance, one can drop generality from Content M and obtain the reflexive content of the specific utterance u.

Content C < [One object x most salient to the speaker of u]
[x is a car], x is yellow>

The reflexive content is a proposition and, hence, a truth-valuable entity. It is also the cognitive value of the utterance (see Perry 2001, p. 15). Different utterances of (3) will have different reflexive contents and, hence, different cognitive values. Different utterances of CDs containing different nominals will also differ in cognitive value because the nominals are different and introduce different conditions in Content C. This fits our intuition that different CDs, because they contain different nominals, have different cognitive values. It also captures the Fregean intuitions that there is mode of presentation under which the speaker thinks of the object referred to by the CD, for example, as being a car. The nominal has more than a pragmatic role because it contributes to the cognitive value of the utterance. This is not a role assigned to the nominal by Larson and Segal. It is also useful to help the hearer identify the designated object. This is the role assigned to the nominal by Larson and Segal. The nominal preserves its standard semantic contribution, a condition, and contributes to the truth-conditions of a proposition an utterance of (3) expresses, i.e., the Content C. According to the Singular Reference Assumption, the referring term introduces an object into the official truth-conditions or Content D, and the latter contains an object as well as the condition determined by the predicate. The utterance of "that" introduces an object into the truthconditions of the utterance of (3): one object x most salient to the speaker of u. How salience is indicated in specific cases (gesture, intention, and what not) is not part of the semantics of bare demonstratives and is irrelevant to my point. The bare demonstrative is actually mute on how salience is indicated. Suppose that you know enough about the context to identify the relevant object, a specific car. It is introduced into the Content D. The referring term, "that car," has completed its referring role and brought in its contribution to the Content D. We now have the official truth-conditions of my utterance of (3),

Content D <CAR, being yellow>.

CAR is the object introduced into Content D. On hearing an utterance of (3) and on reaching the Content D, one knows under what conditions my utterance is true. The nominal contributes to the Content C, but is not found in the Content D: the object designated by the utterance of "that" fills the gap opened by the CD, and the nominal is semantically inert with respect to the Content D, not contributing anything to the Content D. If CDs are complex referring terms and if the Singular Reference Assumption is correct, then the nominal in a CD introduces an element for which there is no room in Content D, because the form of the proposition expressed by a referring-term sentence does not make room for the condition determined by the nominal. I emphasize that the nominal brings in its standard semantic contribution, a condition, and that the latter is part of Content C. However, the condition contributed by the nominal is excluded from the Content D by the very form of the singular proposition. I will say that the nominal in a CD overarticulates a constituent. Let me explain.

8 Overarticulating Constituents

A constituent is articulated if it is both provided by a lexical element and part of the truth-conditions of an utterance. As I understand it, articulation is about the official content or Content D. It does not concern reflexive truth-conditions, but what in the *world* makes an utterance true. My utterance of (I) expresses a proposition D having all its constituents articulated because each echoes a lexical item. All versions of the Articulated View take the condition determined by the clause of a CD to be an articulated constituent, part of the truth-conditions of the utterance. The Character View does not. Unarticulation recently entered the philosophical landscape. A constituent is unarticulated if it is not provided by a lexical item in the sentence but it is required to have a truth-valuable entity or proposition D. Unarticulation is also about Content D. For example, the Content D expressed by an utterance of "It is raining" contains an unarticulated constituent, a place, because there is no term for a location in this sentence (Perry 2001), and a place is required to have a truth-valuable nonreflexive proposition, the Content D. That constituent, the place, does not echo a lexical item in the sentence uttered. I want to introduce the notion of overarticulation. Let us say that a constituent is overarticulated if it is semantically given by a lexical element in a sentence, is part of Content C but is not part of the truth-conditions or Content D of an utterance of that sentence. The lexical item finds no echo in the Content D. Let us go back to complex demonstratives.

The linguistic meaning of the nominal is not ignored by anyone understanding the meaning of (3), and the condition determined by the nominal is part of Content M. We do not want to say that a nominal is not cognitively significant. A speaker uttering (2) and a speaker uttering (3) are making utterances differing in cognitive value. The Content C contains no object and echoes the linguistic meaning of the terms occurring in a sentence. The nominal in a CD introduces a condition into Content C, hence preserving semantic stability and making clear the difference in the cognitive value of utterances of (2) and (3). The cognitive value of an utterance is the Content C of the utterance. The Content D is the aspect of the world making my utterance true. It contains objects connected to referring terms. Content D is what philosophers have in mind when they say that utterances of sentences containing referring terms express singular propositions containing the object referred to by the referring term. Complex demonstratives are referring terms having a structure and components, and the Singular Reference Assumption leaves room for only one truth-conditional element in the Content D expressed by an utterance of a CD sentence. This element is the object introduced by a referring term, the CD, and not a condition introduced by a nominal. The nominal in a CD introduces an overarticulated constituent: it is semantically relevant and is echoed in the cognitive value of the utterance. The nominal semantically contributes a condition (to Content C) and in that sense semantic stability is preserved. However, it does not introduce any constituent or condition in Content D. The reason why it does not has nothing to do with the semantics of CDs, but follows from CDs having a structure, echoed in Content C, and the Singular Reference Assumption, a view on the official truth-conditions of utterances of sentences containing referring terms. Let me rephrase what I wrote earlier: if complex demonstratives are complex referring terms, and if the nominal semantically contribute a condition, then the Singular Reference Assumption implies that the nominal in a CD introduces an overarticulated constituent, that is, an element for which there is no room in Content D or official truth-conditions of an utterance of a CD sentence. I want to emphasize that the nominal is both cognitively significant and helpful in identifying the designated object.[7]

9   Back to Misdemonstrations

Suppose that I utter (4) and designate a faculty member. In understanding the language, you grasp the meaning of the sentence.

Content M < [One object x most salient to the speaker of "that" in c]
[x is a student], x is smart>, u

Focusing on the specific utterance u, you get reflexive truth-conditions.

Content C < [One object x most salient to the speaker of u]
[x is a student], x is smart>

Knowing more about the context of utterance, you reach nonreflexive truth-conditions, the official content.

Content D < MARY , being smart>

You know that I am wrong because the object in the Content D does not fit what I think about it, the Content C. There is a mismatch between my cognitive life (Content C)—I believe that one object x most salient to me is a student, and has the property of being smart—and the world (Content D)—I say of Mary, who is not a student, that she is smart. The Content D my utterance expresses is true. My utterance does not express a false proposition or no proposition at all. I am just wrong about a property of Mary.

I need no extra referring intentions to designate the speaker, even if the latter does not satisfy the condition determined by the nominal, and you need not identify extra referring intentions to identify the object I designated, even if she [Mary] does not satisfy the condition determined by the nominal. This picture also explains why on hearing a speaker uttering "That *Claraveriadelphus truncatus* is great" and designating an object, one can identify the singular proposition or Content D expressed even if one does not understand the meaning of "*Claraveriadelphus truncatus.*" Consider my

---

[7] Now the phenomenon of overarticulation is not confined to complex demonstratives; it is also characteristic of terms like "but," "however," and so on. These expressions are conventional implicature devices (see Frege 1892 and Grice 1989) famous for having a linguistic meaning—hence, on the present picture, introducing a component in the content M of an utterance containing a conventional implicature device—but lacking truth-conditional relevance—introducing no constituent into the content D expressed by an utterance. Unfortunately, I cannot explore this topic here, and I leave it for another occasion (see my "Conventional Implicature Revisited" manuscript).

utterance of "That *Claraveriadelphus truncatus* is great." Thanks to linguistic meaning, we have:

Content M < [One object x most salient to the speaker of "that" in c]
[x is a *Claraveriadelphus truncatus*], x is great>, u

You know that "*Claraveriadelphus truncatus*" means something, but you do not know what it means. Focusing on the utterance *u*, you reach the reflexive content.

Content C < [One object x most salient to the speaker of *u*]
[x is a *Claraveriadelphus truncatus*], x is great>

As far as the Content D is concerned, you can ignore the meaning of the nominal and its cognitive value and, from "one object x is most salient to the speaker of u," you can reach an object, whatever the nominal:

Content D < Î , being great>

where Î is the mushroom. From your point of view, the cognitive value, or Content C, of the utterance is poor because you do not understand the meaning of "*Claraveriadelphus truncates*" and the cognitive significance of that expression. You would neither accept nor reject the Content C. Still, you have the Content D of the utterance.

10 Subcontents

Philosophers working on this topic want to capture some intuitive relations. For example, from an utterance of (4) one can infer that one object salient to the speaker is a student. This is a proposition captured by the Articulated View. One can get it from the subject term in Content C. I call it the sub-Content C of the utterance

Subcontent C of (4) <[One object x most salient to the speaker of *u*]
[x is a student]>

Placing that subpart of C in a context, and identifying the referent of "one object x most salient to the speaker of *u*," you get a false singular proposition. I will say that one can extract such a proposition and I call it the Sub-content D of the utterance.

Subcontent D of (4) <Mary, being student>

This is not the official content or the Content D of (4). Notice also that because it is extracted from Subcontent C, it is not on a par with Content D. My view coheres with Corazza's, Dever's, and Richard's, (who contend that this is the background proposition). One can obtain that proposition by semantic, rather than syntactic, means. The extracted singular proposition is not the official content of the utterance, and that is why the utterance has clear truth-conditions. The Content D contains the object referred to by the utterance of the demonstrative and the conditions determined by the predicate.

Content D of (4) < MARY, being smart>

This is what Corazza calls the principal proposition, and what Perry calls the official content of the utterance.

Let us compare the Character View, the Articulated View, and my suggestion. The Character View preserves the Singular Reference Assumption and the intuition that COs are complex referring terms. However, it does not satisfy the Semantic Stability Assumption and does not clearly capture the cognitive significance of CD utterances. My suggestion takes COs to be complex referring terms and captures the Singular Reference Assumption and semantic stability. It also gives a Fregean account of the cognitive significance of utterances of CD sentences. The Articulated View preserves the Singular Reference Assumption and semantic stability, and captures the cognitive significance of CD utterances. Unfortunately, it rejects the intuition that COs are lexically complex referring terms. My picture preserves that intuition. Finally, the Articulated View does not account for the idea that the nominal is helpful to identify the object referred to. My view does. As distinct from the Articulated View and the Character View, it requires no modification in our intuitive understanding of COs and CD sentences. My suggestion does not require abandoning the idea that COs are lexically complex referring terms, or the idea that the bare demonstrative and nominal do not semantically behave in a standard way when occurring in a CD. My picture also follows from a comprehensive picture of context-sensitive referring terms. Dever's Articulated View is committed to a "many-propositions" stand, where these propositions are logically independent. The Reflexive-Referential View also introduces many propositions. However, the latter are not logically independent, accounting for the intuitive semantic cohesion found in CD sentences, and one single proposition plays the role of official truth-conditions of the utterance. I have a preference for logical dependence, semantic cohesion, and "one single proposition as official truth-conditions of utterances" theories.

11 Conclusion

Following the Singular Reference Assumption, an utterance of (3) ex- presses a singular proposition containing the designated object and the condition determined by the predicate. On my view, the utterance of "That" introduces an object filling the gap in the singular proposition, and there is no room for the condition determined by the nominal. If the Singular Reference Assumption is true, the form of the proposition expressed by a CD utterance blocks the condition contributed by the nominal from entering the Content D. According to the view I am suggesting, the bare demonstrative in a CD introduces an object into the official truth-conditions of the utterance, and the Singular Reference Assumption is preserved. The nominal introduces a cognitively significant, but overarticulated, constituent because it fails to introduce a condition in Content D or official content. Still, semantic stability is preserved and the condition introduced by the nominal is truth-conditionally relevant because it is relevant to the truth-conditions of Content C.

Suppose that you hear an utterance of (3) and an utterance of

(7)   That piece of junk is yellow,

where in both cases the same object is designated: your car. The Content C of these utterances will differ because the nominal are different. The Content D will be the same, even if you disagree with the nominal and can extract a false singular proposition from Content C. The same mechanism explains why on hearing my utterance of (4), you smile. You identified both Content C and Content D, and saw the mismatch between my cognitive life and the world.

The Lexical Simplicity Assumption is false: CDs are complex referring expressions. The falsity of the Lexical Simplicity Assumption is compatible with the truth of the Singular Reference Assumption. I did not offer arguments in favor of the Singular Reference Assumption, and one may want to reject it. My cautious conclusion is that if one takes CDs to be syntactically complex referring terms, and if one wants to preserve the Singular Reference Assumption, then my suggestion is a serious, natural option. My view abandons the Lexical Simplicity Assumption. I prefer to say that it emphasizes and takes seriously the complexity of the referential devices in natural languages. Finally, it assumes an account of the semantics of bare demonstrative. My view on CDs is designed to fit the accounts on the market, and requires only that bare demonstratives are referring terms.

My article has not discussed problems connected to quantifiers, anaphora, and complex demonstratives (see Davies 1982). For instance, I do not examine sentences like "*The woman next to Paul* likes that man talking to *her*" or "That man talking to *Mary* admires *her*." I leave this topic for another occasion.[8]

---

[8] I would like to thank Brendan Gillon, John Perry, and Arthur Sullivan for discussions. Catherine Wearing made very detailed comments on an early version of this article, and Rob Stainton sent me a heavily annotated later version. I am sure that I did not answer all their questions. The usual disclaimers apply. I dedicate this article to the memory of Nicolas Kaufmann.

References

Borg, Emma. 2000. "Complex Demonstratives." *Philosophical Studies*, 97: 229-49.

Braun, David. 1995. "Structured Characters and Complex Demonstratives." *Journal of Philosophical Logic*, 24: 227-40.

Corazza, Eros. 2002. "'She' and 'He': Politically Correct Pronouns." *Philosophical Studies*, 111: 173-96.

Davies, Martin. 1982. "Individuation and the Semantics of Demonstratives." *Journal of Philosophical Logic*, 111: 287-310.

Dever, Josh. 2001. "Complex Demonstratives." *Linguistics and Philosophy*, 24: 271-330.

Frege, Gottlob. 1892. "On Sense and Reference." In *Philosophical Writings of Gottlob Frege*. Oxford: Basil Blackwell.

Grice, H. P. 1989. "On Sense and Reference." In *Studies in the Ways of Words*. Cambridge, MA: Harvard University Press.

Johnson, Ken and Ernest Lepore. 2002. "Does Syntax Reveal Semantics? A Case Study of Complex Demonstratives." In *Philosophical Perspectives*. Vol. 16, *Language and Mind*. Edited by J. Tomberlin. Atascadaro, CA: Ridgeview Press.

Kaplan, David. 1989a. "Demonstratives." In *Themes from Kaplan*. Edited by Joseph Almog et al. New York: Oxford University Press, pp. 481-563.

Kaplan, David. 1989b. "Afterthoughts." In *Themes from Kaplan*. Edited by Joseph Almog et al. New York: Oxford University Press, pp. 565-614.

King, Jeffrey. 2001. *Complex Demonstratives*. Cambridge, MA: MIT Press.

Larson, Richard and George Segal. 1995. *Knowledge and Meaning*. Cambridge, MA: MIT Press.

Lepore, Ernest and Kirk Ludwig. 2000. "The Semantics and Pragmatics of Complex Demonstratives." *Mind*, 109: 199-240.

Perry, John. 1996. "Indexicals and Demonstratives." In *Companion to the Philosophy of Language*. Edited by Robert Hale and Crispin Wright. Oxford: Basil Blackwell, pp. 586-612.

Perry, John. 2000. *The Problems of the Essential Indexical and Other Essays*. Expanded ed. Stanford, CA: CSLI Publications.

Perry, John. 2001. *Reference and Reflexivity*. Stanford, CA: CSLI Publications.

Predelli, Stefano. 2001. "Complex Demonstratives and Anaphora." *Analysis*, 61: 53-59.

Récanti, François. 1992. *Direct Reference*. London: Basil Blackwell.

Récanti, François. 2004. *Literal Meaning*. New York: Cambridge University Press.

Richard Mark. 1993. "Articulated Terms." In *Philosophical Perspectives*. Vol. 7, *Logic and Language*. Edited by James Tomberlin. Atascadero, CA: Ridgeview Press, pp. 207-230.

4

Unarticulated Comparison Classes

1 Relative Gradable Adjectives

Attributive adjectives such as "tall," "short," and "big" are subsective (see Chierchia and MacConnell-Ginet 1990: 463) in that tall men are men, short pants are pants, and big ants are ants.[1] These adjectives are also gradable. A person can be very tall, a pair of pants can be too short, and an ant can be rather big. They can likewise form comparatives such as "taller," "shorter", and "bigger," and superlatives, such as "tallest," "shortest", and "biggest." They are sometimes called comparative (Lepore and Cappelen 2005; Maitra 2007) or gradable adjectives (Glanzberg 2007). They are also known in the linguistic literature as relative gradable adjectives (Kennedy 2007).[2] Relative gradable adjectives share features with indexicals and demonstratives in that relative gradable adjective sentences can change in truth-value from utterance to utterance. For example,

(1)   Monica is tall.

is a complete sentence and utterances of this sentence can differ in truth-value. Suppose that Monica is five years old. I see Monica playing with children of her age, notice that she is slightly taller than most of the others, and make an utterance of (1). Given her height, most people would say that my utterance is true. However, if I see Monica in a group of adults and make an utterance of (1), a standard reaction would be to reply that my utterance is simply false (Stanley 2007; Corazza and Dokic 2007;

---

[1] The list of adjectives I am interested in also includes "fast", "slow", "rich", "poor", "young", "old", and so on.

[2] See also Leslie 2007.

Clapp 2007; MacFarlane 2007). Likewise, it is quite common to assign a truth-value to a relative sentence utterance after taking into account a salient comparison class. The sentence (1) or utterances of (1) are true or false depending on what or whom Monica is compared to, that is a comparison class. It is true if Monica is tall when she is compared to a group of five-year-old children, and it is false when compared to human adults.[3] The adjective "tall" in (1) is the only lexical item such variability can be traced back to. It is natural to think (contra Lepore and Cappelen 2005) that "tall" and other relative gradable adjectives are context-sensitive items (see especially S.-J. Leslie 2007).[4]

In contrast with standard, automatic context-sensitive items, such as "I", relative adjectives, as type, lack linguistic meaning determining an utterance-variable, truth-conditionally relevant item such as a comparison class component of the truth conditions of an utterance (See also Corazza and Dokic 2007: 171 fn. 3). Different utterances of (1) can differ in truth-value, but there is no simple semantic explanation as to why the truth conditions of each utterance can differ, that is, how different comparison classes can be introduced into the truth conditions of different utterances of (1). That being said, relative adjectives are the main suspect for the variation in truth-value and in truth conditions of different relative adjective sentence utterances, such as utterances of (1), and seem to be context-sensitive. The difficulty, however, is that our current view on context sensitivity as being connected to linguistic meaning has no application here. The present paper is about the supposed context-sensitivity of relative gradable adjectives and comparison classes. I want to suggest that the context-sensitivity of linguistic items is not only due to linguistic meaning, and that the relative adjective category itself encodes an aspect making these adjectives sensitive to context. It is not my intention here to critically assess alternative views about relative gradable adjectives but rather to provide a positive alternative. As is usual in philosophy of language, I

---

[3] See also Hawthorne (2004: 53–54). I focus on the positive form of the adjectives.

[4] Add to that picture of relative as context-sensitive terms that these expressions clearly pass Lepore and Cappelen's Intercontextual Disquotation test (Lepore and Cappelen 2005: 135), a noncontroversial test for detecting context-sensitive terms

(ICD) There are (or can be) false utterances of "S" even though S

For example, there are false utterances of "Monica is tall"—when she is compared to adults—even though Monica is tall—when I am comparing her height to the height of five years old children. (see also Leslie 2007: 138).

focus on relative gradable predicates, that is, predicates containing relative gradable adjectives such as "is tall" rather than on adjectives.

First, I want to explore a few intuitions about relative gradable predicates and to clarify some points. Second, I propose a multipropositionalist, Perry-inspired, perspective on relative gradable predicate utterances. Perry's version of multi-propositionalism introduces many different propositions or contents, including indexical content, referential content and designational content, which are carried by the utterance of a single sentence. It also offers a new approach to relative gradable predicates, and suggests an explanation for the way relative predicates work in linguistic communication and for the divergent intuitions about these predicates. Or so I shall argue.

2   Intuitions about Relative Gradable Predicates

Let me introduce a first set of intuitions. It is widely[5] acknowledged that nothing is tall *simpliciter*. Call the idea that nothing is tall *simpliciter* an ontological intuition. The ontological intuition is not specifically about "is tall" and it easily generalizes to all relative gradable predicates, such as "is short" "is big", or "is fast": nothing is short *simpliciter*, nothing is big *simpliciter*, nothing is fast *simpliciter*, and so on. This intuition gives a defining feature of relative gradable predicates and it captures an important aspect of that category of terms. Let me rephrase it in a more general way:

> *Ontological intuition*: If "F" is a relative gradable adjective, then nothing is F *simpliciter*.

The Ontological intuition is a general negative view on relative gradable adjectives or predicates, not a metaphysical theory on what tallness is for example; it does not imply anything specific with respect to what tallness really is or is not. There is simply no metaphysics of tallness underlying the idea that nothing is tall *simpliciter*. The Ontological intuition is not about relative predicates with a comparison class. It does not apply to "is tall for an Inuit" for example.

It is also common place that specific relative gradable predicate sentence utterances vary in truth-value, and a comparison class is standardly invoked to explain differences in truth conditions and in truth-value.[6] Let

---

[5] But not universally. See Cappelen and Lepore 2005: 170 ff.

[6] See, for example, Ludlow 1989: 321; Chierchia and McConnell-Ginet 1990: 463–464; Clapp 2001: 237; Clapp 2007: 253; Recanati 2004; Stanley 2005, 2007; Borg 2007; Maitra 2007; Corazza and Dokic 2007. I follow commonsense and tradition in assigning a comparison class. It can be argued that the comparison class is provided by the category of object designat-

us return to Monica and my utterance of (1). According to the intuition we are examining, my utterance is true if and only if, say, she is *tall for a five-year-old*, not tall for a human being or tall for a hockey player. My utterance is false if the height of Monica is compared to the height of adult human beings or hockey players: Monica is not tall compared to adult human beings or hockey players. Let us call the idea that a comparison class is required for the truth-valuation of specific relative gradable predicate utterances the Pragmatic intuition.[7]

> *Pragmatic intuition*: If "F" is a relative gradable adjective, then an utterance u of "a is F" is true if and only if a is F relative to the comparison class specific to u, where u is a specific utterance.

According to the Pragmatic intuition, no truth-value can be assigned to a relative predicate sentence utterance without considering, implicitly or explicitly, a comparison class. From this perspective, the problem resides in accounting for how a specific comparison class can be introduced into the truth conditions of an utterance of (1) for example. It also lies in explaining how different comparison classes, relevant for different utterances of the same relative predicate, can be introduced in different utterances.[8]

---

ed by the head noun phrase—a human being for instance. However, objects belong to many different categories: teenagers, human beings, males, and so on.

[7] It is often put by saying that the context, not a lexical item, provides a comparison class for the relative gradable predicate used in the context (for example, Maitra 2007). This detail is irrelevant to my main point.

[8] In the relevant cases, the comparison class is not provided by a lexical item in the sentence, and it is not a semantically determined constituent of the truth conditions of utterances. No lexical item in my utterance of (1) introduces a truth-conditionally relevant comparison class into the truth conditions of the utterance. According to Perry (2000, 2001, 2007), a non-lexicalized truth-conditionally relevant component of the truth conditions of an utterance is an unarticulated constituent. Unarticulated constituents were introduced to account for the truth-conditions of some utterances of "rain" sentences. An utterance of "It is raining" is true or false depending on a location. An utterance of "It is raining" can be true if and only if it is raining in Paris. The location, Paris, is not articulated in the uttered sentence, "It is raining", since no lexical item in the sentence refers to that city. The location could be articulated by "in Paris". The proposition expressed by an utterance of "It is raining" with Paris as an unarticulated constituent, and an utterance of "It is raining in Paris", where the location is articulated, have the same truth conditions and the same truth-value. The unarticulated constituents we are interested in here can vary from utterance to utterance. The proposition expressed by a different utterance of "It is raining" can be true if and only if it raining in San Francisco, and contains San Francisco as an unarticulated constituent. In that respect, the truth conditions of relative gradable utterances are similar to the truth-conditions of "rain" sentences: the unarticulated constituent, a comparison class, can vary from utterance to utterance. My utterance of (1) is true if five-year-old children are taken as a comparison class, and can also be true if Monica's brothers and sisters are taken as the relevant comparison class. Accordingly, what is truth-valued is not a sentence but an utterance, and different utterances of the same relative gradable predicate sentence can vary in truth conditions and in truth-value. I propose an account of relative predicates based on Perry's view on unarticulated constituents, and accounting for

The Ontological and the Pragmatic intuitions are fairly robust and cannot be rejected without an argument.

Let us consider a second set of intuitions. Tradition in the philosophy of language assumes that one-place predicates, such as "is square" and "is blue" are echoed in ontology by properties, such as being square and being blue. On that picture, what the predicate "is square" means linguistically also plausibly determines the property of being square. Consider relative predicates ("is tall", "is short", "is big", and so on). Following this model, "is tall" is a one-place predicate, and it semantically determines a property, being tall. "Is tall" is prima facie a context insensitive expression, since, as distinct from "I", its linguistic meaning does not render it reactive to aspects of the context (Lepore and Cappelen 2005; MacFarlane 2007: 247; Corazza and Dokic 2007). "Is tall" thus semantically determines the same property for all utterances. This picture can be generalized. Let us call it the Syntactic intuition.

Syntactic intuition: If "F" is a relative gradable adjective, then "is F" is a one-place predicate determining a property.

The Syntactic intuition is based on the *prima facie* syntactic category of "is tall" and relative gradable predicates, not on a metaphysical view concerning tallness for example. The Syntactic intuition is not supported by a strong metaphysical view of what tallness is or of what tall objects have in common, nor does it not imply any.[9] Furthermore, it does not suggest any specific view of what tallness is or of what tall objects have in common — except being tall. The intuition simply assumes that the linguistic meaning of all relative gradable predicates, just like the linguistic meaning of regular one-place predicates, determines a property. The Syntactic intuition nourishes the view that there is something akin to the property of being tall, whatever that property is, and that all relative gradable predicates determine properties.

An assertive sentence is true or false. (1) is an assertive sentence and it is *prima facie* true or false: "Monica is tall" is true if and only if Monica, the object referred to by the name, is tall. In other words, it is true if and only if she exemplifies the property of being tall (Lepore and Cappelen 2005; Corazza and Dokic 2007; MacFarlane 2007). Schema T applies smoothly and it also applies to all relative gradable predicate assertive sentences. Let us call this the Semantic intuition.

Semantic intuition: If "F" is a relative gradable adjective, then "a is F" is a true or false sentence.

---

their role in the determination of truth-conditions and assignment of truth-value to utterances. See Neale 2007 for an exploration of Perry's view on unarticulation.

[9] See especially Lepore and Cappelen (2005: 170–171).

The Semantic intuition does not reflect a metaphysical view or empirical knowledge concerning tallness, but arguably results from the fact that relative gradable predicate sentences like (1) are assertive sentences and an application of schema T. In keeping with the intuition, and in accord with what Bach (2002) calls the Syntactic Correlation Constraint, a relative gradable predicate sentence utterance does not convey a comparison class: none is conveyed by meaning, none is articulated by a lexical item, and hence no such class can be extracted from the sentence. If a comparison class is introduced, it is on the ground of nonlinguistic factors. The Syntactic and the Semantic intuitions thus dovetail. Not only are these intuitions also robust, but they require a strong argument to be rejected. I will come back to these two sets of intuitions further on.

3   Relativity and Vagueness

I want to make clear from the outset that the issue I am concerned with differs from vagueness. A predicate is vague if it has no clear application in some cases. Yul Brynner clearly exemplifies baldness, Sean Connery does not clearly exemplify baldness, and Lenny Kravitz clearly does not exemplify baldness. Is Sean Connery bald? Yes and no. "Is bald" has no clear application in the case of Sean Connery. Correlatively, some "is bald" sentences are neither determinately true nor determinately false. "Yul Brynner is bald" is true, "Lenny Kravitz is bald" is false, and "Sean Connery is bald" is neither clearly true nor clearly false. The vagueness of the predicate is echoed in an assignment of truth-value to the vague predicate sentence. Vague predicates lack clear application *in some cases* and vague predicate sentences, even if having truth conditions, cannot be assigned a truth-value *in some cases*. "Is bald" is a vague predicate without being a relative gradable predicate. *Prima facie*, the problem with relative gradable predicates is not that they have no clear application in some cases. Likewise, the problem with relative gradable predicate sentences or utterances is not that some are neither clearly true nor clearly false. Following the Ontological intuition, they have no application in any case: nothing is tall *simpliciter*. Following the Pragmatic intuition, relative predicate sentence utterances cannot be assigned a truth-value *in any case* without taking into consideration a comparison class. *Prima facie*, it is simply false that "is tall" can have an application without considering a comparison class, and that utterances of (1), or "tall" sentences, can be assigned a truth-value without taking a comparison class into account. Adding a comparison classes is a semantic issue involving the addition of material required for the predicate to have an application, and of truth-conditionally relevant material needed for the assignment of truth-value to utterances. This does not mean that a relative gradable predicate with a comparison class cannot be vague. "Is tall for a man" is a relative gradable predicate supplemented with a comparison class, and yet it is vague.[10] Michael Jordan is tall for a man, Danny Devito is not tall for a man, and Kevin Costner is neither clearly tall for a man nor clearly not tall for a man. But that is a different issue which does not concern relative gradable predicates.

The view that relative gradable predicates are vague lumps lacking a clear application and the comparison classes required for the predicate to have an application. It likewise brings together the idea of not being determinately true nor determinately false and the lack of truth conditions. Most discussions on the vagueness of these predicates assume a comparison class, implicitly or explicitly. I will come back to vagueness at the end of the paper.

4 Multipropositionalism

The recent discussions on relative gradable predicate sentences take place in monopropositionalist frameworks.

> Monopropositionalism: a complete sentence or an utterance of a complete sentence is associated with one and only one proposition.[11]

Monopropositionalism is a traditional viewpoint in semantics in which one proposition usually plays many different roles, such as truth conditions, bearers of truth-value, thought contents, and so on. Multipropositionalism adopts a quite different approach.

> Multipropositionalism: an utterance of a complete sentence carries many different propositions—excluding presuppositions and implicatures.

The multipropositionalist framework is utterance oriented. It assumes that the utterance of a single sentence can convey many different propositions whose identification depends on what is taken into consideration. It also takes into account various features of utterances: linguistic meaning, nonlinguistic facts, cognitive significance, context-sensitivity, truth conditions, and various types of context. I want to argue that it also explains the *prima facie* features of relative gradable adjective sentence utterances—

---

[10] See Graff 2000.

[11] This definition is inspired by Corazza and Korta ("Two dogmas of Philosophical Linguistics", forthcoming).

their context-sensitivity, their inclusion of a comparison class, and their *prima facie* vagueness—in a manner that makes it clear how these predicates work in linguistic communication. Let me first provide a short sketch of Perry's multipropositionalism.

From this point of view, the conventional linguistic meaning of a lexical item understood as type is a rule that determines the propositional component expressed by an utterance of that item. Meaning is not propositional. The linguistic meaning of a sentence as type is compositional, and it respects the meaning of the words occurring in the sentence as well as the syntactic structure of that sentence. It also determines a proposition semantically carried by an utterance of that sentence. A proposition or content is a truth-valuable abstract entity, and meaning is not. Multipropositionalism introduces a manifold of propositions or contents conveyed by a single utterance. I will mainly consider three in the present paper: indexical content, referential content, and designational content, which have a special relevance in the present debate.[12]

Suppose that I make an utterance **u** of "I like Sponge Bob" and assume that we have the linguistic meaning of this sentence as type. Thanks only to your linguistic competence, you understand that

> the utterance **u** of "I like Sponge Bob" is true if and only if *the speaker of* **u** likes the person the convention exploited by **u** designates with *"Sponge Bob"*.[13]

I use boldface to indicate that the constituent is an object—here, an utterance. I use italics to indicate that the constituent of the proposition is not an object but an identifying condition. The indexical content of the utterance is

> *the speaker of* **u** likes *the person the convention exploited by* **u** *designates with "Sponge Bob"*

It is also a reflexive content because it contains the utterance itself as a constituent. The indexical content of an utterance is a property of a specific utterance and it contains only the semantically determined contribution of each word to a proposition expressed by the utterance of a sentence. For that reason, indexical content is grasped through linguistic knowledge only. Given the utterance, any semantically competent speaker knows the indexical content *a priori*.

---

[12] See Perry and Korta 2006, 2007 for the relationship of that framework to Minimalism.
[13] I assume knowledge of Perry's view on proper names.

In making my utterance, I do not want to communicate that *the speaker of* **u** *likes the person the convention exploited by* **u** *designates with "Sponge Bob"*. The indexical content does not give the intuitive truth conditions of my utterance. Knowing the context of utterance, you can identify the speaker of the utterance and obtain the referential content. The referential content is the content obtained once facts about the context of utterance needed to determine what is designated by indexicals are taken into consideration:

> **RV** likes *the person the convention exploited by* **u** *designates with "Sponge Bob"*.

RV stands for me. This referential content is still reflexive and it does not provide the official truth conditions of the utterance. The designational content does however. The designational content is the content obtained once facts about the utterance and other facts needed "to fix the designation of the terms that remain (definite descriptions in particular, but also possessives, etc.)" (Perry 2001: 83) are taken into account. I want to convey that I like Sponge Bob. What I want to convey is not reflexive and it does not contain the utterance as a constitutent. Moreover, it does not contain identifying condition. Indexical content provides what is needed to give the intuitive truth conditions of an utterance. The indexical "I" does not contribute a condition, *being the speaker of the utterance*, but an object, the referent of the utterance of "I" or the speaker himself, to the intuitive truth conditions or designational content of the utterance. The name "Sponge Bob" does not contribute an identifying condition but an object, Sponge Bob himself, to the designational content of the utterance. Given indexical content, and taking extralinguistic features of the specific utterance u into consideration, namely who the speaker of the utterance is and the referent the convention governing "Sponge Bob" in that utterance determines, one can identify the object referred to by that utterance of "I", me, and the referent of the name: Sponge Bob, the cartoon character. One then arrives at a nonreflexive content containing objects rather that identifying conditions:

> **RV** likes **SB**.

SB stands for Sponge Bob. It is the designational content carried by my utterance of "I like Sponge Bob". It is the non reflexive content obtained after determining—by relying on extralinguistic, contextual information—to what the indexical and the proper name refer. Designational content fits what we call the intuitive truth-conditions of the utterance.

In the case of indexical utterances, like first-person sentence utterances, indexical and referential content always differ. Suppose that I am organizing a party, leave home for an hour, and find a message on my answering machine when I come back: "I will bring beer". *I understand that the speaker of the utterance* **u** will bring beer. However, I cannot identify the speaker and cannot get the referential content of the utterance. Who will bring beer? The distinguishing of indexical and referential content accounts for the fact that I understand the note but do not grasp its intuitive truth conditions.

In that framework, there are many propositions a hearer can grasp. In the "Sponge Bob" example, a hearer can grasp only the indexical content of my utterance. One can also understand the indexical content of the utterance, and grasp its referential content without grasping its designational content. One can also understand the indexical content and grasp both the referential and the designational content.

5   Cognitive Significance

Frege (1892: 56) underlines the idea that sentences have cognitive value: some hold a priori while others do not, and "contain very valuable extensions of our knowledge". Truth conditions and thought contents are being emphasized in recent philosophy of language, while cognitive value, as well as the cognitive aspects of words, are being downplayed in semantics. Nonetheless, the latter have a major role in linguistic communication. Perry (2000) rightly refocused the debate and draws attention to the cognitive significance of utterances. I think, moreover, that this is an underestimated aspect of his multipropositionalist approach. Perry mentions that "if there is some aspect of meaning, by which an utterance u of S and an utterance u 'of S' differ, so that a rational person who understood both S and S' might accept u but not u', then a fully adequate theory of linguistic meaning should say what it is" (Perry 2001: 194). In this approach, cognitive significance is defined in terms of acceptance of utterances—or accepting an utterance as true (Perry 2000: 193)—without taking extralinguistic facts into considerations. Perry also gives conditions on the cognitive significance of an utterance:

   a.   The cognitive significance of an utterance S in language L is a semantic property of the utterance.
   b.   It is a property that a person who understands the meaning of S in L recognizes.
   c.   The cognitive significance of an utterance of S in L is a proposition.

d.   A person who understands the meaning of S in L, and accepts as true an utterance of S in L, will believe the proposition that is the cognitive significance of the utterance (ibid.: 194).

Perry focuses on utterances of two different sentences S and S' in his contention. His view is more in line with different utterances of the same sentence type, where the relevant sentence is an indexical or a demonstrative sentence. In his 1988 paper, he examines the difference in cognitive significance of two utterances of "you are spilling coffee". An utterance **u** of that sentence is true if and only if *the addressee of* **u** is spilling coffee; an utterance **u**' of the same sentence is true if and only if *the addressee of* **u**' is spilling coffee. These two utterances carry two different indexical contents. The indexical content is reflexive and fits cognitive significance: (i) it is a semantic property of the utterance, (ii) it is a property that a person who understands the meaning of the sentence recognizes, (iii) it is a proposition, and (iv) a person who accepts as true an utterance of the sentence will believe the proposition that is the cognitive significance of the utterance. The cognitive significance of different utterances of "you are spilling coffee" differs because the meaning of "you" refers to different utterances. Different utterances of the same indexical sentence can differ in cognitive significance, even if they share the same intuitive truth conditions. For example, we can both address Perry and say "you are spilling coffee". Our utterances differ in cognitive significance—Perry can reject the first one, hear the second one and, after a moment of hesitation, accept it—but they share the same referential content. Both are true if and only if **JP** is spilling coffee. By the same token, the cognitive significance of utterances of sentences such as "I like Sponge Bob" differs from the designational content or intuitive truth conditions of these utterances because cognitive significance contains the utterance itself as a constituent, while designational content does not. Going back to the previous example, the cognitive significance of my utterance of "I like Sponge Bob" is that *the speaker of* **u** likes *the person the convention exploited by* **u** *designates with "Sponge Bob"*. Its designational content is that **RV** likes **SB**. We can now employ multipropositionalism and examine relative gradable predicates.

6   Relative Gradable Predicates and Monopropositionalism

Suppose that we are watching the news. I see Sarkozy and say:

(2)   The President of France is tall.

You know the syntax of the sentence uttered and its linguistic meaning. According to the philosophical tradition, thanks to your knowledge of syntax and semantics, and whatever tallness is, you know that:

(I)   The utterance **u** of "The President of France is tall" is true if and only if the unique person having the property of being President of France is tall.

I set aside problems raised by proper names to focus on relative predicates. (I) fits both the Syntactic and the Semantic intuitions. Now, if, for an utterance of (2),

>   the unique person having the property of being President of France is tall

is the only available content, then different utterances of (2) will have the same truth conditions. Many competent speakers will reply that they do not. Following the Ontological intuition, (I) does not give the intuitive truth conditions of the utterance. Nothing is just tall. My utterance of (2) might be true if Sarkozy is compared to jockeys, but another utterance might be false if Sarkozy is standing beside a basketball team and I compare his size to that of the team members. Following the Pragmatic intuition, my utterance is true if and only if the unique person having the property of being President of France is tall with respect to a specific comparison class such as jockeys. According to the last intuition, (I) misses something in the assigned truth conditions of the utterance: an utterance specific comparison class.[14] Lepore and Cappelen (2005)—and anyone sharing the Syntactic and the Semantic intuition—would reject the Ontological and the Pragmatic intuitions. However, these intuitions are widely accepted, and many linguistically competent speakers will stick to their position and argue that a comparison class is missing. Nonetheless, the topic is still very controversial.

If we stay within the limits of a monopropositionalist framework and continue to focus on linguistic meaning, truth conditions, truth-value, and comparison classes we merely create room for divergent intuitions and do not clarify the debate. Let us put multipropositionalism, and Perry's notion of cognitive significance of utterances, to work. We will then stay clear from highly debated truth-conditions and truth-value.

---

[14] Just like utterances of "It is raining" miss something in their official truth-conditions to get a truth-valuable proposition, a location. The location is not articulated in the sentence.

7 Relative Gradable Predicates and Cognitive Significance

If

> the unique person having the property of being President of France is tall

is the only available content, as it is according to the monopropositionalist framework, then it is also the only possible candidate for the cognitive significance of the utterance. As a consequence, different utterances of (2) have the same cognitive significance. However, a rational speaker can accept an utterance **u** of (2), and reject another utterance, **u'**, of the same sentence. I see the President of France walking with jockeys and utter (2). You accept my utterance. You add "Compared to these guys, who isn't?". I see the President of France talking to a group of basketball players and utter (2). You reject my utterance of (2). You look at me and say "No, the other guys are tall". The linguistic meaning is the same, and the facts about the President of France did not change. These data are very hard to deny (see also Corazza and Dokic 2007) as the two utterances **u** and **u'** of (2) can clearly differ in cognitive significance.

Now, my argument need not invoke the actual truth conditions and truth-value of different utterances of (2), nor the intuitions that concern the actual truth-conditions and truth-value of specific utterances of (2), nor comparison classes. It is grounded on the fact that you can rationally accept an utterance of (2) and reject a different utterance of the same sentence. Moreover, you would be quite irrational in accepting all utterances of a relative gradable predicate sentence, whatever the context, such as an utterance of (1) when talking about children of Monica's age, when seeing Monica walking next to a team of professional basketball players, or when talking to the coach of that team during a conversation on who should be signed. It is clearly false that a speaker accepting an utterance of (1) or (2) would also accept any other utterance of (1) or (2), and be rational in doing so. My argument takes, as it starting point, differences in cognitive significance, whatever the intuitive truth conditions and truth value may be, and is based on the cognitive aspect of utterances, not on what explains divergence in truth conditions and in truth-value of different specific utterances. The argument is also grounded on something speakers know without the help of extralinguistic information and without knowledge of intuitive truth conditions and truth-value: different utterances of (1) or (2) can differ in cognitive significance, whatever their intuitive truth conditions and truth-value. This divergence in attitude, and its rationality, deserves an explanation. Any view on relative predicate utterances assigning the same cognitive significance to different utterances of the same relative predicate sentence lacks plausibility. In this respect, the monopropositionalist framework fails to account for the cognitive significance of utterances of (1) or (2). What accounts for the fact that different utterances of (1) or (2) can differ in cognitive significance? Any explanation should satisfy a "knowable *a priori*" desiderata, because cognitive significance is known *a priori*.

8   Back to the Intuitions

Let us reconsider our second set of intuitions with cognitive significance in mind. Ordinary speakers learn that "tall" is an adjective, plausibly take "is tall" to be a one-place predicate, the meaning of which determines a property, and use that knowledge in their understanding of an utterance of (2). In this, they follow the Syntactic intuition—with all the metaphysical puzzles connected to the property of being tall supposedly expressed by the predicate. I do not wish to question the Syntactic intuition or the enigmas about properties that come with it. The latter are metaphysical enigmas, and I am not concerned here with metaphysics, but with the cognitive significance of utterance, which is not a metaphysical issue. The Syntactic intuition has an impact on the cognitive significance of utterance when paired to a semantic view on the propositions expressed by relative predicate sentence utterance. This brings us to the Semantic intuition.

Speakers apparently follow the Semantic intuition and know that the sentence (2) is true if and only if the unique person having the property of being President of France is tall. I do not want to argue that the Schema T has no application here. It does. One might argue that it focuses on sentences, and we are concerned with utterances. But let us set that worry aside. Does this content,

the unique person having the property of being President of France is tall,

give the intuitive truth conditions or designational content of the utterance? In answering that question, we enter familiar controversies we want to avoid. Let me ask a different question. Does the semantically determined content of sentence (2) give the cognitive significance of an utterance of (2)? Suppose that the answer is yes. All utterances of (2) then have the same cognitive significance. This content cannot account for the difference in cognitive significance of different utterances of (2). If two utterances of (2) have the same cognitive significance, no rational, semantically competent speakers can have divergent cognitive attitudes toward different utterances of (2). Linguistically competent speakers know that they can accept an utterance of (2) and reject a different utterance of the same sentence. *Eo ipso* they know that different utterances of (2) can differ in cognitive significance even if they share the same conventional linguistic meaning. If I am right, then, the semantically determined truth conditions are too poor to account for the cognitive significance of specific utterances of (2) and/or to explain divergences in cognitive attitudes. The Syntactic and Semantic intuitions are legitimate. However, the Syntactic intuition has an ontological scope that leaves no room for comparison classes and the Semantic intuition does not explain cognitive significance enigmas. Sticking to these intuitions simply ignores cognitive aspects of language. Let us move on to our first set of intuitions.

The Ontological intuition is a negative view, not a positive suggestion, and it provides no explanation for differences in cognitive significance. However, I do not think that we do justice to the Ontological intuition in saying that it is merely a negative view.

This intuition is clearly not about the linguistic meaning of "is tall" or the meaning of any relative gradable adjective as type. Is the intuition about facts? Is it empirical in nature? Plausibly not. A competent speaker need not conduct an empirical inquiry to realize that nothing is tall *simpliciter*, large *simpliciter*, or rich *simpliciter*. It would also be very surprising if more empirical research showed that the Ontological intuition is false, or that contrary to intuitions things are tall *simpliciter*. A speaker relying only on the material that is semantically determined *prima facie* by the relative predicate "is tall", and hence excluding comparison classes, would most certainly have a cognitively defective life: with the same facts in hand, and the same description of the world, one can accept an utterance of (2) and reject another one. Most of us have an accurate cognitive relationship to the world as far as relative predicates are concerned. For the same reasons, this speaker would not qualify as linguistically competent as far as relative gradable predicates are concerned. Most of us use these predicates appropriately. The Ontological intuition is not about linguistic meaning, metaphysics, or facts. It is more plausibly understood as being about the cognitive value of relative predicates. Moreover, it does not relate to the contribution of the conventional linguistic meaning of specific terms of that category to designational content or intuitive truth conditions. It concerns the contribution of any relative gradable predicate to the cognitive significance of utterances: there is more to it than what is contributed by the linguistic meaning of specific predicates. This suggests that the category of relative gradable predicates is not just a syntactic category that involves syntactic modes of composition of terms brought together to produce sentences and that disregards meaning. It is, arguably, a cognitive category dealing with the contribution of any terms of that category to the cognitive significance of utterances. "Nothing is tall *simpliciter*" is a remark echoing the difference an expression of the category of relative gradable predicates, whatever the specific predicate, makes to the cognitive significance of a relative gradable predicate sentence utterance. Being an F does not represent the whole story about the contribution made by a relative predicate such as "is F" to the cognitive significance of an utterance of a relative predicate sentence.

Following the Ontological intuition, the specific relative predicate "is tall" on the right hand side of "if and only if" in (I), like any relative predicate, requires something that accounts for its contribution to cognitive significance. Knowledge of the difference an expression of the category of relative predicates makes to the cognitive significance of an utterance, not the syntax or the conventional linguistic meaning of specific relative predicates, motivates the addition of a component to (I).

Let us now look at the Pragmatic intuition while keeping multipropositionalism and cognitive significance in mind.

Pragmatic intuition: If "F" is a relative gradable adjective, then "a is F" is a sentence and an utterance **u** of "a is F" is true if and only if *a is F* relative to the comparison class specific to **u**.

This is a general principle which simply says that there is a comparison class connected to the utterance. It does not mention any specific comparison class. The Pragmatic intuition is a positive viewpoint. But on what? Multipropositionalism offers at least two options. Suppose that the Pragmatic intuition is about the designational content or intuitive truth conditions of utterances. This option is a non starter: the intuition is general, no mention is made of any specific comparison class, and speakers making utterances of (2), for example, do not want to convey that their utterance u is true if and only if *the unique person being President of France is tall relative to the comparison class specific to* **u**. They have a specific comparison class in mind. It makes sense to assume that the Pragmatic intuition is not about the designational content or intuitive truth conditions of the utterance, but rather about a reflexive content playing the role of its cognitive significance. Let me develop this option further.

Following the Pragmatic intuition understood as concerning cognitive significance, a linguistically competent speaker hearing an utterance of a relative gradable predicate sentence knows that a comparison class is a relevant addition, and knows that different utterances of the same relative gradable predicate can be assigned different specific comparison classes. Moreover, according to the intuition seen from a cognitive perspective, if one uses "is tall" without knowing that a comparison class is needed and that the comparison class can vary with utterances, then one is confused about "is tall". The source of the confusion is that one does not know that "is tall" is a relative gradable predicate, or that one does not know what relative gradable predicates are and what their contribution to the cognitive significance of utterances is. This is linguistic ignorance concerning a category of terms, not metaphysical perplexity. Following the Pragmatic intuition, one then has a defective cognitive relationship to the world as far as relative predicates are concerned, assigning an incorrect cognitive significance to all utterances of (2)—assigning them the same cognitive significance—and wrongly assigning to all utterances of (2) the same truth-value—because they all then have the same truth conditions. The Pragmatic intuition captures both the conventional linguistic meaning contribution to cognitive significance of specific one-place predicates, like "is tall", *is F*, and more importantly a general feature of the category of relative predicates, that is their connection to utterance specific comparison classes: relative to the comparison class specific to **u**. If properties of language obtained without considering extralinguistic facts are linguistic properties, then carrying the idea that an utterance specific comparison class is relevant to cognitive significance is a linguistic property of any relative gradable predicate utterance. If cognitively relevant properties of utterances are semantic properties, then the property of conveying the idea that an utterance-specific comparison class is needed is a semantic but not a lexical-item specific property of utterances of expressions of the category of relative gradable predicates. The Pragmatic intuition understood as concerning cognitive significance coheres with the Ontological intuition understood as concerning cognitive significance.

We used to think that meaning rules are the only cognitively relevant rules of language. However, there is no compelling argument backing the idea that only the conventional linguistic meaning of a term carries cognitive significance and contributes to what is linguistically conveyed by an utterance. It is also wrong to think that the use of a term from a specific category, such as the category of a relative gradable predicates, in an utterance does not provide information about that utterance. The Ontological and the Pragmatic intuitions capture generalizations about relative predicates with respect to the impact that the use of a term from that category, whatever the term is, has on the cognitive significance of utterances and communication. The idea that an utterance specific comparison class is relevant is general knowledge of that category of predicates and is not conveyed by the conventional linguistic meaning of specific lexical items. It is not something we learn when learning the conventional meaning of specific relative gradable predicates. It is something we learn when learning what that category is. For instance, philosophers arguing in favor of the Syntactic intuition are not wrong about the conventional linguistic meaning of "is tall"; but they are wrong about its ontological implications. In addition, they do not take into account the impact on cognitive significance of utterances of use of that category of terms. Those arguing for the Ontological intuition do not have a clearer and better grasp of the linguistic meaning of relative gradable predicates. They simply consider the impact of the use of these predicates on cognitive significance of utterances. Knowledge of this aspect of relative gradable predicates is not knowledge of part of the conventional linguistic meaning of a relative gradable predicate, nor is it a feature we learn in a piecemeal fashion when we learn the meaning of a specific relative gradable adjective or predicate. It is an aspect of a predicate you know when you know its category, and an aspect you can predict if you know its category. If it was part of the conventional meaning of the expression, then "Monica is tall" and "Monica is tall for an utterance specific comparison class" would be synonymous. They are not. Adding a mention of an utterance specific comparison class to the conventional meaning of all relative gradable adjectives also neglects a pattern found in natural language and misses an important generalization. Bach (2002: 22–23) is right in recommending caution with semantic intuitions. The Semantic intuition is misleading and it underestimates different aspects of language. It ignores what the use of a category of terms conveys in linguistic communication.

9 Relative Gradable Predicates and Multipropositionalism

I want to suggest that belonging to the category of relative gradable predicates carries cognitively relevant information, and that linguistically competent speakers are sensitive to the use of this category of terms in communication. I also submit that "relative to *the comparison class specific to* **u**" is encoded in all relative gradable predicate utterances. Knowledge of that information builds on the category of terms used by the speaker, not on the conventional meaning of specific predicates.

Let us call the cognitive significance of an utterance of a relative gradable predicate when that category of term is taken into account its category bound cognitive significance. "Is tall relative to *the comparison class specific to* **u**" is the category bound cognitive significance of an utterance of "is tall". I propose the following principle, a principle very close to the Pragmatic intuition:

Category Bound Cognitive Significance of Relative Gradable Predicates: The contribution of an utterance **u** of a relative gradable predicate "is F" to the cognitive significance of **u** is *is F* relative to *the comparison class specific to* **u**.

The category bound cognitive significance of a relative predicate utterance registers the fact that different comparison classes can be constituents of intuitive truth conditions of specific utterances. It is obtained without extralinguistic information by considering only facts about language and knowledge of language, including facts about this category of predicates and knowledge of this category. If I am right, "relative to *the comparison class specific to* **u**" is a general, category dependent, and cognitively motivated reflexive component of the cognitive significance of any relative gradable predicate utterance. A semantically competent speaker mastering this category of predicates already knows enough to identify it with no need of contextual information. Are relative predicates context-sensitive? If context-sensitivity is confined to the conventional meaning of lexical items, they are not. However, if it extends to the difference made by the use of a category of terms—in the present case the category of relative predicates—to the cognitive significance of an utterance, then they are context-sensitive terms.

The statement (I) (see above, Section 6) echoes, for **u**, the Syntactic and the Semantic intuitions and cannot account for differences in cognitive significance of different utterances. However, adding the cognitive significance of relative gradable predicates and making the content reflexive will. Following my suggestion, (I) should be replaced by:

(II)   The utterance u of "The President of France is tall" is true if and only if *the unique person having the property of being President of France* is tall relative to *the comparison class specific to* **u**.

Accordingly,

> *the unique person having the property of being President of France* is tall relative *to the comparison class specific to* **u**

is the indexical content of my utterance of (2). It has a semantically determined, lexical-item-specific component—given in the indexical content by "is tall"—and a category bound component—given in the indexical content by "relative to the comparison class specific to **u**"—which is not specific to the conventional linguistic meaning of the lexical item as type. It is also true or false and it satisfies the conditions for cognitive significance given by Perry. Given the utterance **u**, the biconditional (II) is known *a priori*. No empirical investigation is needed to arrive at (II). (II) is understood by a speaker who ignores what the specific, relevant comparison class is, and who does not know the intuitive truth conditions of my utterance of (2). The natural approach to relative gradable predicates is not syntactic in nature, and it does not alter the syntactic category—they are one-place predicates—and/or the conventional meaning of a specific relative predicate. It does not imply properties, like the property of being tall, that are determined by their meaning and part of the intuitive truth conditions of utterances. It focuses on their non syntactic, cognitive category and the category's contribution to the cognitive significance of any utterance.

Suppose that I make an utterance **u** of (2). The indexical content of my utterance is reflexive and it contains the utterance itself as a constituent: *the unique person having the property of being President of France* is tall relative to *the comparison class specific to* **u**. Suppose that I make a different utterance **u'** of (2). The indexical content of my second utterance is also reflexive and it contains a different utterance, **u'**, as a constituent: *the unique person having the property of being President of* France is tall relative to *the comparison class specific to* **u'**. My suggestion explains the fact that different utterances of relative predicate sentences differ in cognitive significances: they have different indexical content. Now, no one making an utterance **u** of (2) wants to convey *that the unique person having the property of being President of France* is tall relative to *the comparison class specific to* **u**. One usually has a specific comparison class in mind. This is the topic of the next section.

10 Designational Content

Semantics, knowledge of language, and linguistic generalizations, stops at (II). It is not the business of semantics to give the designational content of different relative predicate sentence utterances. However, differences in the cognitive significance of utterances of (2) are good starting points to account for why different utterances of (2) can differ in intuitive truth conditions and truth-value.

Let us go back to my utterance of (2). Using non-linguistic information, you identify the object designated by the definite description, and obtain:

(III)   The utterance u of "The President of France is tall" is true
          if and only if **NS** is tall relative to *the comparison class
          specific to* **u**.

NS is Nicolas Sarkozy. (III) is still a reflexive content. Resolving problems with the relative predicate requires more information about the context.

Let me distinguish between a narrow and a wide context. A narrow context contains the appropriate items for accounting for standard indexicals and demonstratives: speaker, hearer, time, place, objects, and so on. A wide context contains other relevant elements. Different nonlexicalized, unarticulated comparison classes can be fitted into the intuitive truth conditions or designational content of an utterance of a relative predicate sentence.[15] Given that this component of the designational content is not determined by conventional linguistic meaning and is not part of the narrow context, it would seem that any component could be introduced. This cannot be right however. It is simply part of the wide context, and tools other than linguistic meaning are used to reach a specific comparison class. What is it that makes one focus on a specific comparison class when hearing an utterance of (2)? Speakers making utterances follow Grice's Maxim of Quality, "Try to make your contribution one that is true" and Grice's Maxim of Relation, "Be Relevant" (Grice 1989: 27). These maxims concern designational contents, not reflexive contents. What makes my utterance of (2) true and relevant? What do I have in mind? To arrive at the designational content of (2), you need extralinguistic, contextual information on the speech situation. We were talking about the President of France and there was a group of jockeys around. I have jockeys in mind. Hearers rely on wide context—including their knowledge of the speaker and the situation—and the maxims to focus on the contribution of relative predicate utterances to designational content. The description designated **NS** (Nicolas Sarkozy), and I had jockeys in mind.

(IV)   The utterance **u** of "The President of France is tall" is true if and
         only if **NS** is tall relative to <u>jockeys</u>.

I have underlined the specific comparison class. (IV) gives the designational content of my utterance of (2): **NS** is tall relative to <u>jockeys</u>. Knowledge of the designational content goes well beyond knowledge of meaning and linguistic competence. The comparison class is not a lexically determined, articulated part of this content. However, the introduction of a specific comparison class is not the result of what Recanati calls free enrichment (Recanati 2004: 23–24). It is not optional but mandatory, being required by the category of expression, and it does not rest simply on what is naturally understood when hearing (2). The specific comparison class is an unarticulated but cognitively-motivated (by the relative gradable predicate category) and pragmatically-constrained part of the designational content of the utterance. An utterance of:

---

[15] See note 8 on unarticulation.

(3)   The President of France is tall relative to jockeys

contains the same, articulated, comparison class in its designational content. Since it is articulated, utterances of (2) and utterances of (3), however, differ in cognitive significance.

Focusing on a specific comparison class is sometimes difficult due to lack of information about the speaker, the context of utterance, and so on, and one can consequently fail to grasp the designational content of an utterance of a relative predicate sentence. However, even if one is unable to identify its designational content, one can always grasp the cognitive significance of an utterance of a relative predicate sentence. Suppose that you read "Monica is tall" in a letter written in 1960. You understand the cognitive significance of what you read:

> The utterance u of "Monica is tall" is true if and only if *the person the convention exploited by* **u** *designates with "Monica"* is tall relative to *the comparison class specific to* **u**.

But you do not know which Monica the speaker is designating, you do not know the relevant comparison class, and you cannot identify the designational content. Years later, you read a different utterance **u'** of the same sentence in a letter written in 1975. You understand its cognitive significance, but again you do not know which Monica the speaker is talking about and cannot identify the comparison class. It may be the same as or different from the class relevant to the first utterance. You know that:

> The utterance **u'** of "Monica is tall" is true if and only if *the person the convention exploited by* **u'** *designates with "Monica"* is tall relative to *the comparison class specific to* **u'**.

Suppose now that you know who the speakers were designating when using "Monica" on both occasions. Suppose also that it is the same person. You know, for the first utterance, that:

> The utterance **u** of "Monica is tall" is true if and only if **MONICA** is tall relative *to the comparison class specific to* **u**.

You know, for the second utterance, that:

> The utterance **u'** of "Monica is tall" is true if and only if **MONICA** is tall relative to *the comparison class specific to* **u'**.

Knowing that Monica was born in 1955, you know that different comparison classes are probably relevant. These two utterances then plausibly differ in designational contents, and might be assigned different truth-values. Speakers need more than linguistic competence to grasp the designational content of these utterances, and cannot know that they have the same designational content before considering the wide context.

It is worth mentioning that the framework I am relying on to account for relative predicates differs from Speech Act Pluralism (Lepore and Cappelen 2005) in an important respect. According to Lepore and Cappelen (2005: 190), an utterance carries many different contents, but "there can be no systematic theory of speech act content". I agree with the first part of this picture but strongly disagree with the second part. I argue that belonging to the category of relative gradable predicate carries the idea that an utterance specific comparison class is required, and that it is part of the contribution of a specific relative predicate to the cognitive significance of an utterance. Consequently, a systematic theory on how relative predicate sentence utterance carries content can be stated.

11 Thought Content

The view I am presenting here does not capture thought contents expressed by utterances of relative predicate sentences like (1). Reflexive content is about the utterance, while the thought content is not, and for that reason the former cannot be the specific thought content the speaker has in mind and expressed by the utterance. Designational content contain a specific comparison class and for that reason do not qualify as thought content. The thought content expressed by an utterance of a relative gradable predicate sentence would contain a mode of presentation of the relevant comparison class, not that comparison class itself. Neither reflexive content nor designational content contain a representation of a comparison class. To arrive at a thought content, one must go beyond what is given by semantics, rely on wide context, find the comparison class the thought is about, and identify a sentence including the relevant, lexically-articulated comparison class, like "Monica is tall relative to children of her age". As a consequence, one cannot decide on the ground of semantic competence only whether two speakers making utterances of (1) are expressing the same thought content. By the same token, one cannot decide on the ground of semantic competence only whether a speaker making an utterance of (1), and another making an utterance of "It is false that Monica is tall" are expressing contradictory thought contents.

12 Conclusion

Monopropositionalism does not consider all the semantically relevant features of the category of relative gradable predicates; it does not take into account the cognitive significance of utterances of relative gradable predicates, and it does not introduce context-sensitivity in a proposition expressed by a relative gradable utterance. It assumes the context-sensitivity of relative gradable predicate sentence utterances, such as utterances of (1) or (2), but does not explain it, and adds, with no explanation, a specific comparison class for different utterances. The Syntactic and Semantic intuitions leave no room for comparison classes and cannot account for difference in cognitive significance. We once saw comparison classes as implicit arguments in the truth conditions of utterances and tried to articulate them. I see comparison classes as unarticulated components in the designational content of utterances that are introduced as follows: they are category bound, cognitively motivated, and pragmatically constrained elements in the designational content of utterances. Now, if I am right, the vagueness of relative predicate sentences or utterances does not stem from their linguistic meaning or the cognitive significance of the utterances, but rather from the designational content of relative gradable predicate sentence utterances. This is where questions concerning truth value assignment can be introduced. Take an utterance of "Sarkozy is tall", assume that the unarticulated comparison class is the class of men, and compare the size of Sarkozy to the size of many different men in a line up. Is Sarkozy tall for a man?

Acknowledgements

I want to thank Bernie Linsky, Martin Montminy, and Rob Stainton for helpful comments. The audience at the Vancouver CPA meeting asked me very good questions. I hope that I answered some of them here. Finally, the referees for *Pragmatics & Cognition* made very fruitful suggestions. Research for this work has been made possible thanks to the Social Sciences and Humanities Research Council of Canada (SSHRC).

References

Bach, K. 2002. "Seemingly semantic intuitions". In J.K. Campbell, M. O'Rourke, and D. Shier (eds), *Meaning and Truth: Investigations in Philosophical Semantics*. New York: Seven Bridges Press, 21–33.

Borg, E. 2007. "Minimalism versus contextualism in semantics". In G. Preyer and G. Peter (eds), 339–359.

Chierchia G. and S. McConnell-Ginet. 1990. *Meaning and Grammar*. Cambridge, MA: The MIT Press.

Clapp, L. 2001. "What unarticulated constituent could not be". In J.K. Campbell, M. O'Rourke, and D. Shier (eds), *Topics in Contemporary Philosophy: Meaning and Truth*. New York: Seven Bridges Press, 231–256.

Clapp, L. 2007. "Minimal (Disagreement about) semantics". In G. Preyer and G. Peter (eds), 251–277.

Corazza, E. 2007. "Contextualism, minimalism, and situationalism". *Pragmatics & Cognition* 15(1): 115–137.

Corazza, E. and Dokic, J. 2007. "Sense and insensibility". In Preyer, G. and G. Peter (eds), 169–193.

Corazza, E. and Korta, K. Forthcoming. "Two dogmas of philosophical linguistics". In P. Stalmaszczyk (ed), *Philosophy of Language and Linguistics*. Frankfurt Ontos Verlag.

Frege, G. 1892/1970. "On sense and reference". In M. Black and P. Geach (trans), *Philosophical Writings of Gottlob Frege*. Oxford: Blackwell, 56–78.

Glanzberg, M. 2007. "Context, content and relativism". *Philosophical Studies* 136: 1–29.

Graff, D. 2000. "Shifting sands: An interest-relative theory of vagueness". *Philosophical Topics* 28: 45–81.

Grice, H.P. 1989. *Studies in the Ways of Words*. Cambridge, MA: Harvard University Press.

Hawthorne, J. 2004. *Knowledge and Lotteries*. New York: Oxford University Press.

Kennedy, C. 2007. "Vagueness and grammar: The semantics of relative and absolute gradable adjectives". *Linguistics and Philosophy* 30: 1–45.

Lepore, E. and H. Cappelen. 2005. *Insensitive Semantics*. Malden, MA: Wiley-Blackwell.

Leslie, S.J. 2007. "Moderately sensitive semantics". In G. Preyer and G. Peter (eds), 133–168.

Ludlow, P. 1989. "Implicit comparison classes". *Linguistics and Philosophy* 12: 519–533.

MacFarlane, J. 2007. "Semantic minimalism and nonindexical contextualism". In G. Preyer and G. Peter (eds), 240–250.

MacFarlane, J. Forthcoming. "Nonindexical contextualism". *Synthese*.

Maitra, I. 2007. "How and why to be a moderate contextualist". In G. Preyer and G. Peter (eds), 112–132.

Neale, S. 2007. "On location". In M. O'Rourke and C. Washington (eds), *Situating Semantics. Essays on the Philosophy of John Perry*. Cambridge, MA: The MIT Press, 251–393.

Perry, J. 1998. "Indexicals, contexts and unarticulated constituents". In A. Aliseda, R. von Glabbeek, and D. Westerstahl (eds), *Computing Natural Language*. Stanford, CA: Center for the Study of Language and Information (CSLI) Publications, 1–11.

Perry, J. 2000. "Cognitive significance and the new theories of reference". In J. Perry, *The Problem of the Essential Indexical and Other Essays (Expanded edition)*. Stanford, CA: Center for the Study of Language and Information (CSLI) Publications, 189–206.

Perry, J. 2001. *Reference and Reflexivity*. Stanford, CA: Center for the Study of Language and Information (CSLI) Publications.

Perry, J. 2007. "Situating semantics: A response". In M. O'Rourke and C. Washington, (eds), *Situating Semantics. Essays on the Philosophy of John Perry*. Cambridge, MA: The MIT Press, 507–575.

Perry, J. and Korta, K. 2006. "Varieties of minimalist semantics". *Philosophy and Phenomenological Research* 73(2): 451–459.

Perry, J. and Korta, K. 2007. "Radical minimalism, moderate contextualism". In G. Preyer and G. Peter (eds), 94–112.

Preyer, G. and Peter, G. (eds). 2007. *Context-Sensitivity and Semantic Minimalism*. Oxford: Oxford University Press.

Raffman, D. 1996. "Vagueness and content relativity". *Philosophical Studies* 81: 175–192.

Recanati, F. 2004. *Literal Meaning*. Cambridge: Cambridge University Press.

Stanley, J. 2005. "Semantics in context". In G. Preyer and G. Peter (eds), *Contextualism in Philosophy*. Oxford: Oxford University Press, 221–253.

Stanley, J. 2007. *Language in Context*. Oxford: Oxford University Press.

5

Conventional Implicature Revisited

1 Introduction

Frege (1892) and Grice (1975) draw attention to what I will call View on Content Devices or VCDs

> "Even", "but", "already", "besides", "anyway", "moreover", "however", "hence", "nevertheless", "therefore", "although", "though", "so", "too", "still", "despite", "yet", etc.[1]

Calling them them VCDs is intended to suggest that they qualify content without being part of it. Frege (1892) put it in a nice way, saying that they "illuminate[s] (the sense) in a peculiar fashion". For example, if I say "Even Paul was seasick", it is arguable that the use of "even" carries the qualification that Paul's being seasick is surprising.[2] The qualifications introduced are fairly simple: "But" means something like in contrast (Rieber, 1997) or except; "moreover" means something like in addition (Rieber, 1997); "so" means something like in consequence (Rieber, 1997); "even" means something like surprisingly or amazingly, and so on. In introductory books to logic, "but" is frequently semantically read as "and", hence ignoring the specific features of "but" as a VCD and blurring the difference between "Paul is sick and Mary went to see a movie" and "Paul is sick, but Mary went to see a movie". "But" raises another issue in that while "Paul is sick and Mary went to see a movie and Peter is watching television" is acceptable, "Paul is sick, but Mary went to see a movie but Peter is watching television" does not fit

---

[1] See Bach (1999) for an extensive list of VCDs.

[2] This is a brute intuition and is not intended as a contribution to the semantics of "even". For a classic examination of the semantics of "even", see Karttunen and Peters (1979).

well with semantic intuitions and is cognitively dissonant.[3] I will come back to that problem and explore the semantics of "but". As a standard rule, VCDs apply to sentences and form new sentences.[4] Some are adverbs and apply to one single sentence ("Even"). I will focus on "even" in the presentation of my view. Some connect two sentences ("but" and "therefore"). Other VCDs can be handled either as adverbs or as sentence connectives ("however"). Here are examples,

> She is rich; however, she is honest.
> However, she is honest.

These are grammatical sentences. This being said, there is no consensus on the syntactic category of most VCDs. VCDs are assumed not to alter the truth conditions of sentences or utterances (see Frege, 1892, 1918; Grice, 1975).[5] For example, it is taken for granted that

(1)   Joan loves Paul.

is a sentence, and

(2)   Even Joan loves Paul.

is a new sentence, and that both have the same truth conditions, or express the same content (Frege, 1892:73; Grice, 1975:167; Karttunen and Peters, 1979:27; Francescotti, 1995:153; Rieber, 1997:51). In addition

(3)   However, Joan loves Paul.

(4)   Nonetheless, Joan loves Paul.

and (1) have the same truth conditions. I make the same assumption, and I will say that VCDs are truth conditionally irrelevant in a sentence or in an utterance.[6] If the truth irrelevance assumption is correct, it implies that one can understand the sentence's truth conditions, even if one fails to grasp the linguistic meaning of the VCD.

I want to suggest a new approach to VCDs. I first set the philosophical background and introduce Frege's and Grice's view. Both views are important to understand the motivations behind my approach. Second, I focus

---

[3] It is a grammatical sentence but, as a referee mentions, it is hard to process.

[4] In "Peter is rich but happy", "but" links two adjectives. However, this sentence should be read as "Peter is rich but Peter is happy".

[5] That feature is argued for on ground of intuitions, and is not given a theoretical or linguistic explanation or justification.

[6] I emphasize that this does not imply that VCDs are not truth conditionally relevant with respect to a proposition different from the one giving the truth conditions of a sentence or an utterance (see Bach, 1999) Neither does it imply their lack of linguistic meaning or cognitive relevance.

on the nature of VCD's semantic contribution to sentences. I then ignore the specifics of each VCD and sketch my own account, using the Reflexive–Referential framework Perry recently introduced (Perry, 2001) in semantics. Third, I examine more fully the semantic behavior of "but" and distinguish it from "and". I then show the fruitfulness and explanatory power of the Reflexive–Referential framework. An examination of the distinction between "but" and "and" makes clear why it is a mistake to read "but" as "and". Intuitively, VCDs are very simple expressions, and my suggestion is designed to capture that prima facie simplicity.

My motivations for exploring this category of expressions, lacking the philosophically interesting aspect of propositional attitudes or modal operators, are very simple. On the one hand these expressions are underexamined in philosophy,[7] even if they motivate strong semantic positions, like the blurring of semantics and pragmatics. On the other hand, these expressions are interesting because of their anomalous semantic behavior: they are clearly meaningful, but are assumed not to contribute to the truth conditions of sentences or utterances (Frege). If the meaning of an expression is identified with its contribution to the truth conditions of sentences, then VCDs lack linguistic meaning. That cannot be true. We have to stop and examine certain very fundamental principles in semantics. Finally, according to some philosophers, VCDs introduce a proposition: a conventional implicature (Grice, 1975). However, as a rule, a sentence, not a word, is a linguistic item fit to introduce a proposition. Once again, a very basic semantic principle is at stake.

2 Background

1 Frege and Cognitive Significance

In "Sense and Reference", Frege writes

> Subsidiary clauses beginning with "although" also express complete thoughts. This conjunction actually has no sense and does not change the sense of the clause but only illuminates it is a peculiar fashion. We could indeed replace the concessive clause without harm to the truth of the whole by another of the same truth value; but the light in which the clause is placed by the conjunction might then easily appear unsuitable, as if a song with a sad subject were to be sung in a lively fashion. (Frege, 1892:73).

As distinct from "necessary" for example, "although" does not alter the truth value of a sentence. If in

Although the children are sleeping, Joan is not watching television.

---

[7] But see Potts's *The Logic of Conventional Implicature* (2005) and *Iten's Linguistic Meaning, Truth Conditions, and Relevance* (2005).

the first clause is true, then any true sentence can be substituted for "The children are sleeping", and we obtain a true clause. For example

It is raining.

can replace "The children are sleeping" in the previous example and we obtain

Although it is raining, Joan is not watching television.

The first clause also expresses a true proposition. What about cases in which "the light in which the clause is placed by the conjunction might then easily appear unsuitable"? Consider a case where John is a student, and the sentences

All the students are sick. Even John is sick.

In the actual example, the use of "even" is appropriate. Consider now

All the students are sick. Nevertheless John is sick.

Why "nevertheless"? Using that term seems inappropriate in the situation.

VCDs bring in a component contributing to the informational aspect or cognitive value of the sentence or utterance. One can argue that the light shed on the clause is cognitively significant: it is appropriate or inappropriate, and makes a difference as to what a speaker conveys by her utterance as well as to what a hearer understands (Frege, 1892; Grice, 1975; Rieber, 1997). In (2), the use of "even" intuitively conveys as part of its linguistic meaning, for example, that the content is surprising. Perry (1986) identifies a useful condition on the cognitive significance or cognitive value of an utterance, a condition tied to the cognitive notion of acceptance:

> If there is some aspect of meaning, by which an utterance u of S and an utterance u' of S' differ, so that a rational person who understood both S and S' might accept u but not u', then a fully adequate theory of linguistic meaning should say what it is. (Perry, 1986:194)

That condition focuses on the cognitive value of utterances rather than sentences. In the present case, one can accept an utterance of (1) and reject an utterance of (2) because one thinks that it is not surprising that Joan loves Paul. One would then write (1) but refuse to write (2) in a letter. One might also think that "even" is just inappropriate in the circumstances (Francescotti, 1995). According to the standard Perry suggests, "Even" is cognitively significant, and makes a difference to the cognitive significance of the utterance.

Frege does not contend that the carried suggestion is a different proposition or content. I will call his view a One Content View. According to that picture, a hearer understanding a sentence containing a VCD does not grasp two or more different senses or propositions, and such a sentence does not carry two or more autonomous senses or propositions. Frege suggests that

VCDs lack sense because they do not make a difference to the truth conditions of the sentences in which they occur, and do not contribute to the thoughts expressed by these sentences. Since Fregean senses, are also linguistic meanings and cognitive values of terms, he is bound to say that they lack linguistic meaning and cognitive value. However, one does not want to argue that "even" lacks linguistic meaning and cognitive value. That is not plausible. I will come back to Frege.

2   Grice and the Many Propositions

Grice (1975) distinguishes, between what is meant by a VCD sentence, what is centrally said and what is conventionally implicated by that sentence.

VCD + sentence

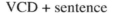

What is meant

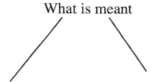

What is said   what is conventionally implicated

He proposes a picture of the semantics of VCDs assuming them to carry conventional implicatures. A conventional implicature is a proposition carried by the meaning of the VCD sentence, and the plausibly suggested view on the content expressed or on what is said in Grice's picture. For example, an utterance of (2) would be true if and only if Joan loves Paul—this is what is said—and the VCD would conventionally implicate, or suggest, in addition to what is said that it is surprising that Joan loves Paul or, according to Karttunen and Peters (1979), that other people besides Joan loves Paul. Sentence (1) and sentence (2) say the same thing, but they do not mean the same thing because of the conventional implicature carried by "even". What is suggested or conventionally implicated by (2) is a proposition different from what is centrally said, or what the speaker centrally meant, and adding to what is centrally said by the sentence. In (2) the proposition that is conventionally implicated would be for example that Joan's love for Paul is surprising or that other people besides Joan love Paul. I will say that Grice proposes a Many Propositions View. Grice writes:

> If I say (smugly), "He is an Englishman; he is, therefore, brave", I have certainly committed myself, by virtue of the meaning of my words, to its being the case that his being brave is a consequence (or follows from) his being an Englishman. But while I have said that he is an Englishman,

and said that he is brave, I do not want to say that I have said (in the favored sense) that it follows from his being an Englishman that he is brave, though I have certainly indicated, and so implicated, that it is so. (Grice, 1975:166–167)

In a diagrammatic form, we obtain,

"He is an Englishman; he is, therefore, brave"

He is an Eglishman; he is brave   *it follows from his being an Englishman that he is brave*

What is conventionally implicated is true or false and hence, strictly speaking, on that theory the VCD is truth conditionally relevant, contributing an implicated truth valuable proposition different from what is said. What is said can be true, and the conventional implicature false (Grice, 1975:167). For instance, it might be true that Joan loves Paul, and false that it is surprising that Joan loves Paul. According to Grice's picture, only what is centrally said qualifies as the truth conditions of the sentence or utterance. I will say that according to Grice, VCDs are proposition introducing devices.

I am reluctant to endorse Grice's approach to VCDs. Prima facie, nothing in a VCD sentence backs the view that VCD sentences express two different, independent propositions, both being truth conditions expressed by the sentence or utterance. In addition, a very basic semantic principle underlies the Semantic enterprise, the Principle of Semantic Cohesion:

PSC: A simple sentence expresses one proposition as its truth conditions.

Grice's framework rejects PSC. Recently, Bach (1999) offered an alternative to that framework. According to Bach's picture, VCD sentences express more than one proposition, both part of what is said. In all cases, the VCD introduces a new proposition. Still, Bach ponders over the importance of each proposition by ranking them (Bach, 1999:353). Bach (1999:350) argues that VCDs force the rejection of the PSC. He contends, for instance, that "Cal is still on the phone" expresses two propositions—and does not express a conjunction:

Cal is on the phone.
Cal has been on the phone.

Barker (2003) states a principle very similar to PSC

SCM: The semantic content of a sentence S—the content S expresses by virtue of linguistic rules and context, and upon which logical particles may potentially operate—is to be identified with S's truth conditional content (Barker, 2003:2)

Barker rejects SCM by invoking the semantic behavior of VCDs. He also draws dramatic consequences for truth conditional semantics like Davidson's. I think that the PCS is sound, and that a semantic theory preserving it would have much in its favor.[8] Finally, Grice's approach is mute on why "Paul is sick, but Mary went to see a movie but Peter is watching television" is at best hard to process or, more appropriately, cognitively dissonant. I will come back to this issue at length.

The literature on the expressions we are concerned with relies predominantly on the notions of what is meant, what is said and what is implicated. These notions are notoriously controversial and I dispense with them in trying to capture the phenomenon we are interested in. I set aside Grice's semantic notions and cast a Fregean net. I argue that VCDs by virtue of their linguistic meaning introduce an element into the cognitive value of the utterance, one illuminating the content or truth conditions in a certain way, but one not part of the truth conditions of the utterance. I will say that it introduces a cognitively relevant view on the content expressed, or the truth conditions, and no truth conditionally relevant content constituent. My suggestion has many advantages. First, it handles conventional implicatures in purely semantic terms. Semantics used to be defined in terms of truth conditions, and pragmatics in terms of the nontruth conditional aspects of sentences. Because VCDs do not alter the truth conditions of sentences, their contribution to sentences is sometimes taken to be pragmatic in nature even if it depends on the linguistic meaning of the expression. I align them to the side of meaning, and do not rely on pragmatics. I use a very conservative view of semantics. The idea that semantics is concerned with the truth conditions of sentences has recently been challenged (see especially Récanati, 2004). I can ignore that debate, which is irrelevant to my main point. Second, my suggestion is not ad hoc: it uses notions already available, and as distinct from Grice's view, it does not require major changes in our picture of how some sentences behave. Finally, on Grice's view, the close relationship between what is said and what is conventionally implicated is not adequately captured. My view exhibits that close relationship.

---

[8] It is important to emphasize that VCDs do not alter the illocutionary force of the speech act then performed. If they did, they would not throw a specific light on the content or illuminate it in a peculiar fashion, but add a new burden to the success condition of the speech act performed. For example, "frankly" is not truth conditionally relevant, but adds sincerity conditions to the successful utterance of (2). "Even", and other VCDs do not. An utterance of "Frankly, Joan loves Paul" does not throw a peculiar light on the expressed content, Joan loves Paul.

3 Features of Conventional Implicatures

Some of Grice's basic ideas shape our view and educate our intuitions on VCDs. I think that these ideas are not controversial and should be accounted for by any theory on VCDs, including more Fregean approaches like the one I propose. Conventional implicatures have characteristic features.

2.3.1 Conventional

A conventional implicature depends on the conventional meaning of a sentence, not on any maxim (Grice, 1989:41) or on the context of utterance. In Grice's view, relying on extralinguistic data is not required to identify or "build" an implicated proposition. According to other authors, it is required (See especially Bennett, Francescotti and Bach). I follow Grice's intuition. This feature draws attention to the fact that what a VCD suggests depends on its linguistic meaning, and not on any contextual aspect of the utterance. This feature is independent from Grice's framework, and it fits within different frameworks.

2.3.2 Detachable

According to the Gricean paradigm, one can say the same thing without carrying the conventional implicature. In so far as what is said is defined by the truth conditions of the sentence and that VCDs do not introduce truth conditional components, this seems to be a trivial feature, resulting from how VCDs are characterized. In a Fregean framework, one will simply say that they are not truth conditionally relevant, and that is exactly what Frege wrote.

2.3.3 Not Calculable

In a plausible understanding of that feature, it simply means that one does not need an argument or extra premises, going beyond the linguistic meaning of the VCD, to identify a conventional implicature or what is suggested, and that one's understanding of the meaning of the words is necessary and sufficient to get the speaker's view on the content. This feature goes hand in hand with the conventional aspect of conventional implicatures. I base my view around that feature.

2.3.4 No Cancellation without Anomaly

I cannot utter (2) and add "it is not surprising that Joan loves Paul", hence cancelling what is suggested, without being incoherent. I want to provide strong reasons for that being the case.

Let me add two more features.

2.3.5 No VCD without Justification

If one expresses an amazing attitude, or illuminates the content in an unexpected way, then a hearer will tend to question the use of that specific VCD. One can follow the maxim "no VCD without justification". For example, I can say "Snow is white, but $2 + 2 = 4$". Why "but"? If "but" introduces a contrast between "snow is white" and "$2 + 2 = 4$", why is a contrast introduced? However, the meaning of the VCD does not carry information on the justification for the idea of the contrast introduced.

2.3.6 Context Insensitive

I want to emphasize that VCDs are context insensitive items. Prima facie, and in contrast with indexicals, nothing in their meaning makes them sensitive to a component of the context of utterance or to the speaker's background belief.

It is important to underline the fact that VCDs do not explain why the speaker uses a specific term and throws a specific light on the content expressed. To repeat, the justification for the use of a specific VCD is not to be found in the meaning of that VCD. Suppose that "even" carries the idea of surprise. This term does not explain why the speaker is surprised or expresses/suggests surprise. Consider (2). Why does the speaker express surprise? There are many options: because an amazing number of people love Paul, because Joan loves no one, and so on.[9] In any case, the reason is not to be found in the meaning of the sentence. Philosophers and linguists are prone to read very rich suggestions conveyed by the VCD. Bennett (1982) and Lycan (1991) are good examples (See also Francescotti, 1995). But this view requires going well beyond the meaning of the VCD.

4   Characterizing VCDs

As previously mentioned, syntactically VCDs are either sentence connectives ("but", "so"), adverbs ("even", "still", "moreover", "nevertheless",) or both ("however"). Semantically, however, they all behave in a very similar way: VCDs suggest a relation between two contents or propositions: a contrast or an opposition, or an addition. For example, in

Peter will come to the party, but Joan has to study for an exam. My flight is scheduled to leave at 2; however, I am asked to be at the gate at 10.

---

[9] Francescotti (1995) introduces very sophisticated conventional implicatures for "even" because he confuses the communication of the attitude of surprise and the communication of an explanation for that attitude.

My flight is scheduled to leave at 2; nevertheless, I am asked to be at the gate at 10.

"but", "however" and "nevertheless" suggest a contrast between the content expressed by the first sentence and the content expressed by the second sentence. Contents contrasted are not confined to those expressed by a simple sentence. For example, "Peter is playing football and Mary is studying, but you can stay" is correct. What is expressed by complex sentences and what is expressed by a simple sentence can be contrasted. In some cases, one content involved in the relation is not part of any sentence used, as in

However Peter will not come to the party.

The content with which "Peter will not come to the party" is contrasted is not part of the sentence and it must be recovered. It can be, for example, that many people will come to the party (see Rieber, 1997). VCDs are called discourse markers. Most authors take VCDs to be connectives on grounds of their semantic behavior—they connect propositions. Rieber (1997) and Blakemore (1989) call them discourse connectives. So will I. Now, in so far as these expressions are blind to truth value and make no contribution to the truth conditions of sentences, they are not truth functional connectives.

3 A Reflexive-Referential Proposal

1 Sense and Suggestion

Frege notes that VCDs lack sense[10] because they are truth conditionally irrelevant. This remark is perplexing. Senses have different roles, among which are linguistic meaning, cognitive value, truth bearer, thought content and referent in oblique context. We have

Sense   (i) Linguistic meaning
          (ii) Cognitive value
          (iii) Truth bearer
          (iv) Thought Content
          (v) Referent in oblique context

Frege's remarks plausibly convey that VCDs are simply truth conditionally irrelevant, not that they lack linguistic meaning or cognitive value. One does not want to argue that "but" has no linguistic meaning. Finally, it is not plausible to believe that VCDs are cognitively irrelevant. The use of a VCD can be appropriate or not, and this fact cannot be explained if VCDs lack cognitive relevance. So, I will preserve these functions of senses for these

---

[10] I remind you that "sense" must be understood as Fregean sense here.

expressions. (iii) is dropped as far as VCDs are concerned. (i)–(ii), and the dropping of (iii) are easily captured in Perry's Reflexive–Referential approach to natural languages. Frege also mentions that the sense of a sentence, a proposition, is a thought content, (iv), and the referent of the sentence in a propositional attitude context, (v). Perry's framework is silent on this topic. I will return briefly to this aspect of Fregean senses at the end of the paper.

2   The Manifold View of Propositions

Let me introduce the framework that supports my suggestion. There are different versions of that theory, and that might be confusing. My version is grounded on Perry's "Individuals in Informational and Intentional Content" (Perry, 1990) and Perry's Reference and Reflexivity (2001). I slightly alter Perry's formulation to make my point clearer. Perry's view focuses on utterances, rather than sentences. An utterance is the use of a sentence by a speaker at a place at a moment of time. He (1997, 2001) introduces a view according to which

Manifold View of Propositions:
an utterance of a sentence expresses many propositions

Consider an utterance of (5)

(5)   Birds have wings.

and suppose that you understand the linguistic meaning of the sentence as type but know nothing about the utterance. Knowing the meaning, you know linguistic rules determining propositions. The linguistic meaning is not a proposition. However, it can determine propositions, and it might determine different propositions for different utterances of the same sentence. Propositions are contents. To make the theory clearer, let me introduce a type of proposition, the proposition S, not found in Perry's but allowing me to emphasize the focus on utterances. Following Perry's picture (Perry, 1990, 1997, 2001), and eliminating possible ambiguities, knowing the linguistic meaning of (5) you know that

Content S
<For any x, if x is a bird, then x has wings; u>

The first component echoes the linguistic meaning of the sentence. It provides the truth conditions of the sentence. The second component is a variable for an utterance. I add this variable at that stage to emphasize Perry's focus on utterances. (5) is utterance insensitive, so on understanding the sentence one understands the truth conditions of any utterance of that sentence. Consider the specific utterance **u** of (5). Focusing on that specific utterance and the linguistic meaning, we can drop the reference to the utterance and get

Content M
<For any x, if x is a bird, then x has wings>

Since that specific Content M is not sensitive to the utterance, and does not contain an utterance as a constituent, all utterances of (5) will have the same Content M. Content M is the cognitive value of the utterance. The first component of the Content S of (5) is then the cognitive value of the utterance, and all utterances of (5) have the same cognitive value. Under what conditions are they true? The truth conditions of this utterance are given by Content D or the official truth conditions of the utterance

Content D
<For any x, if x is a bird, then x has wings>

All utterances of (5) have the same truth conditions that one can identify with their cognitive value. Things do not always work this way.

Consider my utterance of (6)

(6)   I am sick.

Thanks to your semantic competence, you know that

Content S
<The speaker of the utterance is sick; u>

The first part of the Content S is given by the linguistic meaning of (6) and it refers to an utterance. The second part is a variable for an utterance. Suppose that you focus on the specific utterance, **u**. You know that this utterance, **u**, is true if and only if the speaker of the utterance **u** is sick.

Content M
<the speaker of **u** is sick>

Here the Content M contains the specific utterance. Perry calls it the reflexive content of the utterance because it contains the utterance as a constituent. The Content M is arguably the cognitive value of the specific utterance. Different utterances of (6) will have different cognitive values because the Content M will contain a different utterance. Suppose now that you know enough about the context to identify the speaker of the utterance. You have the Content D of the utterance

Content D
<ME, being sick>

The Content D is what we usually take to be the truth conditions of utterance. My utterance of (6) is true if and only if I am sick. Perry calls the Content D the official truth conditions of the utterance. The Content D is obtained once what indexicals, definite descriptions and proper names designate is given.[11]

I emphasize that according to this picture, each proposition is determined by the linguistic meaning of the sentence as type. When features of the utterance are required to obtain truth conditions, they can be introduced into the propositions because utterances are primary in the framework. The overall picture can be summarized in the following diagram

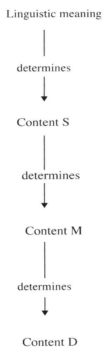

Linguistic meaning

determines

Content S

determines

Content M

determines

Content D

Sometimes, the meaning of a sentence does not fully determine the truth conditions of an utterance—this is the case of nonarticulated constituents (Perry, 2001), or as I prefer to say, unarticulation.

A constituent is articulated if it is provided by a lexical element, and if it is part of the truth conditions of an utterance. In my understanding, articulation is about Content D. My utterance of (6) expresses a proposition D having all its constituents articulated. Unarticulation recently entered the

---

[11] I blur the distinction between Content C and Content D found in Perry's *Reference and Reflexivity*, since this distinction has no use in my paper.

philosophical landscape (Perry, 2001; Récanati, 2002). A constituent is unarticulated if it is not provided by a lexical item in the sentence but it is required to have a truth valuable entity or proposition D. Unarticulation is about Content D. For example, the Content D expressed by an utterance of "It is raining" contains an unarticulated constituent, a place, because there is no term for a location in this sentence (Perry (2001)) and a place is required to have a truth valuable Content D. Rain is always located in space. Following Frege, VCDs lack sense. Under one plausible interpretation, it can be read as the idea that it does not contribute to the truth conditions of utterances. Exegetical evidence backs this interpretation. However, it cannot imply that VCDs lack linguistic meaning or cognitive significance. A semantically competent speaker knows the meaning of VCDs, witness the fact that he/she can select an appropriate VCD, and its cognitive value, witness the fact that one can appreciate the suitability of the "light" thrown by a VCD. So, a VCD sentence does have a Content S and a Content M echoing the linguistic meaning of the VCD. However, the latter is not echoed in Content D. I will say that VCDs do not articulate any constituent in Content D (see also Vallée, 2005).

The Manifold View of Propositions is designed to make semantics sensitive to the reflexivity of indexicals and demonstratives. One feature of this picture is that it distinguishes the linguistic meaning of an utterance, the cognitive value of that utterance and the truth conditions of that utterance. It can also distinguish the contribution of the VCD to the meaning and to the cognitive value of the utterance from its contribution to the truth conditions of the utterance. Let us go back to an utterance of (2). To simplify the presentation, I take "even" to linguistically mean what "surprisingly" means. From the meaning of the sentence we obtain the first component of Content S, and I add the usual second component, a variable for an utterance.

Content S
<Surprisingly Joan loves Paul; u>

We move to the specific utterance and can drop the second component, the variable for an utterance. Because that content, the first component of Content S, is not utterance sensitive, all utterances of (2) have the same Content M:

Content M
<Surprisingly Joan loves Paul.>

All utterances of (2) have the same Content M, and the latter is identical with the first component of Content S. So, in virtue of her understanding of the sentence, and assuming that the meaning of "even" is carried within the meaning of "surprisingly", a speaker understands what Grice takes to be the conventional implicature.[12] Note that the contribution of the VCD is part of the Content S and Content M of the VCD sentence. "Even" does not contribute to the truth conditions of the utterance. Content M is sufficient to get the official truth conditions of the utterance or what Grice takes to be what is said.

Content D
<Joan, Paul, loves>

The relation "loves" is satisfied by Joan and Paul. The cognitive significance or Content M is the mode of presentation of the Content D. The cognitive significance of "even" is part of the mode of presentation of D, even if it does not introduce any component in Content D. Now, according to this picture we go from the cognitive value of the utterance, including the contribution of the VCD, to the truth conditions of the utterance. In Grice's vocabulary, it would mean that we go from the conventional implicature to what is said. I take my picture to be more natural, and to exhibit strong and simple relationships. In addition, according to my picture, one's knowledge of Content D does not require one to understand the specifics of the VCD. Since the latter is truth conditionally irrelevant, one can lack understanding of the meaning of the VCD with no consequence on one's knowledge of the Content D. This is a welcome consequence. To summarize, we have the following determination chain

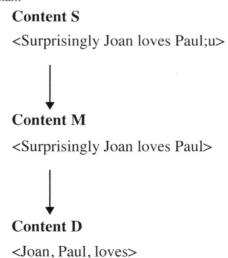

Content S

<Surprisingly Joan loves Paul;u>

Content M

<Surprisingly Joan loves Paul>

Content D

<Joan, Paul, loves>

---

[12] Grice never mentions "even", and here I am just applying my own view.

3   Features of Conventional Implicatures

Let us go back to the celebrated features of conventional implicatures.

3.1 Conventional

The suggestion is carried by the conventional meaning of the VCD and is semantically echoed in a proposition. This is captured by a Reflexive-Referential view on VCD sentences, since the suggestion is determined by the meaning of the VCD and is part of a proposition, the Content M, semantically expressed by a VCD sentence.

3.2 Detachable

The suggestion is detachable, since the VCD can be removed from the sentence and the Content D will stay the same.

3.3 Not Calculable

No calculation is required to obtain the suggestion, since the latter depends only on the meaning of the VCD.

3.4 No Cancellation without Anomaly

Suppose that one utters (2), conveys

> **Content M**
> <Surprisingly Joan loves Paul>

and adds that it is not surprising that Joan loves Paul. That person is incoherent, conveying through the use of "Even" that the it is surprising that Joan loves Paul—this is the Content M—and adding explicitly that it is not—hereby negating the Content M. On my view, the Content M of "Even Joan loves Paul", namely, "Surprisingly Joan loves Paul" or "It is surprising that Joan loves Paul", and the Content M of "It is not surprising that Joan loves Paul" cannot be true at the same time as one is the negation of the other. The problem with cancellation is a cognitive value problem, a problem having to do with the cognitive value of the utterances, not a problem with the truth conditions or Content D of the utterances. The cognitive value of the second utterance is the negation of the cognitive value of the utterance of (2), hence the anomaly. Needless to say that the speaker makes incoherent utterances. My view clearly captures that fact. Notice also that the Content M of an utterance of (2) might be false—it is not surprising that Joan loves Paul—and the Content D of that utterance might be true—because Joan loves Paul. This fits Grice's intuitions.

The last two features of conventional implicature "No VCD without justification" and context insensitivity are also captured. Notice that the use of the VCD must be justified in the context, and that the justification is not given by the VCD itself.

3.4 Presuppositional Analysis

Glanzberg (2005) proposes a presuppositional analysis of "even". That picture is not Gricean in that VCDs are not assumed to introduce a proposition as conventional implicature. Let me sketch that view and compare it to my suggestion. In Glanzberg's picture, sentences and context are distinguished, the context being the information forming the common ground of speakers (Stalnaker, 1974). Let us represent the Sentence S and the Context C as follows

$$S + C$$

Some sentences have presuppositions, the latter being part of the context. If presuppositions fail, that is, when this information is not part of C, then the sentence is infelicitous in the context. Glanzberg contends that syntactic constructions and lexical items trigger presuppositions, that is generate a presuppositional requirement. Sentences containing triggers require the presence of the presupposition. Let us go back to "even". Consider "Even John solved the problem". That sentence's presupposition is something like "Someone other than John solved the problem, and it was unlikely that John might have done so", and "even" triggers that presupposition. In case the presupposition is not part of the context, the sentence is infelicitous.[13]

I tend to prefer my suggestion. First, it is more economical than Glanzberg's, dispensing with the notions of background information and infelicity. In addition, my view does not introduce anything in the common background, and VCD utterances can convey new information, information not part of the background. VCD sentences can build common ground. Second, it approaches "even" in a more standard, Fregean, way in assigning it meaning and cognitive significance, rather than taking it to be a trigger. Thirdly, it does not link "even" to a rich proposition—something Grice's view does—and assigns it the modest role it intuitively has. The presuppositional content Glanzberg provides—"Someone other than John solved the problem, and it was unlikely that John did"—probably motivates the use of "even". However, one does not want what motivates that use to be captured by the semantics of "even".

---

[13] The presupposition can, of course, be introduced in the common ground by accommodation: if an utterance u presupposes a proposition P not part of the context, then the utterance by itself introduces P in the context. (see Stalnaker, 2002 for a recent discussion of accommodation). My view not requiring the notion of common ground, it need not invoke accommodation.

4 "But"

Let us move to the semantic contribution of specific VCDs. I take unary VCDs to be adverbs, and I rely on adverbs to make explicit what they semantically contribute to both Content S and Content M. Binary VCDs are conjunctions. I take this to mean that they semantically contribute a conjunction. But that cannot be the whole story. I want to examine "but", because there is an important literature on that word. My view suggests a new angle on its semantics. I will not pay attention to other binary VCDs. What is characteristic of each VCD is of interest in lexical semantics, and that goes beyond the point of my paper.

4.1 "And" vs "But"

In logic textbooks, "but" is semantically identified with "and". For example, Klenk (1994) asks the reader to symbolize "but" and "however" as "and", since, she contends, they have the same "logical force". I think that this is a mistake.[14] Philosophers of language are wrong in accepting this identification and in neglecting the characteristic features of "but". Consider the following

Paul will come to the movie <u>and</u> Mary will stay home.
Mary will stay home <u>and</u> Paul will come to the movie.

The truth functional connective's only semantic function is to operate on truth values, and the two sentences can be inverted without altering the truth conditions of the complex sentence. Semantically, these two complex sentences are equivalent.[15] In addition, they are also cognitively on a par. The cognitive value of the first one is identical with the cognitive value of the second one: one accepting an utterance of the former and rejecting an utterance of the latter is irrational. One willing to utter the former and refusing to utter the latter, for any reason, is also irrational. Things are different in the following sentences:

Paul will come to the movie <u>but</u> Mary will stay home.

---

[14] I am not convinced that Frege made that mistake (Frege, 1892:73). Frege writes "Subsidiary clauses beginning with 'Although' also express complete thoughts. This conjunction actually has no sense and does not change the sense of the clause but only illuminates it in a peculiar fashion*." In the note he adds "similarly in the case of 'but', 'yet'". If "but" illuminates a clause in a peculiar fashion, it contributes more than "and". In "Thoughts", he clearly writes that "but" differ from "and" (Frege, 1918:39).

[15] I reject the idea that "and" carries tense, and that "and" is responsible for our intuition that "They got married and had children" and "They had children and got married" are not equivalent because intuitively the order of the sequence of events in time is different in each case.

Mary will stay home but Paul will come to the movie.

Paul will come to the movie; however, Mary will stay home.
Mary will stay home; however, Paul will come to the movie.

Paul will come to the movie; nonetheless, Mary will stay home.
Mary will stay home; nonetheless, Paul will come to the movie.

These sentences are prima facie not equivalent. For example, prima facie "Paul will come to the movie but Mary will stay home" is different from "Mary will stay home but Paul will come to the movie". "But", as well as "however" and "nonetheless", each introduce a contrast (see Wilson, 1975), and introduce it whatever the truth value of the sentences it connects. Let us say that in virtue of its linguistic meaning, "but" introduces a cognitively significant contrast between propositions. Now I don't want to suggest that "but" is unequivocal. That term might well semantically be ambiguous. However, that has no impact on my main point. Let me distinguish the base proposition and the contrasted proposition. The contrasted proposition is the one following "but" (see also Rieber, 1997). Consider the following

Paul will come to the movie but (in contrast) Mary will stay home.
Mary will stay home but (in contrast) Paul will come to the movie.

Bach (1999:327) suggests that in the previous examples a contrast is indicated between coming to the movie and staying home. If so, the two previous sentences are cognitively equivalent, because in both cases the same contrast is indicated. If there is a contrast between coming to the movie and staying home, then there is one between staying home and going to the movie. However, the cognitive impact of the first "but" sentence differs from the cognitive impact of the second "but" sentence. Each introduces a proposition meant to be the contrasted proposition, and which proposition is the contrasted proposition matters. Because the contrasted proposition follows "but", inverting the sentences alters the cognitive value of the complex sentence. "But" is both cognitively significant, contrasting cognitive contents, and truth conditionally irrelevant. Consider the following sentences

She is honest, but she is rich.
She is rich, but she is honest.

In both cases, the contrast is clear. These sentences are not equivalent in all respects, even if sharing the same truth conditions, and they are not appropriate in the same circumstances. One might utter the former, and refuse, for any reason, to utter the latter, or vice-versa, depending on the contrast one wants to emphasize: richness, as opposed to honesty, or honesty, as opposed to richness. These sentences differ in cognitive significance: what is contrasted, the contrasted content, differs in both cases. In that respect, theses sentences differ from

> Paul will come to the movie and Mary will stay home.
> Mary will stay home and Paul will come to the movie.

These last sentences are equivalent in all respects, and they are appropriate in the same circumstances.

I want to draw attention to the fact that a "but" sentence contrasts propositions, but does not explicitly state why there is a contrast. To explain the asymmetry between "A but B" and "B but A", one could invoke a conversational maxim like "Be orderly!". This strategy is sometimes used to explain in non semantic terms the intuition that "They got married and had many children" and "They had many children and got married" are different without arguing that "and" carries the idea of time. However, arguing that that maxim, or a similar maxim, establishes a contrast or a priority, or make natural a certain order, is not plausible. There is nothing beyond the contrast introduced by the meaning of "but", contrasting the second component with the first. In addition, were a maxim like "Be Orderly" invoked to make sense of the contrast or emphasis, it would turn a prima facie semantic issue into a pragmatic one, connected to conversational maxims, while a semantic explanation is already available. Another issue should be addressed.

Grice (1975) writes that a "but" sentence has the truth conditions of an "and" sentence, and in addition suggests a contrast. It is not infrequently argued that

A +: "but" = "and" + something else

Wilson (1975), for instance, writes: "It seems to me that sentences containing but are assigned a truth-value as a function of the values of their constituent conjuncts, and that in addition hearers attempt to construe a contrast of some sort between the conjuncts." (p. 119). Gazdar (1979:38) echoes the same intuition and Bach (1999) mentions it when writing, with respect to the following:

(7)   Shaq is huge but he is agile.
(8)   Shaq is huge and he is agile.

"According to common wisdom, the truth of (7) (my numbering) requires nothing more than the truth of (8), although in uttering (7) rather that (8) one is indicating that there is some sort of contrast between being huge and being agile." (p. 327). (8) is true if and only if the two conjuncts are true, and it is false otherwise. "But" is then to be read as containing a hidden conjunction. Should a conjunction be introduced between the sentences? If so, in addition to being a truth functional connective, "but" has a cognitive value "and" does not have. Rieber (1997) offers a similar suggestion. He (Rieber, 1997:58) writes

"For "but" is equivalent in meaning to "and" plus a parenthetical verb."

If so, then "but" is a truth functional connective, in addition to introducing a parenthetical verb. Following Frege, I take "but" to be a truth conditionally irrelevant discourse connective, and for that reason it cannot be a truth functional connective, or contain a hidden truth functional connective in addition to something else. It is blind to truth values. I do not adopt an approach dictated by A+. Let me insist. "But" alters the cognitive value of the sentence, and contrasts contents. By the same token, it does not "add" or "put together" contents by way of the logical connective "and". There is more.

4.2 Blakemore Hypothesis

Diane Blakemore (1989:32) offers the following observation:

"whereas and can conjoin any number of propositions, but can only be used to connect two."

If Blakemore is right, then A+ is not defensible: her observation implies that it is false that "but" can replace any occurrence of "and", or any occurrence of "and" plus something else. She is right in an important way. I want to take a few pages to explore her view. It tells us a lot about the very limited capacities of VCDs as conjunctions. I will conclude by formulating a generalization concerning binary VCDs based on Blakemore's observation. Let me rephrase her view in a slightly different language. The idea that "and" can connect many propositions is ambiguous. It can mean that it can take many simple propositions (or a complex proposition) on its right side and many simple propositions (or a complex proposition) on its left side. It can also mean that it can take one simple proposition on the right side and one complex proposition on the left side, or one complex proposition on the right side and one simple proposition on the left side. Consider the example:

P and Q and R and S and T and U and V.

That sentence is multiply ambiguous, and must be disambiguated, one way or another as in

((P and Q) and ((R and S) and T)) and (U and V).

Different disambiguation will result in different assignments of truth value to the complex proposition if the truth values of the simple sentences differ. In long conjunctions, brackets should be introduced to get a clearly truth valuable conjunction with no impact on the linguistic meaning and cognitive value of the sentence. However, things are different with

P but Q but R but S but T but U but V.

or

Peter plays violin but Gary is learning piano, but Mary plays basketball but John swims in his college team but Diane cooks but Alan teaches in a high school but Bob rides horses.

That example is grammatical, but barely understandable. If one introduces brackets as before, one gets the also grammatical but barely understandable

((P but Q) but ((R but S) but T)) but (U but V).

or

((Peter plays violin but Gary is learning piano), but ((Mary plays basketball but John swims in his college team) but Diane cooks)) but (Alan teaches in a high school but Bob rides horses).

What is the problem with these long "but" sentences? Why does "but" have these limited capacities as a conjunction? What limits free bracketing? How can these sentences be made readable? Two options are on the table. Consider again

P but Q, but R, but S, but T, but U, but V.

Q, R, S, T, U, V can each be compared to P, or every proposition can be compared to the preceding simple proposition. These are the only plausible intelligible options. I will call them forced options. Others options are not plausible. For instance, in

Peter plays violin but (Gary is learning piano), but Mary plays basketball)

the last sentence ("Mary plays basketball") is contrasted with the complex sentence ("Peter plays violin but Gary is learning piano").

This way of reading the long sentences is not plausible. One may wonder how a contrast is introduced between the complex sentence and the simple sentence, or how one is supposed to contrast "Peter plays violin but Gary is learning piano" and "Mary plays basketball". Remember that in the long sentence "but"s are introduced, and contrasts identified. I will come back to this dictated by the forced option and the second. A better reading of the sentence is given by

Peter plays violin but Gary is learning piano.
Gary is learning piano but Mary plays basketball.

"P but Q, but R, but S, but T, but U, but V.", in the interpretations we examined, are predicted as semantically incorrect by Blakemore Hypothesis. I will replace "proposition" with "sentence" and restate

Blakemore Hypothesis 1:
"But" can only connect two sentences.

For example

((P but Q) but ((R but S) but T)) but (U but V).

or

P but (Q but (R but (S but (T but (U (but V)))))).

where simple and complex sentences are contrasted. However, these options are not plausible—they are barely understandable—and are excluded. Blakemore's hypothesis is more specific than she states. "But" can connect a simple sentence to a simple sentence, a simple sentence to a complex sentence containing logical connectives or a complex sentence containing logical connectives (like "and") to a complex sentence containing logical connectives (like "and"). In these cases, the result is intelligible. For instance

Peter plays violin and John is learning piano, <u>but</u> Mary plays basketball.
Peter plays violin <u>but</u> Mary plays basketball and John swims in his college team.
Peter is rich <u>but</u> he is unhappy and he is depressive.
Peter plays violin and Gary is learning piano, <u>but</u> Mary plays basketball and John swims in his college team.

"But" can connect simple and complex sentences, but it can not connect a simple sentence to a complex sentence containing many "but"s, or a complex sentence containing "but" to a complex sentence containing "but". The following are cognitively dissonant and not acceptable, unless the third simple sentences is contrasted with the first simple sentence or contrasted with the simple sentence immediately preceding it.

Peter plays violin <u>but</u> John is learning piano, <u>but</u> Mary plays basketball.
Peter plays violin <u>but</u> Mary plays basketball <u>but</u> John swims in his college team
Peter is rich <u>but</u> he is unhappy <u>but</u> he is depressive.
Peter plays violin <u>but</u> Gary is learning piano, <u>but</u> John swims in his college team.

On the other hand, the following are perfectly acceptable

Peter plays violin *but* John is learning piano and Mary plays basketball.

Peter is rich and he is unhappy *but* he is depressive.

Let me rephrase the hypothesis.

Blakemore Hypothesis 2:
"But" can only connect simple sentences to simple sentences, simple sentences to complex sentences not containing "but", or complex sentences not containing "but" to complex sentences not containing "but".

The Hypothesis can be generalized, since it applies to

Peter plays violin; *however*, John is learning piano, *but* Mary plays basketball.
Peter plays violin; *but* Mary plays basketball; *however*, John swims in his college team.

These sentences are cognitively dissonant and not acceptable, unless the second and third simple sentences are compared to the first simple sentence or to the sentence immediately preceding it. BH 2 also applies to "however". For instance, it predicts that

Peter plays violin and John is learning piano; *however*, Mary plays basketball.
Peter plays violin; *however*, Mary plays basketball and John swims in his college team.
Peter is rich; *however*, he is unhappy and he is depressive.
Peter plays violin and Gary is learning piano; *however*, Mary plays basketball and John swims in his college team.

are acceptable and that

Peter plays violin; *however*, Mary plays basketball *but* John swims in his college team.
Peter is rich; *however*, he is unhappy *but* he is depressive.

are hard to process and cognitively dissonant. So, I suggest

A binary VCD can only connect simple sentences, simple sentences to complex sentences not containing binary VCDs, or complex sentences not containing binary VCDs to complex sentences not containing binary VCDs.

Let us go back to the initial example:

Mary will stay home, but Paul will come to the movie.

We have the following contents:

Content S

<Mary will stay home, in contrast Paul will come to the movie; u>

Content M

<Mary will stay home, in contrast Paul will come to the movie>

Content D

<Mary will stay home>   <Paul will come to the movie>

I contend that "but", like "however" and "nonetheless", does not introduce a truth functional conjunction. I also contend that it semantically introduces contrasts between contents in Content M. The semantic value of these terms separate contents and operate on cognitive contents, not on truth values. Neither "but" nor "however" leaves a trace in Content D. Blakemore offers no explanation for the principle she offers. Let me suggest one for BH2: binary VCDs do not operate on truth values but on cognitive contents, and they contrast propositions in Content M.

What is wrong with "Peter plays violin but Gary is learning piano, but Mary plays basketball"? The model predicts the following:

Content S

<Peter plays violin in contrast Gary is learning piano, in contrast Mary plays basketball; u>

Content M

<Peter plays violin in contrast Gary is learning piano, in contrast Mary plays basketball>

Content D

<Peter plays violin>   <Gary is learning piano>   <Mary plays basketball>

Content M, the cognitive content, contrasts a proposition and two contrasted propositions, not a proposition and a proposition. Contrasting with contrasted propositions does not make much sense. For example, using brackets, "Peter plays violin in contrast (Gary learns piano, in contrast Mary plays basketball)" does not make much sense. Of course, the forced options are still available. My view captures the intuition that there is something wrong with the example. It also provides an appropriate explanation, identifying the problem as having to do with the cognitive value of the utterance and as having nothing to do with the truth conditions of the sentence or the utterance.

Now remember that Content M is the mode of presentation of Content D. In the mode of presentation of Content D, the propositions are contrasted. Someone saying "Mary will stay home, but Paul will come to the movie" and adding "Mary's staying home is not in contrast with Paul's coming to the movie" would contradict herself, even if expressing the same Content D. The Content M expressed by her utterance of the "but" sentence and the Content M of her utterance of "Mary's staying home is not in contrast with Paul's coming to the movie" cannot be true at the same time.

Now, what about
If P but Q, then R

Where P and Q seems to be joined by a conjunction?

If P. Q then R

It is easy to obtain a conjunction. Take "P but Q". You get P and Q as Content D, and then use

Conjunction Rule

P

Q

P. Q

and then go back

If P. Q then R

I do not think that there are deep semantic differences between "however", "nonetheless" and "but". Piling them up creates redundancy, as in "Peter is sick, however, nonetheless Mary went to the movie". I will not explore that aspect of binary VCDs I let the reader put together unary and binary VCDs, as is "Peter is sick, but even Mary doesn't care".

5   Conclusion

Is there a range of views on contents? Do different VCDs express different views on contents? I leave this question open. It requires investigations in the lexical semantics of specific languages, and this is beyond the scope of this paper (but see Iten, 2005). Let me go back to thought content and content reported in oblique context. Frege assumes that "but" makes no difference to the thought. He writes

> The way that "but" differs from "and" is that we use it to intimate that what follows it contrasts with was was to be expected from what preceded it. Such conversational suggestions make no difference to the thought. (Frege, "Thoughts", p. 39)

Assume that "thought" here is not read as truth conditions but thought content, reported by a propositional attitude sentence. Frege's view on the relationship between VCDs and thought is then negative: VCDs make no contribution to thoughts. Frege fails to provide an explanation for the role of what VCDs express in the cognitive life of the speaker. Consider now

Paul believes that even Mary is kind.
Paul believes that Mary will stay home but Paul will come to the movie.

What is reported in propositional attitudes? If propositional attitudes report thoughts, then Frege suggests that VCDs make no difference to what is reported. The thought reported cannot be the Content M, since that latter contains the semantic contribution of "even" and "but". However, "even" seems to make a difference to thought. The Reflexive–Referential framework does not take into account thought contents. If we follow Frege, that framework implies that VCDs do not contribute to thought contents and reported thought. These are very difficult questions. I leave this topic for another paper.

Acknowledgements

I want to thank Catherine Wearing and Arthur Sullivan, and the audiences at the SEP meeting in Toronto and the *Principia* symposium in Florianopolis. The referees made very useful suggestions and, thanks to them, the paper is better than the previous version. One of them made very detailed comments, and made me see many problems I did not notice. Suzanne Deschênes shared with me her linguistic intuitions on "but".

References

Bach, Kent, 1999. The myth of conventional implicature. Linguistics and Philosophy 22, 327–366.

Barker, Stephen, 2003. Truth and conventional implicature. Mind 112, 1–33.

Bennett, Jonathan, 1982. Even if. Linguistics and Philosophy 5, 403–418.

Blakemore, Diane, 1989. Denial and contrast: a relevance theoretic analysis of But. Linguistics and Philosophy 12, 15–37.

Francescotti, Robert M., 1995. Even: the conventional implicature approach reconsidered. Linguistics and Philosophy 18, 153–173.

Frege, Gottlob, 1892. On sense and reference. Philosophical Writings of G. Frege, vol. 1952. Basil Blackwell, pp. 56–78.

Frege, Gottlob, 1918. Thoughts. In: Salmon, N., Soames, S. (Eds.), Propositional Attitudes, Oxford University Press, 1988, pp. 33–55. There is an alternative translation: The Thought; A Logical Inquiry. In: Strawson, P.F. (Ed.), Philosophical Logic, Oxford University press, 1976, pp. 17–38.

Gazdar, Gerald, 1979. Pragmatics. Implicature, Presupposition and Logical Form. Academic Press, New York.

Glanzberg, Michael, 2005. Presuppositions, truth values, and expressing propositions. In: Preyer, G., Peter, G. (Eds.), Contextualism in Philosophy: On Epistemology, Language, and Truth. Oxford University Press, Oxford, pp. 349–396.

Grice, Herbert Paul, 1975. Logic and Conversation. In: Cole, P., Morgan, J. (Eds.), Syntax and Semantics 3: Speech Acts, Academic Press, New York, pp. 43–58. Also in Grice, 1989. Studies in the Ways of Words, Harvard University Press, Cambridge.

Grice, Herbert Paul, 1989. Studies in the Ways of Words. Harvard University Press, Cambridge.

Iten, Corinne, 2005. Linguistic Meaning, Truth Conditions and Relevance. Palsgrave MacMillan, Houndsmill.

Karttunen, Lauri, Peters, Stanley, 1979. Conventional implicature. In: Oh, C.-K., Dinnen, D. (Eds.), Syntax and Semantic 11: Presupposition. Academic Press, New York, pp. 1–56.

Klenk, Virginia, 1994. Understanding Symbolic Logic, third ed. Prentice Hall, Englewood Cliffs, New Jersey.

Lycan, William, 1991. Even and even if. Linguistics and Philosophy 14, 115–150.

Perry, John, 1986. Cognitive Significance and New Theories of Reference. In Perry, J. 2001, 189–206.

Perry, John, 1990. Individuals in informational and intentional content. In: Perry, J. 2000. The Problem of the Essential Indexicals and Other Essays, CSLI, Stanford, California.

Perry, John, 1997. Indexicals and demonstratives. In: Hale, B., Wright, C. (Eds.), Companion to the Philosophy of Language. Blackwell, Oxford, pp. 586–612.

Perry, John, 2001. Reference and Reflexivity. CSLI, Stanford, California.

Potts, Christopher, 2005. The Logic of Conventional Implicature. Oxford University Press, Oxford.

Récanati, François, 2002. Unarticulated constituents. Linguistics and Philosophy 25, 299–334.

Récanati, François, 2004. Literal Meaning. Cambridge University Press, Cambridge.

Rieber, Steven, 1997. Conventional implicatures as tacit performatives. Linguistics and Philosophy 20, 51–72.

Stalnaker, Robert, 1974. Presupposition. In: Munitz, M., Unger, P. (Eds.), Semantics and Philosophy. University Press, New York, pp. 197–213.

Stalnaker, Robert, 2002. Common ground. Linguistics and Philosophy 25, 701–721.

Vallée, Richard, 2005. Complex demonstratives, articulation and overarticulation. Dialogue 97–121.

Wilson, Deirdre, 1975. Presupposition and non-truth-conditional semantics. Academic Press, London.

6

On Local Bars and Imported Beer

1 Contextuals

"Imported" is a member of a large family of adjectives including "enemy," "domestic," "local," "exported," "foreign," "alien," "native," "indigenous," and "exotic," and common nouns, including "immigrant," "emigrant," and "foreigner" (See also Mitchell 1986; Hall Partee 1989, 1995; Nunberg 1992; Perry 2001, 2006; Récanati 2002; Vallée 2003; Lepore and Cappelen 2005; Marti 2006; Neale 2008). Let us call these terms contextuals. Contextuals are *prima facie* context-sensitive expressions in that the same contextual sentence can have different truth-values and, hence, different truth conditions from utterance to utterance. The sentence

(1)   Stella Artois is an imported beer.

is complete, and utterances of (1) are true when talking about the U.S., and false when talking about Belgium, since Stella Artois is brewed in Belgium. Moreover, the sentence (1), or utterances of (1), cannot be assigned a truth value if no country is taken into consideration. The sentence

(2)   Luisa is a foreign student.

is also complete and utterances of (2) are true when talking about the U.S., and false when talking about Columbia, since Luisa is from Columbia. Similarly, if no country is taken into account, the sentence (2), or utterances of (2), cannot be assigned a truth value. Other examples include "Bananas are imported fruits." The sentence "Bananas are imported fruits" is true when talking about Canada, and false when talking about Nicaragua, and it, or utterances of it, cannot be assigned a truth value if no specific country is taken into consideration. When in the U.S., I make an utterance of (1) with the U.S. in mind and say something true. Suppose that later on I travel to Belgium. When stopping there for a beer and talking to a friend, with Belgium in mind, I say

(3)   Stella Artois is not an imported beer.

What I say is also true. Sentence (3) is the negation of (1). If (1) and (3) are context-insensitive sentences, then these sentences, or utterances of these sentences, cannot both be true. Thus, (1), (2) and (3) are not context-insensitive sentences.

Contextuals do not belong to a unique syntactic category. Common nouns ("foreigner," "immigrant"), adjectives ("foreign," "imported," "exported," "domestic") and verbs ("to immigrate") can all be contextuals. There is no syntactic characterisation of such terms as forming a unique class of expressions. They share a simple feature: when they are part of sentences, these sentences can change their truth value from utterance to utterance, and if a nonlexicalized component is not taken into account—a country in the case of (1)—they cannot be assigned a truth value. These terms are not captured by any simple generalisation, and identifying them proceeds in a piecemeal fashion

From now on, I will focus on predicates containing contextuals, and I will call predicates like "is imported" and "is foreign" contextual predicates. Predicates are not referring expressions.[1] Given their syntactic category, they contribute conditions, not objects, to the truth conditions of utterances. For example, predicates such as "is blue" and "is sick" contribute the condition of being blue and the condition of being sick to the truth conditions of utterances. As such, predicates, including contextual predicates, differ from indexicals and demonstratives. The latter contribute objects to the truth conditions of utterances.[2] If I am right about (1) and (2), the contribution of contextual predicates to the truth conditions of sentences may vary from utterance to utterance; witness how the truth value of (1) can change depending on the country under consideration. Notice however that an object is needed to explain this variation in truth conditions and in truth value. The utterance of (1) is true if the speaker is talking about the U.S., and false if the speaker is talking about Belgium. A specific object, a country, is needed for the truth conditions of the utterance, and the rele-

---

[1] From here on, I will disregard thense when discussing such predicates.

[2] I am setting aside discussion of sentences like "This color" where the demonstrative is apparently used to designates a condition.

vant unarticulated[3] country is the one the speaker is talking about. I want to account for how sentences like (1) and (2) can vary in truth-value from utterance to utterance by making it clear how the contribution of contextual predicates to the truth conditions can vary from utterance to utterance depending on what speakers have in mind.

In the next section, I make clear that contextuals are context sensitive expressions, and also draw attention to some non context-sensitive occurrences of contextuals. The third section examines options. The fourth introduces Perry's multipropositionalist framework, used in the fifth section to account for the semantics of contextuals. I contend that the meaning of these predicates introduces a complex constituent into the truth conditions of utterances, a constituent complex enough to explain differences in cognitive significance and in intuitive truth conditions of contextual sentence utterances.

2   Contextuals, Context-Sensitivity, and Context Insensitivity

1   Context-Sensitivity

Let me provide a brief reminder of how context-sensitive terms are introduced and defined, negatively, by their lack of a Fregean sense (Perry 1977, 1979).[4] Following the Fregean tradition, sentences express propositions, and the same proposition has many different functions in Frege's semantics, among which are meaning, cognitive value, thought content, thought reported in oblique context, and truth conditions.

	Meaning
	Cognitive value
Proposition	Thought content
	Thought reported in oblique context
	Truth conditions

Let us call these functions Fregean roles. Basic context-sensitive terms ("I," "you," "here," "now") have no Fregean sense (Perry 1977, 1979) and the thoughts they are used to express are controversial, resisting capture in belief reports (Castaneda 1967; Perry 1977, 1979). These expressions are also unfit for reporting thought contents in an oblique context (Castaneda 1967). "I" keeps the same linguistic meaning as type in different utteranc-

---

[3] An unarticulated constituent is an element which is required in the truth conditions of an utterance for the utterance to have a truth value but which does not correspond to any morpheme in the sentence uttered (see Perry 2001).

[4] I intend my presentation of Frege's view to be very conservative. Call it the standard Fregean picture. The latter is controversial and some philosophers disagree with it. However, I do not want to address the various interpretation of Frege's view in the present paper.

es. "I," however, does not have a Fregean sense: it may refer to different people for different utterances. The sense of a term cannot refer to different objects depending on the utterance. Different utterances of

(4)   I am sick.

may differ in truth conditions and in truth value. It is true when I say it, and false when you do. If that sentence had a sense, it would not differ in truth conditions and in truth value from utterance to utterance. Different utterances of (4) also differ in cognitive value and do not carry the same information: after uttering "I am sick," I go to the hospital; after hearing your utterance of the same sentence I recommend you to go to the hospital. If "I" had a Fregean sense, all the utterances would carry the same information. Moreover, I can accept as true my utterance of that sentence and reject as false your utterance of the same sentence. Finally, the thought content one expresses by an utterance of (4) is controversial (Castaneda 1967; Perry 1979) and the use of "I" cannot report that thought content in an oblique context (Castaneda 1967; Perry, 2008). For example, the thought I expressed by an utterance of "I am sick" is contentious, and it cannot be reported by "Richard believes that I am sick." Nonetheless, the thought content you communicate by uttering that sentence is no doubt different from the thought content my utterance carried. Contextuals share these features with indexicals, suggesting that they also lack Fregean sense.

Contextual sentences such as (1) and (2) have the same linguistic meaning as type[5], but they cannot have the same Fregean sense. If they had the same Fregean sense, they would also have the same truth conditions and the same truth-value. Sentence (1) has the same linguistic meaning in different utterances, but some utterances of (1) are true and others are false. By the same token, these utterances cannot have the same truth conditions. If sentences like (1) have a Fregean sense, then all utterances of (1) have the same cognitive value. If having a cognitive value means carrying information, then all utterances of (1) carry the same information. If they all carry the same information, then believing an utterance of (1), or what is expressed by an utterance of (1), and not believing a different utterance of the same sentence, or what is expressed by that utterance, is irrational. However, it is rational to believe some utterances of (1), when talking about the U.S., and not to believe some others, when talking about Belgium. Moreover, it is irrational to believe all utterances of this sentence—for example, to believe all utterances of (1), whatever the speaker is talking about. Utterances of (1) do not all carry the same information. If

---

[5] I am setting aside the semantic ambiguity of contextuals for now.

they had a Fregean sense, they would also express the same thought content. Assume that utterances of (1) express thoughts. Suppose that I make two utterances of (1), one in the U.S. and the other in Belgium. If my two utterances of (1) express the same thought content, then this thought content is both true and false. This thought is true when I am in the U.S. and false when in Belgium. Thought content cannot be true and false. Let us go back to my utterances of (1) and (3). I had a true belief in the U.S. and stick to that belief when going to Belgium. I also had and expressed a true thought when uttering (3) in Belgium. What accounts for the fact that I do not have contradictory thoughts even while uttering a sentence and its negation? The thought content cannot be read from the linguistic meaning of the sentences uttered. As a consequence, one needs more than meaning to identify the thoughts expressed by utterances of (1) and (3). I assume that the contextual occurring in (1) is responsible for these features, and that it lacks a Fregean sense.

Reporting the thought expressed by my utterance of (1), you tell a friend,

(5)   Richard believes that Stella Artois is an imported beer.

The sentence in the belief report does not tell the whole story about my belief. Do you have the U.S. or Belgium in mind? If it is the U.S., your belief attribution is true; if it is Belgium, your belief attribution is false. I do not believe that Stella Artois is an imported beer in Belgium. The country my thought content is about is not articulated in the belief report, and sentence (5) does not fully report my thought content. You could also truly report

(6)   Richard believes that Stella Artois is not an important beer.

If you have the U.S. in mind, it is false; if you have Belgium in mind, it is true. I really believed that Stella Artois is not an imported beer when making my utterance in Belgium. Do you have the U.S. or Belgium in mind? Once again, the country my thought content is about is not articulated in the belief report and (6) is not specific enough to report a true thought content. Finally, you can truly say (5) and (6), without attributing contradictory beliefs to me. What explains the fact that these belief reports can both be true?

2   Grasping Contextuals

According to philosophical tradition, standard one-place predicates contribute conditions to the truth conditions of a sentence or an utterance. Let me state what I will call the Syntactic-Semantic Correlation Principle.

Syntactic-Semantic Correlation Principle
One-place predicates only contribute conditions to the truth conditions of sentences.

This principle is not controversial and is widely accepted. It is assumed to apply to any standard one-place predicate, whatever its linguistic meaning. It applies to "is blue," "is sick," and so on. The linguistic meaning of these predicates contributes, respectively, the condition of being blue and the condition of being sick to the truth conditions of sentences. Recently, it has been argued that some predicates, namely relative gradable predicates ("is tall," "is big," etc.) and taste predicates ("is fun," "is tasty"), raise certain issues. A comparison class is plausibly carried into the truth conditions of utterances by relative gradable adjectives (Kennedy 2007). For example, an utterance of "Secretariat is fast" is true if Secretariat is fast compared to horses, not to race cars. It is true if the comparison class is the set of horses, and false if the comparison class is race cars. It cannot be denied that the predicate is responsible for introducing such a truth-conditionally relevant comparison class. The contribution of taste predicates to the truth conditions of utterances prompts modifications in semantics (Lasersohn 2005). For example, the sentence "Licorice is tasty" is true, according to me, and false according to my wife. The same nonindexical sentence, or utterances of the latter, can have intuitive differences in truth value. Taste predicates have features motivating alterations in semantics to account both for intuitions concerning the contribution of these predicates to the truth conditions of utterances and for the assignment of truth value to the latter (Lasersohn 2005; MacFarlane 2006). Some one-place predicates are not standard. Given the problems contextual predicates raise, it can be argued that contextual predicates are not standard either.

The linguistic meaning of standard predicates determines conditions, satisfied or not by objects (the extension of the condition), and all utterances of the same standard predicate determine the same condition, which is satisfied or not by objects. Contextual predicates are not typical standard predicates in that respect. The meaning of "is imported" does not determine a simple condition satisfied or not by objects: pineapples can simultaneously have the property of being imported (in Canada) and lack that property (in Nicaragua). They can be simultaneously imported and not imported. Moreover, if contextual predicates have an extension, it cannot be a set of objects satisfying a condition they semantically determine, because that set may satisfy and not satisfy that condition. To assume that contextual predicates determine mere conditions is a far too simple description of predicates such as "is imported." There is more.

Treating contextual predicates as standard does not account for uncontroversial intuitions concerning the truth conditions of contextual sentences. If contextual predicates are standard predicates, and if the linguistic meaning of "imported," and more precisely the meaning of the predicate "is imported," contribute the condition of being imported or something similar, then the truth conditions of an utterance of (1) are

(A)   An utterance of (1) is true only if Stella Artois is an imported beer.

Or, in a language closer to a formal representation, if and only if Stella Artois is a beer and is imported. These are context-insensitive truth conditions. The latter do not cohere with intuitions concerning these utterances. If utterances of contextual sentences vary in truth value then they vary in truth conditions, and their linguistic meaning does not and cannot determine a simple, context-insensitive condition, such as *being imported*, which is a component part of the truth conditions of utterances. In fact, on that picture, *being imported* is a feature any beers can have—it depends on the country you are in—and does not state a specific characteristic of that beer. When saying that Stella Artois is an imported beer, you are saying something rather specific about that beer. In contrast with some other beers, it is brought into the country you are talking about. The speaker making an utterance of (1) must have a specific country in mind for his utterance to have a truth value. Likewise, the truth conditions of his utterance depend on which specific country it is: the U.S. or Belgium? If utterances of contextual sentences like (1) are context-insensitive, there is, for instance, no explanation for why and how specific countries are required and truth-conditionally relevant for utterances of (1), and no room for introducing a specific country into these truth conditions. The Syntactic-Semantic Correlation Principle does not clearly apply to contextual predicates, and the meaning of such terms does not *prima facie* determine a simple condition, part of the truth conditions of a sentence or an utterance.

Speakers have clear and fine-grained linguistic intuitions about contextual predicates. These intuitions are difficult to account for if contextual predicates are standard predicates. You are in Canada talking with a friend about a student and say (2). Your friend asks where Luisa is from. He knows that you are talking about a person coming from a country different from Canada. He needs no extra sentential, factual information to ask his question. Were he to suggest that that person is probably from Winnipeg or Vancouver, then he would have failed to understand the linguistic meaning of your remark, or does not know that Winnipeg and Vancouver are in Canada. He would be wrong about the semantics of the sentence, or confused about facts. I assume that he is right about facts. What would he have wrong about the meaning? In (2), the idea that she comes from a different country can be grasped by any semantically competent speaker, and "foreign" carries this idea. The same goes for "imported." For your utterance of (2), Canada is the relevant country. For my utterance of (1), the U.S. is the relevant country. The idea that Stella Artois is brought into a country is grasped by any semantically competent speaker. It is a semantic fact about "imported" that a country is truth-conditionally relevant, and it is also a semantic fact about "imported" that the beer is brought into that country. Extralinguistic information is needed to identify the specific, truth-conditionally relevant country the speaker is talking about in uttering (1). Contextual predicates are *prima facie* context sensitive expressions, and they are not standard in not determining a simple condition.

3 Contextuals and Context-Insensitivity

Unfortunately, things are not so simple. In contrast with utterances containing indexicals and demonstratives, utterances of contextual sentences are not all context-sensitive. Consider

(7)   Imported beer is expensive.

Utterances of this sentence are not always about a specific country. An utterance of (7) might be about any country and convey that in any country, beer brought into this country is expensive. All utterances of (7) then have the same linguistic meaning, the same truth conditions, and the same truth value. The speakers' intentions and/or what they have in mind has no role as far as truth conditions of these utterances of (7) are concerned. Context-insensitivity is also reflected in the cognitive value of utterances. All utterances of (7), under the interpretation we are concerned with, have the same cognitive value and carry the same information. Of course, believing what is expressed by an utterance of (7) and not believing what is expressed by a different utterance of the same sentence is irrational. Finally, all context insensitive utterances of (7) express the same thought content. The latter is echoed in belief attribution. All utterances of "Richard believes that imported beer is expensive" plausibly report context-insensitive thought contents, this sentence itself being context-insensitive. I share this belief with many people. Any semantic account of "imported" has to make room for such context-insensitive reading.

A plausible view of contextual predicates must account for both their *prima facie* context-sensitive occurrences, as in (1), and their context-insensitive occurrences, as in the utterance of (7) we just saw. Similarly, it should explain how they let what the speaker has in mind play a role in the determination of the truth conditions of utterances of some sentences, as in (1), and sometimes make what he has in mind semantically irrelevant, as in some utterances of (7). Now, if some contextual sentences are context-sensitive and some are context-insensitive, then contextuals cannot be either indexicals, such as "I," or standard predicates such as "is blue." Taking them to be of one of those categories does not account for the facts. Indexicals are never context-insensitive,[6] and standard predicates are never context-sensitive. Nonetheless, contextual predicates are very systematic and have the same linguistic meaning in all sentences. Learning the meaning of the predicate occurring in (1) is also learning the meaning of the predicate occurring in (7), and *vice-versa*. The main issue is to account for how "imported" contributes to the truth conditions of utterances of (1) and (7). I wish to suggest an approach for the context sensitivity of contextual predicates. I will come back to (7) after having presented my view. First, I would like to mention a few of the available options in the literature.

3 Options on the Market

Some options emphasize a semantic approach. Hall Partee writes that "large numbers of open-class lexical items act as though their meaning includes something like a bound-variable part" (1989: 343). She adds that "Ignoring the sense of *local* which contrasts with *regional*, *national*, *international*, etc., we can say that *local* has to be anchored to some reference location, and means something like 'in the vicinity of [the reference location]'" (ibid.: 344; see also Nunberg 1992: 284). Hall Partee focuses on meaning rather than syntax. Unfortunately, she does not offer a complete analysis of these predicates. I wish to further develop her intuitions, being particularly interested in the differences she downplays.

Récanati (2002) also favors a semantic approach to contextuals. He compares contextuals to indexicals (2002: 311) and writes about relative predicates like "is tall," genitives like "John's car," and contextuals like "local."

> I think that the contextually provided element (the comparison class, or the relation R) is *somehow 'articulated'*, in virtue of the simple fact that its contextual provision is required for the interpretation of the particular linguistic expression. (Récanati 2002: 311)

I understand Récanati as suggesting that the linguistic meaning of contextuals like "imported," *somehow* requires the truth conditions of utterances to contain a country. If Récanati is right, contextuals *somehow* make room

---

[6] I am focusing on standard uses. Sentences like 'Never do today what you can put off until tomorrow' raise issues I cannot deal with in the present paper.

for a constituent thanks to their linguistic meaning. I follow Récanati's lead in thinking that the linguistic meaning of "local" or "imported" strongly suggests a location, and more precisely a country in the case of "imported," and in a sense makes room for a location or a country in the truth conditions of an utterance. This is the basic idea I want to explore.

Perry (1998: 7) also raises the contextual issue. He mentions that "local" calls for a location but argues that it is a one-place argument and that the location is unarticulated. The picture of contextuals he offers remains sketchy. On the other hand, his view on semantics can be used to provide an account of contextuals. I will come back to this point in the next sections.

Other options involve syntax. Stanley (2000: 31) advocates the view that "all effects of extra-linguistic context on the truth conditions of assertions are traceable to logical form" and rejects the idea that "local" or "imported" sentence utterances contain an unarticulated constituent. He adopts a syntactic approach, where "local" becomes "local to x," and "imported" plausibly becomes "imported in x," (ibid.: 58). He turns a *prima facie* syntactically one-place predicate ("is imported") into a two-place predicate ("is imported in x"). The place relevant to the truth conditions of (1) is here articulated by the variable. The latter can be read as a free variable, a demonstrative, or a bound variable. The implicit argument accounts for the utterance variability of a "local" and "imported" sentence. In Stanley's view, the sentence (1) is syntactically complete, and the proposition determined by a token of (1) in a context is gappy, containing a variable needing the assignment of a value. I agree with Pagin in thinking that "speaker intuitions about syntax should count more than speaker intuitions about semantics" (Pagin 2005: 332). Given that people use their knowledge of the syntax and semantics of words and sentences to grasp the truth conditions of utterances, and given that "is local" and "is imported" are *prima facie* one-place predicates, I favor preserving that intuition. In addition, Stanley's strategy applies across the board—to relative predicates, meteorological ("rain") predicates, and so on—and offers no suggestion specific to contextuals. Mine does. Stanley is right in thinking that a free variable, a demonstrative, or a bound variable is relevant. In an utterance of (1), there is a reference to a specific country and that reference is demonstrative-like. However, I think that he is wrong about the location of this variable. Moreover, Stanley's view does not capture the idea that every speaker knows, in virtue of his semantic competence, that a country is relevant for "imported" and "foreign." I want to account for that aspect of linguistic understanding. I will not press on with criticisms, but rather will propose my own explanation.

4   Multipropositionalism

Perry recently introduced a new framework called Reflexive Referential Semantics (Perry 2001, 2006). The latter focuses on utterances and the token-reflexive nature of the meaning of pure indexicals, and it proposes an account of standard context-sensitive terms. It also suggests a picture of the semantics of contextuals and contextual utterances. Let me briefly introduce the framework.

According to Perry, the linguistic meaning of a pure indexical is a property of the indexical as type; it is a rule for determining the contribution of the indexical to the truth conditions of an utterance. The meaning of a sentence is given by the rules governing the components of this sentence. Truth does not apply to the meaning of sentences, because truth is not a property of rules. Truth applies to propositions or contents determined by these rules. The linguistic meaning of indexicals determines a reflexive condition on reference. It is called reflexive because it is a condition containing the utterance as a constituent. For example, the linguistic meaning of "I" is *the speaker of the utterance*, and the meaning of "you" is *the addressee of the utterance*. Suppose that I make an utterance **u** of "I am hungry," Given the meaning of the components of this sentence

(B)   the utterance **u** of "I am hungry" is true if and only if *the speaker of* **u** is hungry

Perry calls this content, *the speaker of* **u** *is hungry*, the indexical content of the utterance. This content is reflexive because it contains the utterance itself as a constituent. The indexical content is the proposition obtained by only considering the linguistic meaning of the sentence uttered, and excluding extralinguistic information. Given the utterance **u**, the biconditional is known a priori and it does not carry information about the world. It carries information about the utterance itself. The indexical content of this utterance of (1) does not give the official content of an utterance of (1), or what is said. The speaker does not want to talk about his utterance. He wants to talk about himself. Exploiting meaning and the context of utterance, you identify the speaker

(C)   The utterance of **u** of "I am hungry" is true if and only if **RV** is hungry.

RV is the speaker himself. Perry calls **RV** *is hungry* the referential content of the utterance. The referential content contains the speaker as a constituent, and no mention of the utterance is made. To identify the referent of that utterance of "I," more than knowledge of language is required, and one needs to use extralinguistic information. The referential content gives the intuitive truth conditions or official content of my utterance.

Reflexive-Referential Semantics is a multipropositionalist framework. In this approach, an utterance of a single sentence determines many propositions or contents, forming a variety of truth conditions that one can identify by exploiting meaning and extralinguistic context. In our example, indexical and referential contents are contents identified by exploiting, respectively, linguistic meaning, and meaning and extralinguistic context.

Let me introduce an important aspect of Reflexive Referential Semantics. As we saw, in the framework we are using, meaning is a property of expressions as type rather than being part of a proposition or content. Perry pays attention to utterances but takes Fregean roles of propositions or contents into account. The referential content of my utterance of "I am hungry" plays the role of intuitive truth condition or official content of my utterance. Thought contents are difficult to deal with, and we can set them aside here. Frege was also interested in cognitive value. While Frege had the cognitive value of sentences in mind, Perry's view takes utterances into consideration and focuses on the cognitive significance of utterances. He mentions that

> If there is some aspect of meaning, by which an utterance u of S and an utterance u' of S' differ, so that a rational person who understood both S and S' might accept u but not u', then a fully adequate theory of linguistic meaning should say what it is (Perry 1988, in Perry 2000:194)[7]

He also gives conditions on cognitive significance of utterances:

(a) The cognitive significance of an utterance S in language L is a semantic property of the utterance.
(b) It is a property that a person who understands the meaning of S in L recognizes.
(c) The cognitive significance of an utterance of S in L is a proposition.
(d) A person who understands the meaning of S in L, and accepts as true an utterance of S in L, will believe the proposition that is the cognitive significance of the utterance. (Perry 1988: 194).

Cognitive significance is defined in terms of acceptance of utterance — or accepting an utterance as true (Perry 1988: 193) — *without taking extralinguistic facts into considerations*. The indexical content of my utterance **u** of "I am hungry" is *the speaker of* **u** *is hungry*. The latter takes charge of the cognitive significance role of that utterance.

---

[7] Actually, Perry is interested in two utterances of the same indexical sentence.

In the case of indexical sentences, semantically determined reflexive content or indexical content can be identified with cognitive significance. However, that strategy will not work for utterances of (1), for example, because none of the lexical items in (1) is reflexive and the semantically determined content of (1) does not contain an utterance as a constituent. *Prima facie*, in that framework, we cannot account for the fact that a speaker can accept an utterance of (1) and reject a different utterance of the same sentence. The framework implies that all utterances of (1) have the same cognitive significance. But it leaves room for manoeuvre. I will come back to the cognitive significance of contextual utterances.

5   A Suggestion

1   Meaning and Complementary Conditions

According to the traditional view, all standard predicates follow the Syntactic-Semantic Correlation Principle and semantically provide a unique, simple condition to the content of an utterance. That common conception fits predicates such as "is black" and "is round" but cannot easily handle "is imported." Now, there is no compelling argument backing the idea that the traditional view and the Syntactic-Semantic Correlation Principle apply to contextual predicates. In fact, it is doubtful that this principle does. Moreover, there is no reason to think that it is the only option in semantics. Reflexive Referential Semantics and contextuals suggest a different perspective. Reflexive Referential Semantics makes a distinction between the linguistic meaning as type and the contribution of meaning to semantically determined content of utterances. Frege does not make a clear distinction between the meaning of a term and its contribution to propositions containing that term. Actually, the meaning of a term, its sense, is part of the proposition expressed by a sentence containing that term. There is no way of distinguishing these two aspects of a term in Frege's framework. Reflexive Referential Semantics clearly separate the meaning of a term, a rule associated to the term as type, and its contribution to the various contents of an utterance. Once meaning and content are distinguished, the Syntactic-Semantic Correlation Principle is less constraining and much more flexible. The Reflexive Referential framework also introduces many different contents having different Fregean roles. Bringing in semantically determined content as the cognitive significance of utterances creates space between meaning of expressions as type and contribution to the official content of utterances in a way that is appropriate for capturing our understanding of various aspects of semantically complex terms such as contextual predicates.

As distinct from "I," the contribution of "is imported" to the official content of utterances of (1), or what is said, is not automatic: it does not always depend solely on linguistic meaning and context. However, it can be argued that, just as the linguistic meaning of "I" as type brings in a complex identifying condition, *the speaker of the utterance*, into the content of an utterance, the linguistic meaning of "is imported" also brings in a complex condition into the proposition or content of an utterance. Any semantically competent speaker knows that imported things are objects brought into a country. This is not knowledge of facts but knowledge of language. The linguistic meaning of "is imported" contributes something like the complex condition *being brought into a country* to the semantically determined content of an utterance.[8] However, the intuitive truth conditions or official content of an utterance of (1) do not contain that condition. Moreover, it contains a specific, nonlexically determined country as a constituent. That country is the one the speaker is talking about. What constrains the speaker of (1) to have a country in mind? And how can the country the speaker is talking about be a relevant component of the official content of an utterance of a complete sentence, such as (1), which *prima facie* leaves no role for intention or what the speaker has in mind, and no room for a country in a content it determines? Intentions or having something in mind play no role in the determination of the official content of a complete, context-insensitive sentence like "The King of France is bald." Intentions play a role in the determination of the official content of an utterance of "This is a fly" thanks to the fact that the referent of the utterance of "this," and hence the contribution of this term to the official content of the utterance, depends on the speaker's intention. However, there is no demonstrative in (1). One way of facing the problem is to explicitly define complex conditions determined by the linguistic meaning of contextual predicates.

We are used to the idea that a predicate semantically introduces a simple condition into the truth conditions of a sentence or an utterance. The Fregean tradition has rendered that idea commonsense in philosophy of language. Some predicates, such as contextual predicates, have a rather complex linguistic meaning, and *prima facie* introduce something richer than a simple condition into the content of an utterance. I wish to explore the idea that the lexical linguistic meaning of contextual predicates as type brings in a complex condition—indeed, a relation and a property—to the indexical content or the semantically determined content of an utterance. I will focus on "is imported."

---

[8] See also Hall Partee (1989) on the meaning of "local." My opinion differs from that of Hall Partee (1989: 344), who argues that the meaning of "local" is something like "in the vicinity of [reference location]." In my view, this is a semantically determined condition given by the linguistic meaning of that lexical item as type.

The meaning of "is imported" determines something like the complex condition of *being brought into a country*. To make things clear, let us say that the linguistic meaning of "is imported" as type semantically determines a relation and a condition to the indexical content of an utterance

(D)   *being brought into y . country y*

I will keep using the term indexical content even if reflexivity is not involved here. The complex constituent semantically contributed to indexical content by the intuitive conventional meaning of "is imported," *being brought into a country*, has a structure, and it is more than a mere juxtaposition of conditions because of the role played by the variable *y* occurring in both the relation and the condition. Call such a conjunction of relations and conditions complementary conditions. Complementary conditions are not conditions, such as *being sick*, which objects can satisfy or not. Of course, not all conjunctions of relation and condition are plausible complementary conditions. For instance, *being raised into y . circle y* is not. That does not mean that complementary conditions do not exist. It only means that it is false that every set of relations and conditions is a complementary condition. The latter echoes the complexity of the conventional linguistic meaning of some lexical items, as is the case with the condition determined by the meaning of "is imported."[9]

I shall generalize this picture by suggesting that predicates containing contextual adjectives semantically bring in complementary conditions to the semantically determined content of utterances

(E)   Being R y . F y

The complementary condition contains a variable, *y*, that does not correspond to any lexical component in the sentence (1). The variable is not part of the syntax of the sentence, and it is carried by the meaning of the contextual. My proposal echoes Récanati's suggestion that a variable is *somehow* articulated by the contextual. This variable is the available tool for letting the speakers' intentions, or what the speakers have in mind, play a semantic role. My view focuses on the complex condition that linguistic meaning as type sometimes semantically determines. It likewise exploits complementary conditions. These conditions are not obtained by decomposition and decompositional analysis of the meaning of terms. Just as is the case for indexicals, they are what you find when you inquire about the meaning of a term by looking it up in a good dictionary.

---

[9] As with "exported", *brought out of a country*, "local", *characteristic of a place* or *in the vicinity of a place*, "enemy", *hostile to a country*, or *hostile to a person,* "national", *characteristic of a country*, and so on. Lexical semantics should tell us more about these expressions.

Consider the semantically determined contribution of "is imported" to semantically determined or indexical content of an utterance, *being brought into y . country y*, and an utterance of (1).

(F)   The utterance **u** of (1) is true if and only if Stella Artois is a beer brought into y . country y.

This content is neither true nor false because it contains a free variable. This is a feature fixed by the meaning of the contextual predicate. Semantically competent speakers take utterances of (1) to have a truth-value: some, such as those about the U.S., are true, and others, such as those about Belgium, are false. How can a speaker make an utterance of (1) truth valuable? Let us focus on cognitive significance first.

If the semantically determined content of an utterance plays the role of the cognitive significance of that utterance, utterances of (1) all have *prima facie* the same cognitive significance. However, a rational person can accept an utterance of (1) about the U.S. as true and reject a second utterance of the same sentence about Belgium as false. By the same token, any speaker accepting as true all utterances of (1)—about the U.S. and Belgium for instance—would be linguistically incompetent or irrational. I assume that speakers are linguistically competent and rational. Given the linguistic meaning of (1), whatever the extralinguistic facts, semantically competent speakers could have divergent cognitive attitudes toward different utterances of (1) without being irrational and would be wrong to adopt only one of these attitudes toward that content. Competent speakers know that different utterances of (1) can differ in cognitive significance, whatever their actual official content and their actual truth value.[10] Linguistic meaning does not tell the whole story about the cognitive significance and the truth conditions of utterances of (1), or about our understanding of utterances of (1). Now, utterances offer many different aspects speakers exploit to convey and grasp contents. Meaning contributes to cognitive significance, and speakers exploit cognitive significance in linguistic communication.

To account for the cognitive significance of an indexical utterance, Perry uses the semantically determined reflexive content of that utterance. His claim that the semantically determined reflexive content is the cognitive significance of an utterance is slightly misleading. For indexical utterances, the semantically determined reflexive content accounts for differ-

---

[10] Now, one could rely on free enrichment (Récanati) and arrive at something like "The utterance **u** of (1) is true if and only if Stella Artois is a beer imported in Mexico." If so, one neglects the systematicity connected to "is imported" and contextual predicates. One also fails to account for the difference in the cognitive significance of different utterances of (1).

ences in cognitive significance. However, there is no reason to believe that what accounts for differences in cognitive significance is always a semantically determined reflexive content; utterances of (1) bear witness to this. In the case of some contextual utterances, such as utterances of (1), identifying the content having the role of cognitive significance is done by focusing on the relevant variable, y. This variable can be used to explain differences in cognitive significance, in official content, and in truth-value.

2   Selecting a Reading—Context Sensitivity

A variable can be free or bound. In the semantically determined content of an utterance of (1), *Stella Artois is a beer brought into y . country y, y* is a free variable. Speakers are not passive in their understanding of utterances: they do not always simply mechanically follow the meaning of words and their syntactic relationship. They also focus on cognitive significance, official content and truth value. Speakers know, in virtue of their semantic competence, that not identifying a country, or not assigning y a value, results in the utterance having no truth conditions and lacking truth value. They also know that the utterance of (1) has truth conditions and truth-value, whatever they are. The fact that y is a free variable requiring an assignment of value makes room for the speakers' intentions, or what they have in mind, to play a role in determining the official content of an utterance of this complete, nonindexical, nondemonstrative sentence. It also opens up room to account for cognitive significance.

On hearing my utterance **u** of (1), and grasping its semantically determined content, you know that you can neither accept that utterance as true nor reject it as false. If a speaker thinks that she can neither accept an utterance of (1) as true nor reject it as false that speaker does not qualify as semantically competent. You understand that the utterance **u** of (1) is true if and only if Stella Artois is a beer brought into y . country y. Thanks to your semantic competence, you know that there is an element in the semantically determined content of that utterance needing a value assignment to determine the official content and a truth-value. You also know that a country should be assigned to the variable. You furthermore know that the assigned value can differ from utterance to utterance and that a device appropriate for assigning a value needs to be attached to the variable.

Knowing that a free variable needs an assignment of value, you understand that

(G)   The utterance **u** of "Stella Artois is an imported beer" is true if and only if Stella Artois is a beer brought into y . country y and y = the object the speaker of **u** has in mind.

Let us call it the enriched content. This content is reflexive. It plays the role of the utterance's cognitive significance, something one can accept as true. The condition of being a country is cognitively significant, and it is part of what accounts for the cognitive significance of the utterance: *Stella Artois is a beer brought into y . country y*. A value assignment is needed to obtain a truth value for the utterance.

I do not wish to endorse one view or the other on how the referent of a free variable is selected. Views on the assignment of value to free variables, such as "that", are complex and controversial. I do not need to join that controversy to make my point. I prefer to keep options open with the vague *the object the speaker of* **u** *has in mind*.[11] There is no demonstrative in the sentence, and "y = *the object the speaker of* **u** *has in mind*" is not semantically provided. However, this clause reiterates the fact that the complex condition determined by the contextual predicate contains a free variable, and that the speaker says something true, or false, on the assumption that he has something in mind and must be talking about a country in order to do so. Moreover, the speaker knows that he needs to assign a value to obtain a truth-valuable official content and knows that the relevant value is a country. The nonsemantically determined clause, *the object the speaker of* **u** *has in mind*, is required due to the fact that there is a free variable in need of an assignment for the utterance to have cognitive significance, official content, and truth value. The biconditional (G) is known *a priori* and it is cognitively significant. A different utterance **u'** of (1) would have a different cognitive significance: *Stella Artois is a beer brought into y . country y* and y = *the object the speaker of* **u'** *has in mind*. The specific country itself is not part of the cognitive significance of the utterance.

One may wish to dispense with what the speaker has in mind and to let the context of the utterance decide what the value of the variable is. This is counterintuitive. Speakers have something in mind when making utterances of (1) and what they have in mind motivates their utterances. Moreover, we understand speakers of (1) as having something in mind, and that something makes the utterance true or false. Why am I uttering (1)? Because I think that I am in the U.S. A speaker may think about something which is not part of the physical context of utterance—say, make an utterance of (1) in a discussion about The Netherlands in Houston—or might be

---

[11] I thank Maite Ezcurdia and Eleonora Orlando for discussions on this issue.

wrong about the context of utterance—one might think that one is in The Netherlands and make an utterance of (1) while one is actually in Belgium.[12] Still, what the speaker is thinking about is at the foreground of his mind when producing and understanding the utterance. Letting the context decide the value of the variable does not allow the speaker to speak about a country that is not part of the physical context. Introducing "having in mind" does. That does not mean that *Stella Artois is a beer brought into y . country y and y = the object the speaker of* **u** *has in mind* is my thought content. This content is not my thought content, because it is reflexive and my thought content is not. My thought content is not about the utterance. It is about a country. Moreover, in no case is it the content motivating my utterance and a thought content motivating what I want to express. The specific country I am thinking about, whether it is the country I am in or the country we are talking about without ever mentioning it, partly motivates the utterance, is truth-conditionally relevant, and is part of the official content of my utterance. This is what *"the speaker of* **u** *has is mind"* is designed to capture. Were the beer not brought into that specific country, my utterance would be false (See Perry 2008).

Suppose that I am in Belgium, but think that I am in The Netherlands, a neighbouring country, and make an utterance of (1). Is my utterance true? If the country I am in is relevant, then my utterance is false: I was talking about Belgium, the country I am in. If the intended location or what I had in mind is relevant, then my utterance is true: I was intending to talk about The Netherlands.[13] Whatever the argument in favour of one answer or the other, I take this dispute to assume my basic point: contextual predicates are context-sensitive terms containing a free variable, y, which is assigned a value. Whatever position one takes on that issue, it presupposes my approach as a general framework. This puzzle echoes Kaplan's famous Spiro Agnew puzzle. Discussing it more fully here would involve assuming that my view is correct, and would require a new paper. For obvious reasons, I shall not pursue this issue here.

The utterance would not communicate the intended specific content were this content—*Stella Artois is a beer brought into y . country y and* y = *the object the speaker of* **u** *has in mind*—to give the official content of the utterance or what is said. I want to talk about a specific country in making the utterance. We were in the U.S., and I had the U.S. in mind when I uttered (1). Under what conditions is my utterance of (1) true? My utterance is true if and only if Stella Artois is a beer brought into that

---

[12] I thank Jeff Pelletier for raising this issue.

[13] I thank Jeff Pelletier for this example.

specific country. The truth conditions of my utterance **u** of (1) contain the U.S.

(H)   The utterance **u** of "Stella Artois is an imported beer" is true if and only if Stella Artois is a beer brought in **THE U.S.**

THE U.S. stands for the U.S. itself. Call the content *Stella Artois is a beer brought into* **THE U.S.** the referential content of my utterance[14] or what is said. It gives the official content of the utterance, or what is said. The condition of being a country is truth-conditionally relevant, constraining a component part of the referential content of the utterance. Because of the linguistic meaning of "imported," I cannot really be intending to talk about the 19th century. If intentions are invoked, then the intentions relevant for contextual predicates are postsemantic. They are not about meaning selection, they play a role after meaning is given, and are constrained by descriptive linguistic meaning. What I have in mind is semantically constrained by the meaning of the contextual.

The idea that Stella Artois is brought into a country is part of the cognitive significance of the utterance, but it is not part of its referential content. The country itself is. Further more, the property of being a country is not part of referential content of the utterance. The speaker did not say that the U.S. is a country. However, his utterance conventionally implies that it is (Grice 1975).

The referential content depends on the intended object, not on a representation of that object—namely, a representation of the U.S. Making an utterance **u** of (1) and talking about the U.S., the utterance **u** is about the U.S. and it is true if and only if Stella Artois is a beer brought into the **U.S.** Making an utterance **u'** of (1) and talking about Belgium, the utterance **u'** is about Belgium and it is true if and only if Stella Artois is a beer brought into **Belgium** The utterance is also false. Two utterances of (1) about the U.S. differ in cognitive significance, because of the reflexive content of these utterances. Nonetheless, they have the same nonreflexive designational content, containing the U.S. as a constituent. Like indexical utterances, contextual utterances exhibit a gap between indexical and referential content, or cognitive significance and official content. Sentence (1) and "Stella Artois is a beer brought into the U.S." are not synonymous. My utterance **u** of (1) about the U.S. and the utterance of "Stella Artois is a beer brought into the U.S." differ in linguistic meaning and in cognitive significance. However, they cannot differ in referential content and in truth value. The sentence "Stella Artois is a beer brought into the U.S."

---

[14] I call it 'referential content' because the free variable is used in a way very similar to a demonstrative.

expresses in a context-insensitive way what is said in a context-sensitive way when uttering (1) about the U.S. A speaker making an utterance of this context-insensitive sentence and another making an utterance of (1) say the same thing.

3 Selecting a Reading—binding

The relevant variable is sometimes bound, as in some utterances of

(7)   Imported beer is expensive.

Suppose that you hear an utterance **u** of (7). All utterances of (7) have the same linguistic meaning as type. *Prima facie*, the speaker is not thinking or talking about any specific country. In a plausible reading, the speaker means that wherever one is, imported beer is expensive. Variable y is then plausibly not a free variable in need of a value assignment. Adopting this interpretation, one can accept the utterance of (7) and accept any utterance of the same sentence. Actually, one would then be irrational in accepting some utterances of (7) and in rejecting other utterances of the same sentence. In addition, all utterances of (7) can have the same truth value. Finally, every speaker of (7) shares the same thought content: they all then believe that imported beer is expensive.

Given linguistic competence, you understand that

(I)   The utterance **u** of (7) is true if and only if (x) beer (x) x is brought into y and country y $\to$ x is expensive.[15]

The condition in the complementary condition introduces a variable fit for binding. It also gives a constraint on the value of that variable: y is a country. The utterance is about any country. No quantifier binds that variable, but given cognitive significance, universal quantification is required. The variable cannot be existentially quantified and the utterance meaningful. Hence

(J)   The utterance **u** of (7) is true if and only if (x) beer x (y) country y, x is brought into y $\to$ x is expensive.

Reading a contextual as containing a free or a bound variable depends on the linguistic context. One reading or another is also prompted by the cognitive significance of the utterance containing it and the context of utterance in a wide understanding of that notion. Identifying the relevant reading is motivated by the acceptability as true of different utterances of the sentence containing it.

---

[15] There is some simplification here. I treat "beer" as a count noun, not as a mass term, to make the presentation of my view easier. Such a simplification does not impact my main point.

4   Cognitive Dissonance

Now let us consider

(8)   Stella Artios is an imported beer in San Francisco.

This sentence is perplexing. What is the problem here? Beer is not imported in cities. The cognitive significance of an utterance of (8) is

(K)   The utterance **u** of (8) is true if and only if Stella Artois is a beer
           brought into y . country y and y = San Francisco.

The problem with (8) is not only that it is false. No true designational
content can be reached, unless one focuses on the country San Francisco is
in: the U.S.[16]

5   Back to Beliefs and Belief Reports

Sentences (1) and (3) do not contradict one another and can both be true.
In the U.S., my utterance of (1) has a reflexive content

(M)   The utterance **u** of (1) is true if and only if Stella Artois is a beer
           bought into y . country y and y is the object the speaker of **u** has
           in mind.

From reflexive content and information on the speaker, one can easily obtain

(N)   The utterance **u** of (1) is true if and only if and only if Stella Ar-
           tois is brought into **the U.S.**

In Belgium, my utterance of (3) has a different reflexive content.

(O)   The utterance **u'** of (3) is true if and only if Stella Artois is not a
           beer brought into y . country y and y is the object the speaker of
           u' has in mind.

It also has a different referential content

(P)   The utterance **u** of (3) is true if and only if Stella Artois is not a
           beer brought into **BELGIUM**.

Both reflexive contents, as well as both referential contents, are true.
The thought my first utterance expresses is about the U.S.; the thought my
second utterance expresses is about Belgium. The place the thought is

---

[16] The idea that imported goods are brought into a country might raise issues. My understanding is intended to capture a very common understanding of "imported". One could argue
that they are brought into a different jurisdiction, a country, a state or a city. Our linguistic
intuitions concerning contextuals are underexplored. I want to leave options open here, and
adopt a very standard view on 'imported'.

about is implicit, being articulated neither in the sentence nor in the thought, but it is a constituent of the official of the utterance. Consider

(9)   Richard believes that Stella Artois is an imported beer.

(10)   Richard believes that Stella Artois is not an imported beer.

Both attributions can be true, depending on the country the belief attribution is about. Both attributions are underinformative about what the speaker has in mind when making the attribution, and about the country my belief is about. On the other hand

(11)   Richard believes that Stella Artois is an imported beer in Canada.

carries a linguistic representation of the country my belief is about. The country is articulated in the belief attribution.

6   Ambiguity

Semantic ambiguity is about having two distinct unrelated meanings. "Crane" is semantically ambiguous, being a word for a piece of machinery and a word for a bird. There is no connection between the relevant meanings. A speaker learning the word as having one meaning may not know its other, different meaning. Sentences containing these terms may also have very different truth conditions. For examples, "Cranes are tall" is ambiguous, being true if and only if some sort of machinery is tall or true if and only if some sort of bird is tall. The conditions determined by ambiguous predicates are both part of the cognitive significance and the official content of utterances. A speaker understanding the meaning of an expression and not knowing its other meaning cannot identify the cognitive significance of the other expression as well the contribution to official content of utterances of that other expression. It would be surprising not to find semantically ambiguous contextual predicates. And, indeed, they do exist. In the case of contextual predicates, lexical ambiguity is a little more complicated. *Prima facie*, lexical ambiguity can be created by the relation or by the property. "Local" means either *characteristic of a place* (as in "local beer") or *in the vicinity of a place* (as in "local bar"). "Local" is semantically ambiguous. Semantic ambiguity is reflected in truth conditions. The relation, *being characteristic of* for instance, is reflected both in the cognitive significance and in the official content of the utterance. The property, *a place*, is reflected in cognitive significance, but it is not reflected in the official content. An object satisfying that property is. An utterance of "The local bars are weird" is true if and only if the bars *in the vicinity of* **P** are weird, or if and only if the bars *characteristic of* **P** are weird, where **P** is a place. Taking official content into account, "local" is semantically ambiguous even if a place is relevant in both readings because the relation differs. "Enemy" means either *hostile to a country* (as in "enemy ship"), or *hostile to individuals* (as in "enemy player"). The relation *enemy of* is the same, while the properties differ, and can be satisfied by differing objects: countries or people. If semantic ambiguity is echoed in official or referential content, then "enemy" is not semantically ambiguous because the property is not part of the referential content of the utterance. The problem with "local" is in the relation, while in the case of "enemy," it is in the property.

Consider Geoff's utterance of

(12)   Local bars are great.

"Local" is semantically ambiguous. In one reading, it semantically contributes a complementary condition like *being in the vicinity of y. y is a place* (similar to Hall Partee 1989: 344). Hearing his utterance **u** of (12) you know that

(Q)   The utterance **u** of (12) is true if and only if (x) bar x (y) place y (x in the vicinity of y → x is great).

In another reading, "local" means something like "characteristic of a place," and determines the complementary condition *characteristic of y . y is a place*.

(R)   The utterance **u** of (12) is true if and only if (x) bar x (y) place (x is characteristic of y → x is great).

You can quantify over the variable. Let us set aside the way a hearer can disambiguate the utterance, and assume that in the relevant reading, (12) means something like *whatever the place, bars characteristic of that place are great*. It means that Geoff does not like big hotel bars. Under that interpretation, all utterances of (12) have the same meaning, the same official content, the same truth-value, and the same cognitive significance. They also express the same thought content. The latter is reported by "Geoff believes that local bars are great." It does not express a singular proposition, as is expected from a context-sensitive utterance, but rather a general proposition, as expected from a context-insensitive utterance. We then have the belief report

Geoff believes that (x) bar x (y) place y (x is characteristic of y → x is great)

You and Geoff can also have the same thought content, that both of you would express by uttering (12). The same goes for

(7)   Imported beer is expensive.

Under the reading mentioned earlier, you and Geoff believe the same thing when uttering that sentence. All utterances of (7) have the same official content. We can explicitly define the official content of an utterance of (7)

(J)   The utterance **u** of (7) is true if and only if (x) beer x (y) place y (x is brought into y $\rightarrow$ x is expensive).

7   A Test

I introduce my view by using a clear and simple example. However, I have neither provided a complete list of contextuals in English, nor have I provided a test to detect contextual predicates. I wish to propose something like the following as a test. Suppose that F is an adjective. Some contextuals are *prima facie* intersective, non-gradable adjectives. In addition, they do not form comparatives and superlatives. Furthermore, they are not evaluative. Take any adjective F that has these properties.

If the sentence "a is F" changes truth-value from utterance to utterance, and if an object can simultaneously satisfy both F and not F then F is a contextual adjective.

6   Conclusion

A semantically competent speaker of (1) knows that a country is under consideration. Assuming that "imported" contributes the condition of being imported to the truth conditions of an utterance, and adding an unarticulated constituent to these truth conditions downplays the descriptive meaning of "imported" and abandons the requirement of a country. It also neglects the contribution of the linguistic meaning of that term to the cognitive significance of utterances of "imported." My suggestion takes meaning and a multiplicity of contents into account. It assigns contextuals a complex meaning appropriate for determining a rich indexical content, containing a relation, a property and a variable, fit to capture various intuitions concerning cognitive significance and official content of contextual utterances. Contextuals illustrate the complex relationship between language, mind, and the world. My proposal invites philosophers to pay more attention to empirical lexical semantics.

Acknowledgements

I want to thank the audience at the 2010 Society for Exact Philosophy (SEP) conference in Kansas City, at the 2010 meeting of the Asociation Latinoamericana de

Filosofia Analitica in Merida, at the PHILANG 2011 conference in Lodz. The referees of *Pragmatics and Cognition* made very helpful comments, helping me to significantly improve the paper. I want to give special thanks to Eros Corazza, Michael Glanzberg, and Jeff Pelletier. Research for this work has been made possible thanks to the Social Science and Humanities Research Council of Canada.

References

Cappelen, H. and Lepore, E. 2005. *Insensitive Semantics*. Malden, MA: Blackwell.

Grice, H.P.1975. "Logic and Conversation". In *Studies in the Ways of Words*. Cambridge, MA: Harvard University Press (1989), 22-40.

Hall Partee, B. 1989. "Binding implicit variables in quantified contexts". *Papers from the Chicago Linguistic Society* 25: 342-365.

Hall Partee, B. 1995. "Lexical semantics and sompositionality". In Osherson, D., *Invitation to Cognitive Science, Part 1, Language*. Cambridge, MA: MIT Press, 311-360.

Kennedy, C. 2007. "Vagueness and grammar. The semantics of relative gradable adjectives". *Linguistics and Philosophy* 30: 1-45.

Korta, K. and Perry, J. 2007. "How to say things with words". In S.L. Tsohatzidis (ed), *John Searle's Philosophy of Language: Force, Meaning, and Thought*. Cambridge: Cambridge University Press, 169-189.

Lasersohn, P. 2005. "Context dependence, disagreement, and predicates of personal taste". *Linguistics and Philosophy* 28: 643-686.

MacFarlane, J. 2007. "Relativism and disagreement". *Philosophical Studies* 132: 17-31.

Marti, L. 2006. "Unarticulated constituents revisited". *Linguistics and Philosophy* 29: 135-166.

Mitchell, J. 1986. *The Formal Semantics of Point of View*. PhD dissertation, University of Massachusetts, Amherst.

Neale, S. 2008 "On location". In O'Rourke and C. Washington (eds), *Situating Semantics, The Philosophy of John Perry*, Cambridge, MA: The MIT Press, 251-393.

Nunberg, G. 1992. "Two kinds of indexicality". In C. Baker and D. Dowty (eds.) *Proceeding of the Second Conference on Semantics and Linguistic Theory*. Columbus, OH: Ohio State University, 283-301.

Nunberg, G. 1993. "Indexicality and deixis". *Linguistics and Philosophy* 16: 1-43.

Perry, J. 1988\2000. 'Cognitive significance and the new theory of reference'. In J. Perry, *The Problem of the Essential Indexical and Other Essays*, 2nd edition. Stanford, CA: CSLI Publications, 189-206.

Perry, J. 1998. "Indexicals, contexts and unarticulated constituents". In A. Aliseda, R. von Glabbeek, and D. Westertal (eds.) *Computing Natural Languages*. Stanford, CA: CSLI Publications, 1-11.

Perry, J. 2001. *Reference and Reflexivity*. Stanford, CA: CSLI Publications.

Perry, J. 2006. "Using indexicals". In *The Blackwell Guide in the Philosophy of Language*. Oxford: Blackwell, 314-334.

Perry, J. 2008. "Directing intentions". In Almog, J. and P. Leonardi (eds.), *The Philosophy of David Kaplan*. Oxford: Oxford University Press, 187-201.

Récanati, F. 2002. "Unarticulated constituents". *Linguistics and Philosophy* 25: 299-345.

Stanley, J. 2000. "Context and logical form". *Linguistics and Philosophy,* 23 (4): 391-434.

Vallée, R. 2003. "Context-sensitivity beyond indexicality". *Dialogue* 79-106.

7

Slurring and Common Knowledge of Ordinary Language

1 Ethnic Slurs

Ethnic slurs ("chink", "nigger," "kike," "boche," and so on) have recently raised interest in philosophy of language (Kaplan, 2005; Richard, 2008; Hom, 2008; Williamson, 2009; Anderson and Lepore, 2013), and rightly so. Lexical items have many features that speakers take into consideration in conversation, and one of these is the display of contempt. Natural language expressions do not all have the same impact in linguistic communication. By all accounts, slurs convey hatred and negative attitudes toward the groups they designate (see especially Hom, 2008, 2010). "Kike" conveys prejudices whatever the attitude of the speaker, and it carries them whether or not they are intended. I do not want to focus on the details of stereotypical properties and negative features connected to these groups, on the intensity of some slurs such as "nigger," or on what backs the introduction of specific slurs in a language. Sociology, more than philosophy, can inform us about these aspects of slurs. Rather, I wish to examine some of the puzzles these expressions raise in philosophy of language, and to suggest a view on the semantics and pragmatics of such words[1] that fits how they convey hatred toward groups. I will use an outdated word, "boche" (Dummett's example) and a not so outdated word, "chink" (Hom's example), as my main examples. Because we are examining philosophy of language problems, it is not a good strategy to put the most

---

[1] I am interested in literal utterances of slur sentences. My approach will base intuitions on non-literal utterances, such as "Jean is a boche," where clearly Jean is not German but rather French.

offensive words such as "nigger" at center stage. We would then risk losing the focus on semantics.

Section 2 of the paper introduces two important semantic puzzles to which slurs give rise. Any view on such terms must account for both of them and for the communication of prejudices. Section 3 proposes a multipropositionalist perspective on the semantics of slurs and the puzzles introduced in Section 2. Multipropositionalism is a new approach that assigns meaning to lexical items as type, focuses on utterances, and assigns many different propositions, contents, or truth conditions to theses utterances (Perry, 2012). This section also suggests an account of two new puzzles, the first one concerning propositional attitudes and the second, tautologies. Section 4 proposes a mechanism explaining how specific insulting contents are communicated by slur sentence utterances. The view offered in Section 3 stands even if the suggestion concerning how specific prejudices are communicated is rejected. Section 5 makes a short presentation of Hom's view, Williamson's view, and of an expressivist perspective on slurs. Each is briefly critiqued and contrasted with my own.

2   Semantic Problems with Slurs

"Boche" is a slur introduced and initially used to designate Germans. It is arguable that any speaker competent in the use of this term knows that it is a word designating Germans. A person who use this term literally to talk about Chinese or Canadians does not really master it. Moreover, if "boche" did not designate Germans, then there would be no explanation as to why the contempt and stereotypes associated with the word initially targeted only Germans and not Canadians or Chinese. "German" is the neutral counterpart of the derogatory term "boche." "Boche" is not just an expression designating a group. It is a term prejudiced speakers use to replace a nondenigrating, neutral expression designating that group, namely, "German." If there is no neutral term corresponding to a candidate slur, then prima facie, that term does not qualify as a slur, and there is no argument for arguing that it is a slur rather than an ordinary term, be it derogatory like "bastard," or not. I accordingly assume that

> If S is an ethnic slur in language L, then there is a nonderogatory expression G in L such that G and S have the same extension.

Let us call it the Decent Talk Principle. The principle does not imply that S and G have the same linguistic meaning or the same Fregean sense, just that they have the same extension. For example, the extension of "German" is the set of German people, as is the extension of "boche," and the extension of "Chinese" is the set of Chinese people, as is the extension of "chink."[2] As such, we wish to capture and explain the intuitive difference between a slur and its neutral counterpart.

Consider

(1)   Hans is German,

and

(2)   Hans is a boche.

If I am right about "German" and "boche," these terms have the same extension. If they have the same extension, then (1) and (2) have the same truth-value (see also Anderson and Lepore, 2013). If these expressions have the same linguistic meaning, (1) and (2) have the same truth conditions. Do "German" and "boche" have the same meaning? Do they make the same contribution to truth conditions of sentences? Do (1) and (2) have the same truth conditions? These are the main questions I will address in the next section.

Next, let us consider

(3)   Hans is not German,

and

(4)   Hans is not a boche.

If "German" and "boche" have the same extension, these sentences have the same truth-value. "Boche" in (4) is as offensive as it is in (2), and it has the same cognitive impact in both sentences (see also Hom, 2008; Anderson and Lepore, 2013; Croom, 2011; McReady, 2010 on slurs and negation). Negation does not alter the derogatory aspect of a slur, even though it changes the truth conditions of slur sentences. The negative features carried by slurs are not lessened by negation.[3] If the meaning of a sentence determines its truth conditions and if negative aspects of slurs are not altered by negation, then *prima facie*, such aspects are not carried by

---

[2] Richard (2008, p. 28) accepts a weak version of the principle, writing that "every slur, so far as I can tell, has or could have a "neutral counterpart" which co-classifies but is free of the slur's evaluative dimension" (2008, p. 28) (see also Hornsby, 2001 for a similar stand). Hom (2008, note 4) states that some slurs have a nonderogatory correspondent. He does not go so far as to say that they all have one, but he does not deny the Decent Talk Principle either. Croom (2011) and Jeshion (hand out, Winnipeg) assume that the principle is true. Anderson and Lepore (2011), Bach (2012), and Whiting (2013) also endorse the principle. One could argue that the relevant neutral term is a description like "those living on the other side of the river." Such a neutral expression does not designate an ethnic group, nor does an ethnic slur, designating an ethnic group, replace such expression.

[3] This phenomenon is known as scoping out.

linguistic meaning and they are not part of the truth conditions of slur sentences. This characteristic suggests that it is plausible that the negative aspects conveyed by slurs are not semantically communicated. Prejudices, however, are communicated by slur sentences. What accounts for this intuition? And how are they communicated? In Section 4 of the paper, I will put forward a suggestion concerning the way utterances of slurs convey specific prejudices. Now if "boche" designates Germans, then (1) and (4) are *prima facie* contradictions. However, a speaker can make an utterance of (4) and add (1) with no contradiction. Suppose that I make an utterance of (2). You look at me and say: "He is not a boche! He is German." This is a perfectly fine and justified reply. The fact that "boche" and "German" have the same extension is prima facie irrelevant to the negation here. How can we account for this fact? The impact of a negation in slur sentences calls for an explanation.

I wish to explain the difference between (1) and (2), taking into account that the specific prejudices carried by slurs are not *prima facie* conveyed by linguistic meaning, and the intuition that (1) and (4) are not always contradictions. Let me first give the general framework I will be using, and then address specific semantic issues.

3   A Suggestion

1   Multipropositionalism

Different frameworks are used in philosophy of language. Two should be contrasted here. Kaplan's monopropositionalist semantics (Kaplan, 1989) focuses on tokens and logic. It introduces character, or linguistic meaning, and truth-valuable contents determined by sentences in context. A sentence in context determines one single content. Perry's multipropositionalist approach (Perry, 2012) also introduces linguistic meaning and truth-valuable contents, but it emphasizes utterances and communication. An utterance, as distinct from a token, is an action performed by a speaker. From Perry's perspective, an utterance does not determine one but many different contents or truth conditions. (1) and (2) have, prima facie, the same truth value, but differ in cognitive significance: a person can make an utterance of (1) and refuse to make an utterance of (2), even if (1) and (2) have the same truth value. Moreover, prejudices are not, prima facie, tied to tokens of slurs and are arguably carried by speakers making utterances. I wish to capture in terms of content the cognitive difference between (1) and (2), as well as the similarities that explain why they can be assigned the same truth value. A one-content, monopropositionalist framework like Kaplan's does not make room for the necessary distinctions between contents. Given the role of utterances in the examination of slurs, a semantic view giving them a major role is appropriate. I will therefore employ Perry's multipropositionalist framework.[4]

Following multipropositionalism, linguistic meaning, just as in Kaplan's framework, is a property of lexical items as type, something we can learn. The linguistic meaning of an expression as type is a rule determining the contribution to content of utterances of that expression. Setting aside semantic ambiguity, the linguistic meaning of a lexical item is the same for different utterances of that item. Semantics focuses on the meaning of linguistic expression as type, and how it contributes to different contents of utterances. It first emphasizes content determined only by meaning and known a priori by competent speakers. Let us call it the semantically determined content of an utterance. The latter faithfully echoes sentences, including semantic and syntactic rules, and is extracted from lexical items in sentences. Ambiguities must be solved at that level because an ambiguous expression is assigned many linguistic rules which in turn can introduce at least two different content constituents.

Consider my utterance **u** of "I am short." "I" designates the speaker of the utterance. The linguistic meaning of "I" is reflexive in that its designation depends on the utterance itself. For that reason, the semantically determined content or truth conditions of a first-person sentence utterance is reflexive.

(5)   Given that the sentence is in English, the utterance **u** of "I am short" is true if and only if the speaker of **u** is short.

*The speaker of **u** is short* is the relevant semantically determined content of the utterance. Perry (1988) draws attention to an important role of contents or truth conditions, namely the cognitive significance of utterances, and sets conditions for it.

(a)   The cognitive significance of an utterance S in language L is a semantic property of the utterance.

(b)   It is a property that a person who understands the meaning of S in L recognizes.

(c)   The cognitive significance of an utterance of S in L is a proposition.

(d)   A person who understands the meaning of S in L, and accepts as true an utterance of S in L, will believe the proposition that is the cognitive significance of the utterance." (Perry, 1988:194).

---

[4] I refer the reader to Perry (2012) for a detailed presentation of that perspective in semantics.

(5) gives the content playing the role of cognitive significance of my utterance of "I am short," namely *the speaker of **u** is short*. This content is captured by considering meaning only. Cognitive significance is propositional and is appropriate as belief content. After hearing my utterance, you can believe that the speaker of u is short even without knowing who the speaker is.

Once facts relative to the utterance are taken into account, including who the speaker is, we have a different content.

(6)   Given linguistic meaning and facts about the utterance, the utterance **u** of "I am short" is true if and only if RV *is short*.

RV is the speaker of the utterance himself. These truth conditions, RV is short, are obtained once the semantically determined content and utterance relevant facts are set. They result from semantically determined content in a context, the reflexive meaning of "I" automatically selecting the relevant element in that context. Perry calls it the official content. This singular content is not utterance reflexive. The speaker making an utterance of "I am short" does not want to say that *the speaker of **u** is short*. He is talking about himself, not about his utterance. Clearly, you and I do not say the same thing when making an utterance of "I am short." The official content is what is said (Grice, Perry) by utterances of (1) or what the speaker says.

Perry (1988) notes, rightly, that "a theory of linguistic meaning should help provide us with an understanding of the properties sentences have that lead us to produce them under different circumstances, and to react as we do to their utterances by others" (Perry, 1988, 192). A theory of meaning should take into account the fact that the sentence (2) has the property of containing a slur—a feature plausibly motivating an utterance of (2) rather than (1)—and conveys contempt because it does so. Hearing an utterance of (1) and hearing an utterance of (2) also prompts different reactions. Containing a slur is a linguistically relevant factor. The Decent Talk Principle implies that "German" and "boche" are coextensional, but it does not imply that "German" and "boche" have the same cognitive value and the same impact in linguistic communication. *Prima facie*, utterances of (1) and (2) differ in cognitive significance. According to multipropositionalism, two utterances can differ in cognitive significance, but still have the same official content or say the same thing (Korta and Perry, 2011). Do utterances of (1) and (2) have the same official content? Do speakers of (1) and (2) say the same thing? Let us go back to (1) and (2) with multipropositionalism in mind. In the following pages, I assume basic knowledge of Perry's view on proper names.

2   "German"

You and I are talking about Hans. I ask you where he is from. Making an utterance of (1) would not convey bad feelings. Making an utterance of (2) would. Let us begin by considering (1) or your utterance of (1). Given its linguistic meaning as type, I understand that

(7)   Given that (1) is in English, the utterance **u** of (1) is true if and only if *the person that the convention exploited by* (1) *allows one to designate with the utterance* **u** *of "Hans" is German.*

The content that the person that the convention exploited by (1) allows one to designate with the utterance **u** of "Hans" is German is semantically conveyed by the utterance. It is something a speaker knows thanks only to his linguistic competence. This content is reflexive because it contains the utterance itself as a constituent. The semantically determined reflexive content of the utterance of (1) gives the cognitive significance of that utterance. I can accept as true your utterance of (1) and believe that content. By these standards, different utterances of (1) have different cognitive significances, because the content of each utterance contains a different utterance as a constituent. Suppose that a friend joins us and makes an utterance **u'** of (1). The reflexive content of his utterance, the person that the convention exploited by (1) allows one to designate with the utterance **u'** of "Hans" is German, differs from the reflexive content of my utterance of the same sentence. Believing the cognitive significance of my utterance of (1) does not imply believing the cognitive significance of a different utterance of the same sentence.

The content the person that the convention exploited by (1) allows one to designate with the utterance **u** of "Hans" is German is reflexive and it does not provide the official content or the official truth conditions of the utterance. It is not what you say. You do not want to talk about the name but about what it designates. Identifying who this utterance of "Hans" designates, one gets

(8)   Given linguistic meaning and facts, the utterance **u** of (1)
        is true if and only if Hans is German.

Hans is Hans himself. This content is not reflexive, and it is true or false whether or not you utter (1). It is the official content of the utterance or what you said.

3   Slurs

While "boche" and "German" may both have a conventional meaning, they certainly do not have the same linguistic meaning. "Boche" is not synonymous with "German," and vice versa. If "boche" has a linguistic meaning as type that introduces a descriptive condition into the truth conditions of a sentence, then these two expressions do not contribute the same descriptive condition to the truth conditions of the sentence. If (1) and (2) do not share the same linguistic meaning, they cannot share the same truth conditions. "Boche" is not a simple condition determining description of a group and, furthermore, it does have a slurring aspect. Moreover, learning a slur is not equivalent to learning a word that has meaning that determines a unique negative condition. If a slur semantically conveys a specific prejudice, a sentence attributing that prejudice would be a tautology. For example, if being lazy is a feature attributed to the Chinese, and if being lazy is conveyed by the meaning of "chink," then "Yao is a chink and he is lazy" is a tautology, and "Yao is a chink but he is not lazy" is a contradiction. However, I maintain that the first example is not a tautology nor is the second one a contradiction. *Prima facie*, slurs as type lack conventional, learned linguistic meaning that conveys a simple specific prejudice. In addition, the specific prejudices carried by slurs, like "boche," are not affected by negation, as would be the case if they were semantically conveyed.

Hornsby (2001) observes that a speaker "can know that a word is commonly understood to convey hatred or contempt without being in a position to say exactly what commitments those who see fit to use it may incur" (Hornsby, 2001:137).[5] I assume that she is right and that

> To know that 'S' is a slur for a group G is all that there is to know about 'S.'

Knowing that a word is a slur for a group G is knowing that it conveys contempt toward that group. This does not imply knowing the specific prejudices that term directs against G. Linguistically competent speakers know that "boche" designates Germans and, for that reason, contributes the property of being German to the content of the utterances. A competent speaker also knows that "boche" has a derogatory nature. The presence of a derogatory word in a sentence is cognitively relevant. I wish to suggest that a slur conveys the very general idea that the group it designates is despicable simply because it is that group. "Boche" carries the idea that a person is German and despicable because of it. Despicable because of it, also found in Richard (2008), Hom (2008) and McReady

---

[5] A postcard example makes this clear: reading on a post card that 'chinks are lazy' informs the competent reader that the person who wrote that card does not think highly of Chinese, whatever the reader's specific prejudices.

(2010), is a general, nonspecific prejudice.[6] It captures the intuitive idea connected to slurs: a group is despicable because it is that very group. Despicable because of it is introduced into the cognitive significance of slur sentences by linguistic meaning. Every slur has the common feature of adding this contribution to the cognitive significance of utterances precisely because it is a slur. Since despicable because of it contains a component sensitive to the group a slur designates, *it*, each slur is also specific to a group. The meaning of "boche" contributes German and despicable because of it to the semantically determined content or cognitive significance of an utterance of a 'boche' sentence. The contribution of "chink" is *Chinese and despicable because of it*, of "nigger," *Black American and despicable because of it*, and "kike," *Jew and despicable because of it*. Cognitive significance can be understood by only considering language and without grasping any specific denigrating content.

Most proposals in the literature downplay the fact that slurs, as words, have a cognitive impact and that a linguistically competent speaker knows that a slur, any slur, is degrading, whatever it is used to precisely convey about groups, and whatever the speaker intends to convey. Most proposals also ignore a speaker's intention to select specific words. Once a speaker selects a slur to provide a cognitive fix on a group, more specific intentions to convey negative aspects of the extension are immaterial. The word itself carries prejudice. Knowing that "boche" is a slur for Germans, that is, that it conveys the idea that *Germans are despicable because of it*, namely *because of being German*, is all there is to know about that word to be competent in using it. Knowledge of language is irrelevant to knowledge of the specific prejudices a slur sentence utterance conveys. Let us return to (2).

4 Back to "Boche"

Hearing an utterance of "Hans is a boche," and taking into account that a slur is used, I know in virtue of my linguistic competence that

(9)   Given that (2) is in English, the utterance u (2) is true if and *only if the person that the convention exploited by* (2) *allows*

---

[6] Hom (2008:424) gives an example which I take to be the cognitive significance of an utterance of (2), namely, *the person that the convention exploited by (1) allows one to designate with the utterance **u** of "Hans" is German and despicable because of it as conventionally* implicated by sentence (2). He does not however advocate my position.

> *one to designate with the utterance* **u** *of "Hans" is German and despicable because of it.*[7]

This content gives the cognitive significance of the utterance. There is nothing against Hans personally in (2). He just happens to belong to a group the speaker has prejudices against.

I can accept an utterance of (1) as true, and refuse an utterance of (2). I need not reject the utterance of (2) because of the extension of "boche" or because Hans is not German. I can do so because of the derogatory nature of the word used and the cognitive significance of the utterance.

Identifying the person referred to by that utterance of "Hans," and making explicit what it is anaphoric with, I get

(10)   Given linguistic meaning and facts, the utterance **u** of (2) is true if and only if **Hans** *is German and despicable because of being German.*

Let us call it the slurred singular content. I do not wish to say that you have said that Hans is despicable because of being German. But you certainly suggested it.

Grice (1989a) introduces a distinction, between what is meant by a speaker, what is said, and what is implicated. What is said is "closely related to the conventional meaning of the word (the sentence) he has uttered," (1989:25). What is implicated can be conventionally or conversationally implicated. Let us set aside conversational implicatures for now. What is conventionally implicated depends on the meaning of the words used, and its identification requires no calculation or argument, since it depends on the meaning of the words. According to Grice, the speaker making an utterance of "He is poor but he is honest" says that the person is poor, says that the person is honest, and does not say but conventionally implicates that there is a contrast between being poor and being honest. What is said can be true, and what is conventionally implicated can be false. In the utterance of "He is poor but he is honest," what is said can be true even if it is false that there is a contrast between being poor and being honest (Grice, 1989a:25). Finally, what is conventionally implicated is not cancelable—for example, one cannot make an utterance of "He is poor but he is honest" and deny that there is a contrast between being poor and being honest.

---

[7] More perspicuously, one should write: *that the person that the convention exploited by (2) allows one to designate with the utterance* **u** *of "Hans" is German and despicable because of being German.*

Suppose that you make an utterance of (2). Your utterance arguably means that the person referred to is German and despicable because of it. While you plausibly said that he is German, you did not say that the person is despicable because of being German. However, you certainly suggested it. Following Grice, let us distinguish what you said—**Hans** *is German*—and what you conventionally implicated—**Hans** *is despicable because of being German.* You cannot use (2) and add "and it is false that **Hans** is despicable because of being German." On the other hand, **Hans** *is German* can be true, and **Hans** *is despicable because of being German* can be false. Someone talking about your utterance would be wrong to argue that you said that Hans is German and despicable because of being German. If I am right, **Hans** *is despicable because of being German* is conventionally implicated, and it does not flow into what is said.

Eliminating the slurring aspect of "boche," and considering only the extension of that term, we get the official content or truth conditions of your utterance, or what you said.

(11)   Given linguistic meaning and facts, the utterance **u** of (2) is true if and only if **Hans** *is German.*

A speaker making an utterance of (2) is not *saying* anything negative about Germans. However, the word the speaker uses, a slur, *conventionally implicates* that Hans is despicable because of being German. Speakers of (1) and (2) say the same thing, but the speaker of (2) conventionally implicates a negative picture of Germans. Clearly the speaker making an utterance of (2) accepts the content giving the cognitive significance of the utterance and believes it. My view on the cognitive significance of slur sentences predicts that the speaker of (2) believes that Hans is German and despicable because of it, even if he does not say so.

The utterances of (1) and (2) share the same official content, but they differ in cognitive significance. My suggestion does not call for complex meaning and contents, and it does not imply learning anything specific against Germans when learning "boche."[8] To grasp the official content of the utterance or what is said, one must know the group designated by the ethnic slur. One does not have to figure out specific denigrating contents.

The reader can easily identify both the semantically determined of an utterance of (3), *the person that the convention exploited by (3) allows one to designate with the utterance* **u** *of "Hans" is not German*, and the official content or what is said by that utterance, **Hans** *is not German.* Let us

---

[8] Anderson's and Lepore's speakers know that "boche" is a slur, but this finds no echo in a proposition or content they grasp when hearing (2), and it has no cognitive impact. Their view underestimates the importance of our ordinary knowledge of words.

now consider (4), "Hans is not a boche". If "boche" is offensive, it is also so in (4). Negation does not alter that aspect of slurs. However, speakers using this word do not always want to be offensive. Utterances of this sentence are ambiguous. Consider (4) and its cognitive significance.

(12)   Given that (4) is in English, the utterance of (4) is true if and only if the person that the convention exploited by (4) *allows one to designate with the utterance* **u** *of "Hans" is not German and despicable because of being German.*

Suppose that we are interested in slurred singular content, that is **Hans** *is not German and despicable because of being German*. The slurred singular content of an utterance of (4) has two different readings, depending on the scope of negation.

(13)   Given linguistic meaning and facts, the utterance **u** of (4) is true if and only if **Hans** *is not German and despicable because of being German*,

where despicable because of being German is not in the scope of negation, and

(14)   Given linguistic meaning and facts, the utterance **u** of (4) is true if and only if **Hans** *is German and it is false that he is despicable because of being German*

where *despicable because of being German* is in the scope of negation. The cognitive significance of an utterance of (4) has two readings and two possible slurred singular contents. There are also two corresponding official contents, namely

(15)   Given linguistic meaning and facts, the utterance **u** of (4) is true if and only if **Hans** *is not German*,

and

(16)   Given linguistic meaning and facts, the utterance **u** of (4) is true if and only if **Hans** *is German.*

Suppose that the speaker of (4) keeps the slur but wants to say that Hans is not German. We get (13), which gives the right slurred singular content of the utterance of (4), with (15) giving its official content. The speaker may also want to negate despicable because of being German and his utterance to have the "slurred" singular content given in (14) and the official content or truth conditions given by (16). The slurring aspect of the utterance is denied. What is said is different, depending on the reading of (4). Some speakers uttering (4) take steps to make it clear that they want to cancel what the slur category conveys through air quotes or tone. Quotation marks or other means can be used to make a statement about the nonapplication or nonapplicability of a slur by cancelling its derogatory aspect (see also Hornsby, 2001; Potts, 2007; Williamson, 2009; Whiting, 2013). Careful people do that, or use means to do that, in conversation. (17) is a good rendering of that reading of (4).

(17)   Hans is not a "boche."

You then get the "slurred" singular content given in (14), with the corresponding official content or what the speaker said. An utterance of "Hans is not a boche! He is German" is not designed to be informative but rather to rephrase what has been said without using a slur.[9]

5   Slurs and Propositional Attitudes

What does Joe believe when he makes an utterance of "Yao is a chink" or "Hans is a boche"? Do these beliefs differ from the beliefs that he would express with "Yao is Chinese" and "Hans is German"? Let us consider

(18)   Joe believes that Yao is Chinese,

(19)   Joe believes that Yao is a chink,

(20)   Joe believes that Hans is German,

(21)   Joe believes that Hans is a boche.

Slurs do not fall within the scope of propositional attitude terms and are immune to belief reports: they carry prejudices in both direct and oblique contexts (see also Anderson and Lepore, 2011).[10] But do we report different thought contents with (18) and (19)? Are the beliefs reported by (19) and (21) racist? Is the derogatory aspect of "chink" or "boche" part of the reported belief contents?

If I am right, one can report at least two different propositions after an utterance of (1) or (2). Suppose that Joe makes an utterance of (1). A speaker can make two belief reports, (20) and (21). (20) reports the official content of the utterance or what is said; (21) reports more than the official content (see Anderson and Lepore, 2011). In this case, the speaker of (21) is clearly responsible for the introduction of derogatoriness and for implicating prejudice because he uses a slur in his report. Consider an utterance of the sentence (2) and (20) and (21). The speaker of (20) reports the official content of the utterance of (2), and is responsible for removing derogatoriness. The speaker of (21) plausibly reports the cognitive signifi-

---

[9] A monopropositionalist semantic framework, relying on one content only, does not capture the ambiguity of "Hans is not a boche."

[10] This phenomenon is known as scoping out.

cance of the utterance of (2). Suppose that he makes an utterance of (21). Did Joe utter (1) or (2)? Suppose that he makes an utterance of (20). Did Joe utter (1) or (2)? Is he reporting the official truth conditions of the utterance or is he slurring? His reporting is doubly ambiguous. Slurs in oblique contexts let speakers add material having no impact on the official content of the report. They also make room for the reporter to slur as well.

6 Slurs in Tautologies

Let us now consider

(22)   Chinese are Chinese,

(23)   Chinese are chinks,

(24)   Chinks are Chinese,

(25)   Chinks are chinks.

Just like "war is war," (22) is a tautology. Being a tautology is not, however, the whole story about (22). The speaker making an utterance of (22) is flouting a maxim of quantity—"Make your contribution as informative as is required (for the current purpose of the exchange)"—but is assumed to observe the Cooperative Principle. He is exploiting a maxim of conversation and conversationally implicates (Grice, 1989a, b) at least one proposition, the relevant implicatures being particularized, that is, specific to that utterance. Grice writes

> A man who, by (in, when) saying (or making as if to say) that p has implicated that q may be said to have conversationally implicated that q, provided that (1) he is at least to be presumed to be observing the conversational maxims, or at least the Cooperative Principle; (2) the supposition that he is aware that, or thinks that, q is required in order to make his saying or making as if to say p (or doing so in those terms) consistent with his presumption; and (3) the speaker thinks (or would expect the hearer to think that the speaker thinks) that it is within the competence of the hearer to work t or grasp intuitively, that the supposition mentioned in (2) is required. (Grice, 1989a, b:30—31)

Conversational implicatures are propositions, or contents, which must be assumed to preserve the idea that a speaker is following conversational maxims. A particularized conversational implicature is not conveyed by every utterance of a sentence. Particularized conversational implicatures depend heavily on both conversational maxims and context. They are "cases in which there is no room for the idea that an implicature of this sort is normally carried by saying that p" (Grice, 1989a:37). Moreover, particularized conversational implicatures can be "worked out" and identified through an argument. The speaker of (22) is conversationally implicating a proposition or, more plausibly, some propositions that make the utterance relevant, just as the speaker of "war is war" conversationally implicates a proposition, or some propositions, that make his utterance relevant. He also knows that that these propositions are needed to make his utterance consistent with conversational maxims, and thinks that the hearer can grasp them. If "Chinese" and "chink" have the same extension, and if we substitute "chink" for "Chinese" in one occurrence, then (23) and (24) are also both tautologies.[11] However, it is clear that these sentences are not mere tautologies and utterances of (23) and (24) convey much more than their official truth-conditions. Notice also that while (23) is very offensive, (24) is clearly not as offensive. Things are different with (25). Like (22), (25) is a clear tautology, and a speaker making an utterance of (25) conversationally implicates propositions that make his utterance relevant, and thinks that the hearer can grasp these propositions. As is the case with (22), conversational implicatures are specific propositions the speaker needs to assume for his utterance to be relevant in a given context. Do speakers of (22) and (25) in the same context conversationally implicate the same thing? Prima facie, in contrast with an utterance of (22), the speaker of (25) cannot but conversationally implicate propositions exhibiting prejudices concerning Chinese. Where lies the difference between these two tautologies? Do both these utterances use the same mechanism to implicate content? Any theory assigning the same extension to a slur and its neutral counterpart should tell us about the difference between making utterances of (22), (23), (24), and (24).

Eliminating the slurring aspect of (25), utterances of (22) and (25) have the same official content and are always true: *Chinese are Chinese*. How do they differ? We do not want the relevant particularized conversational implicatures to be simply given by the linguistic meaning of the terms themselves. Making these utterances, the speaker is clearly and knowingly flouting the maxim of quantity. He wants the hearer to grasp, and thinks that the hearer can grasp, some conversationally implicated content to make the utterances relevant. Let us go back and look at the cognitive significance of (22) and (25).

(26)   Given that (22) is in English, the utterance **u** of (22) is true if and only if *Chinese are Chinese*.

(27)   Given that (25) is in English, the utterance **u** of (25) is true if and only if *Chinese and despicable because of being Chinese are Chinese and despicable because of being Chinese*.

---

[11] We are substituting coextensional terms.

Considering the cognitive aspect of utterances of (22), which is identical to their official content, and conversational implicatures, there is no reason to identify specific derogatory contents as conversationally implicated. Considering the cognitive aspect of utterances of (25), which is different from their official content, and conversational implicatures, there are good reasons to identify specific negative contents—such as, following Hom, Chinese are lazy, Chinese ought to be subject to higher college admission standards, Chinese ought to be subject to exclusion from advancement to managerial positions, and so on—as conversationally implicated by the speaker flouting the maxim of quantity. The speaker knows that these or similar contents are required to make his utterance relevant, and also thinks that the hearer can identify these or similar contents. The difference between what these tautological utterances conversationally implicate is explained by the difference in their cognitive significance. Identification of the negative conversational implicatures is grounded on cognitive significance, not official content. My view also explains differences between (23) and (24): they do not have the same offensive impact even though, once again, they share the same official content, namely, Chinese are Chinese. The cognitive significance of an utterance of (23) is given by

(28)   Given that (23) is in English, the utterance **u** of (23) is true if and only if *Chinese are Chinese and despicable because of being Chinese.*

The cognitive significance of an utterance of (24) is given by

(29)   Given that (24) is in English, the utterance **u** of (24) is true if and only if *Chinese and despicable because of being Chinese are Chinese.*

(23) and (24) differ in cognitive significance. The second part of the cognitive significance of (23) adds 'information' to what is conveyed by the first part. The first part of the cognitive significance of (24) includes the *conjunction Chinese and despicable because of being Chinese.* The second part of this content, are Chinese, does not add much to the first part of the cognitive significance of the utterance. Remarkably, the cognitive significance of these utterances is not tautological (though what is said is), no maxim is flouted as far as cognitive significance is concerned, and utterances of these sentences do not carry conversational implicatures. However, utterances of both (23) and (24) conventionally implicate that Chinese are despicable because of being Chinese.

4 Communication and Prejudices

1 Conveying Specific Prejudices

The details of the emotions, prejudices, and negative images that the speaker of "boche," for example, displays are not buried in linguistic meaning or the slur category, and they are not learned when learning a specific slur. Grasping the cluster of negative ideas a slur conveys in an utterance requires nonlinguistic, ordinary knowledge of the underlying prejudices against a community.

Slurs convey prejudices in every context and are context independent. To use Grice's formula, there is no room for the idea that implicatures are not normally carried by saying that word. Suppose that the speaker of (2) follows the Cooperative Principle: make your contribution such as is required, at the stage at which it occurs, by the accepted purpose or direction of the talk exchange in which you are engaged. He is also assumed to follow more specific maxims. Some are about word selection, and manner of speaking is important.[12] Korta and Perry (2011) suggest their own maxim in their discussion of the theory of reference:

> Choose your way of referring according to the cognitive fix you want your hearer to get on the reference, to facilitate the inference of implicatures (Korta and Perry, 2011:136).

We are interested in slurs and the cognitive fix they give on the groups they target. The maxim suggested by Korta and Perry can be applied here.

The speaker who is uttering (2) is choosing a certain way of saying that Hans is German, namely he is employing a derogatory word. He is making an utterance having a certain cognitive significance—*the person that the convention exploited by (2) allows one to designate with the utterance* **u** *of "Hans" is German and despicable because of being German*—and a slurred singular content—**Hans** *is German and despicable because of being German*—and is displaying a certain way of thinking about Hans and Germans. The speaker uttering (2) is not violating a maxim, opting out, or facing a clash. He is not flouting a maxim nor is he exploiting any maxim. That speaker does not need intend to convey specific negative content to preserve the idea that he is respecting the maxims. The hearer can rely on the cognitive fix on a group a slur gives and the cognitive significance of the utterance to start trying to identify generalized conversational implicatures. He must assume that, because he is using a slur, the speaker has specific negative views extracted from common prej-

---

[12] Grice introduces a new maxim of manner in 'Presupposition and Conversational Implicature,' a maxim concerning words and fit for a theory of generalized conversational implicature: Frame whatever you say into the form most suitable for any reply that would be regarded as appropriate (1989b:273).

udices against Germans in the speaker's community—like Germans are cruel, to take Williamson's example, or too respectful of authority. Intuitions about these contents need not be replaced by an argument, as would be the case if they were particularized conversational implicatures. The speaker uses a slur. Suppose that a common prejudice against Germans in the speaker's community is that Germans are cruel, too respectful of authority, and so on. The speaker would not use this slur unless he has these or other prejudices. Another speaker, say, in 1942 France, would plausibly convey different prejudices by using the same slur, because different prejudices were held in that community at that time. Slurs are very flexible with respect to the stereotypes they can carry. Unless the hearer knows negative features associated with Germans in a community, he cannot grasp the generalized conversational implicatures. "Nigger" is used in true utterances about Black Americans to conversationally implicate (and only generalized conversational implicatures are relevant here) prejudices that are intention independent and can vary from time to time, location to location, and, arguably, speaker to speaker. The point of using a slur is to convey prejudice, not to convey the same prejudices in every utterance. In my view, there is no semantic relationship between a slur and the various specific negative views it can carry, and only a loose but persistent, nonsemantic relationship between slurs and the picture they conversationally implicate. These generalized conversational implicatures are open-ended, and they exhibit a certain degree of indeterminacy (Grice, 1989a:40). I want to emphasize that a speaker can cancel a specific generalized conversational implicature (Grice, 1989a:39). Being too respectful of authority might be a negative feature commonly assigned to Germans and carried by any utterance of (2). However, a speaker can make an utterance of "Hans is a boche, but he is not too respectful of authority" without contradicting oneself.[13]

In multipropositionalism, a distinction is made between cognitive significance and what is said. What is said by the utterance of (2)—that **Hans** is German—can be true, and what is conventionally implicated can be false. In the case before us, the speaker could use the neutral counterpart of a slur to say the same thing. He does not. The speaker could also use air quotes—"he is a 'boche'"—or other means to signal that he is distancing

---

[13] Slurs can be appropriated by altering their cognitive value and turned into honorifics. They can then be used to conversationally implicate positive features of a group. For example, "nigger" can be turned into an honorific and convey, as cognitive significance, Black American and admirable because of being Black American. I set aside honorifics in the present paper.

himself from the slur and opting out (Grice, 1989a:39). Once again, he does not.

2   Where Nonlinguistic Facts Fit In

Speakers select slurs precisely because they are slurs. Utterances of this category of words convey negative contents concerning the group it designates. Such expressions are created in linguistic communities for all sorts of reasons to convey a negative view. These words have an impact in virtue of their linguistic meaning and the specific prejudices their utterance implicate. Knowing which words are slurs in a linguistic community is part of our knowledge of the language spoken in that community. Such knowledge does not require knowing details about these prejudices (see Hornsby, 2001 and Hom, 2008).

5   Other Options

1   Hom's View

Hom (2008, 2011) takes into consideration the rich "information" a slur can convey and proposes a monopropositionalist semantic view he calls Combinatorial Externalism, in which: "the meanings of epithets are supported and semantically determined by their corresponding racist institutions." (Hom, 2008:431). The meaning of a term is then fixed by factors external to speakers (Hom, 2008:430). According to Hom, the meaning of "chink" determines a complex condition such as: *ought to be subject to higher college admission standards, and ought to be subject to exclusion from advancement to managerial positions, and.... because of being slanty-eyed, and good-at-laundering, and.... all because of being Chinese.* (Hom, 2008:431). In so far as, according to Hom, "Chinese" and its slurring counterpart "chink" differ in meaning, they are bound to determine different conditions.

Hom suggests that all the prejudices that a slur can convey against a community are carried by linguistic meaning. Standard conventional meaning does not semantically carry such complex information in the truth-conditions of sentences. If meaning also determines a thought content component, prima facie slurs do not determine such a complex thought content component (on this point, see also Croom, 2011 and Nunberg, 2013). Moreover, it is arguable that meaning which would determine such a complex property, or any complex conjunction of conditions, is not learned when one learns a slur, and it is, furthermore, very hard to believe that such a complex meaning can even be learned when learning a slur.[14] Hom also has difficulty accounting for the fact that negation does not affect specific prejudices carried by the utterance of a slur. Finally, according to Hom, the properties associated with slurs have no extension. As a consequence, (1) is true, but (2) is false (Hom, 2008:437). I argue that the specific prejudices Hom mentions are not semantically communicated but are generalized conversational implicatures carried by the use of a slur. My suggestion preserves the intuition that "boche" designates Germans, and that (2) is true even if it is a slurring sentence. Hom assigns much more to the meaning of slurs than what semantics is designed to take care of or can handle. My view does not put such a heavy load on meaning.

2   Williamson's View

Williamson (2009) argues that (1) and (2) have the same truth conditions. He contends that a sentence like (2) conventionally implicates (Grice, 1989a) a derogatory content: Germans are cruel (p. 149). Because (1) does not have conventional implicature, (1) and (2) cannot have the same linguistic meaning. Following this view, slurs, just like conventional implicature terms (like "but" and "however"), have a major, non-truth-conditional meaning. What "boche" semantically conveys, as distinct from what "German" conveys, is truth-conditionally irrelevant (Williamson, 2009:149). In addition, it is neither context-dependent nor speaker-intention-dependent (see also Hom, 2008:426). The negative image that "boche" suggests is also detachable: one can use a different sentence, namely (1), to convey the same truth-conditional content without communicating the implicature. It is not cancellable however: one cannot use (2) without suggesting a negative image of Germans, and one cannot contend that this way of talking does not imply a negative view. Williamson's conventional implicature view depends on the idea that "boche" carries a specific negative content as an implicature in virtue of its linguistic meaning, like "but" carries the idea of a contrast in virtue of its linguistic meaning.

Whatever unique, semantically conveyed, negative content that implicature might be is debatable. Williamson's suggestion concerning "boche"—"Germans are cruel"—like any simple suggested content is ad hoc and poorly motivated. We certainly learn what "but" means and conventionally implicates when learning English. In learning a slur, however, we do not learn a very specific negative feature conventionally implicated

---

[14] Hom (2008) offers a reply to that criticism. His defence depends on his Externalist proposal. But one may prefer a view of slurs that does not depend on such a controversial approach.

by that word. Moreover, hearing a slur, we do not try to identify the single negative feature conventionally implicated by that term. It is unclear to me, and it is not backed by any arguments in the literature, whether "boche," or any slur for that matter, semantically conveys a well-defined, specifiable content as is the case with what "but" conventionally implicates. My suggestion also relies on conventional implicatures. But my conventionally implied content, *despicable because of it*, or, in this case, *despicable because of being German*, is very general.

Slurs exhibit what Potts (2007) calls descriptive ineffability. To paraphrase Potts, when speakers are asked about what negative image is conveyed by the use of a slur, they do not offer a strict definition, suggesting that no paraphrase of "chink," for example, can be offered and no unique specific negative content can plausibly be given for what "you are a chink" semantically communicates. No doubt an utterance of that sentence can communicate a lot. However, the volley of negative features carried by the use of a slur are too poorly structured and open-ended to be captured in a specific semantically determined content. My 'generalized conversational implicature' view accounts for the wide net of prejudices spread by the utterance of a slur.

3 Expressivism

Richard (2008) and Herder (2012, 2013) contend that slurs have no descriptive content, and only an expressive content. For that reason, slur sentences lack truth value (see Nunberg, 2013 for criticisms). In contrast with my suggestion, expressivism is a noncognitive approach to slurs. My suggestion does not reject the idea that slurs have expressive value and strongly display contempt. However, rather than taking display of contempt as a brute fact, it is accounted for via the cognitive significance of slurs and the specific prejudices conveyed by utterances of slur sentences.

6 Conclusion

Using only linguistic competence or knowledge of language, one cannot identify the negative features about groups that slurs convey. To identify them, a speaker needs extralinguistic knowledge of social facts in a slur-using linguistic community: what are the prejudices concerning Germans underlying the use of "boche" in that community? What are the negative features associated with Germans in that community? What are the stereotypes about Germans in that community? My view does not trivialize the negative and emotional features of slurs. It places emotions and prejudices in their proper place, that is, in the nonsemantic aspects of a word, where they have devastating impact on both speakers and hearers. It also elucidates how socially situated and complex linguistic interaction can be. When they know words in this category, speakers know that using them conveys more than the official content, that these words suggest something different from what is said, and that they have a strong impact in linguistic communication. Ignoring that a word belongs to this category, a speaker risks conveying more than he wants to. Some epithets are stronger than others (Hom): "nigger" vs. "boche." Strength depends on social facts, not on meaning or belonging to the slur category. Using such words, a competent speaker cannot but endorse the prejudices and stereotypes underlying them. He has options, and his choosing a slur rather that a neutral term speaks for itself. Slurs have an ineffable aspect that is not related to syntax or linguistic meaning. It relates to the cluster of prejudices about a group in a community. That is why they are hard to translate and cannot be eliminated or tamed by changing language, but only by altering social, nonlinguistic facts. This is also the reason why they have such a deep destructive impact and can hardly receive a mere linguistic reply. With a slur, contempt and prejudice toward a group invite themselves into conversation.

Acknowledgements

I want to thank Eros Corazza, Kepa Korta and the audience at the AMPRAG 2012 meeting, in Charlotte. The referees for Journal of Pragmatics made very helpful comments. They taught me a lot about my paper. Research for this work has been made possible thanks to the Social Sciences and Humanities Research Council of Canada.

References

Anderson, L., Lepore, E., 2013. Slurring words. *Noûs* 47, 25—48.

Bach, Kent, 2012. Mean and Nasty Talk: On the Semantics and Pragmatics of Slurs, (unpublished).

Croom, A., 2011. Slurs. Language Sciences 33, 343—358.

Grice, H.P., 1989a. Logic and conversation. In: Grice, H. Paul (Ed.), *Studies in the Ways of Words*. Harvard University Press, pp. 22—40.

Grice, H.P., 1989b. *Studies in the Ways of Words*. Harvard University Press, Cambridge.

Herder, J., 2012. The semantics of racial slurs: using Kaplan's framework to provide a theory of the meaning of derogatory epithets. *Linguistic and Philosophical Investigations* 11, 74—84.

Herder, J., 2013. Meaning and racial slurs: derogatory epithets and the semantic—pragmatic interface. *Language and Communication* 33, 205—213.

Hom, C., 2008. The semantics of racial epithets. *Journal of Philosophy* 105, 416—440.

Hom, C., 2010. Pejoratives. *Philosophical Compass* 5 (2), 164—218.

Hornsby, J., 2001. Meaning and uselessness: how to think about derogatory words. In: Peter, French, et al. (Eds.), *Midwest Studies in Philosophy XXV.* Blackwell, Notre Dame, pp. 128—141.

Kaplan, D., 1989. Demonstratives. In: Almog, J., et al. (Eds.), *Themes From Kaplan,* pp. 481—563.

Kaplan, D., 2005. *The meaning of 'Ouch' and 'Oops'* (unpublished).

Korta, K., Perry, J., 2011. Critical Pragmatics. *An Inquiry into Reference and Communication.* Cambridge University Press, Cambridge, 178 pp.

McReady, E., 2010. Varieties of conventional implicature. *Semantics and Pragmatics* 3, 1—57.

Nunberg, G., 2013. Slurs Aren't Special (unpublished).

Perry, J., 1988. *Cognitive Significance and the New Theory of Reference.*

Perry, J., 2012. *Reference and Reflexivity, second ed.* CSLI Publications, 332 pp.

Potts, C., 2007. The expressive dimension. *Theoretical Linguistics* 33, 165—198.

Richard, M., 2008. *When Truth Gives Out.* Oxford University Press, Oxford.

Whiting, D., 2013. It's Not What You Said, It's the Way You Said It: slurs and conventional implicatures. *Analytic Philosophy* 54, 364—377.

Williamson, T., 2009. Reference, inference and the semantics of pejoratives. In: Almog, Joseph, Leonardi, Paolo (Eds.), *The Philosophy of David Kaplan.* Oxford University Press, Oxford, pp. 137—158.

Further Reading

Almog, J., Perry, John, Wettstein, Howard, 1989. *Themes from Kaplan.* Oxford University Press, New York.

Boghossian, P., 2013. Blind reasoning. *Proceedings of the Aristotelian Society Supplementary* volume, no. 77, 225—248.

Jeshion, R., 2011. Dehumanizing slurs. In: Korta, Kepa, Ponte, Maria (Eds.), *ILCLI International Workshop on Semantics, Pragmatics and Rhetoric, Book of Abstracts.* Universidad de Pais Vasco, Euskal Herriko Unibertsitalea, pp. 157—161.

Korta, K., Perry, J., 2008. The pragmatic circle. *Synthese* 165, 347—357.

Perry, J., 2000. The Problem of the Essential Indexicals and Other Essays, second ed. CSLI Publication, pp. 189—206.

8

Color Adjectives, Compositionality, and True Utterances

1 Introduction

1 Color Adjectives

Travis (1997) contends that the truth conditions of an utterance of a color adjective sentence are not solely a function of its component parts—or, to put it more simply, are not solely determined by the meaning of its component parts. In support of this position, he gives what has by now become the standard example:

> A story. Pia's Japanese maple is full of russet leaves. Believing that green is the colour of leaves, she paints them. Returning, she reports, 'That's better. The leaves are green now.' She speaks truth. A botanist friend then phones, seeking green leaves for a study of green-leaf chemistry. 'The leaves (on my tree) are green,' Pia says. 'You can have those.' But now Pia speaks falsehood. (Travis 1997: 89)

For simplification, let's assume that there is only one leaf and that both utterances that Pia produces are of the very same syntactically complete affirmative sentence: "The leaf is green". Let's also assume that the world does not change at all during the temporal period that elapses between the two utterances. Evidently, since the sentence contains no semantically ambiguous or indexical terms, it should have the same meaning in both of its utterances, being true in worlds where the leaf is green, and false in worlds where the same leaf is not. So, since the world remains the same in both utterances of the same nonindexical sentence, one could not hold one of them to be true and the other false.

In Travis' example, however, each utterance is truth assessed after considering facts, and, following brute intuitions, with the first one being considered true and the second one being considered false. Prima facie, these utterances should differ accordingly in their truth conditions, in some way or another, but we do not seem to be able to trace any such differences back to meaning. Travis concludes that

> [. . .] one speaking of it may clearly state what is true, while another state what is false. That can only be so if the semantics of [1] ['The leaf is green'][1] on some speakings is substantially richer than that fixed for it by the meanings of its constituents, and richer in different ways for different such speakings. So what [1] says on a speaking, of given leaves, etc., is not determined by what it, or its parts, mean. (Travis 1997: 91).

Discussing the relevant argument, Bezuidenhout notes that "the mainstream view in philosophy of language is that sentence meaning determines truth-conditions" with "a corollary [. . . being] that the truth or falsity of an utterance depends only on what the words mean and how the world is arranged" (2002: 105). Following the color argument, however, both the mainstream view and its corollary seem to be mistaken, as they fail to provide an explanation for why the first occurrence of "The leaf is green" is true, as it is about the color in which the leaf has been painted, and the second is false, on the grounds that it is about the leaf's natural color. Effectively, this leads her to the conclusion that "meaning undermines truth-conditions" (Bezuidenhout 2002: 105).

Suppose now that Pia writes the first token of the sentence under question on a post-it, and later on, while answering her botanist friend's request on Skype, she is just plain lazy and simply reuses her post-it rather than utter the sentence. In this setting, it would be the same token that is taken to be respectively true and false. Yet, there is no explanation for how, in this scenario, the same token can be true on one occasion and false in another. Basic linguistic intuitions call for explanations. Unfortunately, none can be found in Travis' paper. Along the same lines, one can also question the philosophical principle the example is intended to support, namely that natural language sentences have truth conditions determined by factors beyond and above meaning, since this principle is suspiciously silent about what these factors or what truth conditions for specific token sentences are.[2]

---

[1] This is my own, simplified version of the example of course.

[2] To be fair, Travis' argument has prompted some suggestions on the semantics of color terms; yet none offered by him. According to some philosophers and linguists, color adjectives are indexical expressions, like "I" (cf. Szabo 2001; Rotschild and Segal 2009), or contain variables that are assigned values in a context (cf. Kennedy and McNally 2010; Hansen 2011; but, for a critique, see Clapp 2012). It also fuels truth-conditional pragmatics, the view that "truth conditional content depends on an indefinite number of unstated background assumptions, not all of which can be made explicit" (Bezuidenhout, 2002: 105) or, alternatively, that "the information available in the context that is not semantically encoded by an uttered sen-

Now, the argument that I wish to pursue in this paper is that the assessment of the truth of a token of a sentence differs from the assessment of the truth of an utterance of that same sentence. All in all, I contend that accepting that the meaning of a sentence determines its truth conditions does not entail that utterances of sentences have truth conditions that are solely determined by meaning, or that utterances are assessed as true solely by considering linguistic meaning and facts. In this, I agree with Travis when he states that "truth depends on what words mean, the way the world is, and further factors: aspects of the circumstances in which the words were produced" (Travis 1996: 96); but still, I see no argument against truth-conditional semantics here. Travis seems to be making his point by relying on a semantically idle, common-sense notion of truth that connects language to facts and depends on, but does not affect meaning. If that is correct, it seems to me that the assessment of the truth of tokens or utterances has no impact on basic semantic principles, such as semantic compositionality and truth-conditional semantics. What is more, Travis neither presupposes a specific position on the semantics of color adjectives, nor does he draw any conclusions about the semantics of color terms from his example. He simply assumes that color adjectives, like many adjectives, determine a condition that an object either satisfies or not. Against this backdrop, I will argue that color terms have specific features, which can be used to explain the relevant data.

1 Truth Bearers

A token of a sentence is a particular object located in space and time. Written and recorded occurrences can be copied and moved in space and time. One can copy an occurrence of one's score on an exam, or take the paper it is written on back home, much like one can copy a sound signal on a voice recorder, and play it later on at a different location. In this respect, tokens of sentences are structured, complex linguistic entities composed of lexical items. Different tokens of a sentence can be of the same type, like, for example, three tokens of the sentence "Whales are mammals" found in three different books.[3] An utterance of a sentence, on the other hand, is a spatio-temporally located, particular event performed by a speaker. Utterances, in the relevant sense, are individuated by their loca-

---

tence is relevant for determining the truth conditions of, or what is said, by the utterance" (Clapp, 2012: 72). In this paper, however, I set these proposals aside and offer my own suggestion.

[3] Resorting to the abstract entity of type captures what is common to all these three tokens. However, since sentence type does not play a major role in the present argumentation, I will not analyze the term any further here.

tion, the time of the event and their speaker. Once produced, they cannot change location in space or time, that is, utterances cannot be copied or moved to a different location in space, say, next door, or in time, say, the following day.

So, one can clearly copy the written or acoustic trace left by an utterance (i.e. a token), but cannot do so for the utterance itself. One can even read and understand a token and know nothing about the utterance it is a trace of. Consider, for example, a token of "I am sorry for the scratch on your car" on a piece of paper you find on the street. You do not know who wrote it, when it was written and even who the addressee was; yet, you understand its linguistic meaning. Similarly, the same token can be used to make many different utterances, like when a token of "I will be back in five minutes" on a post-it on your office door is borrowed by the person in the office next door in order to be put on his/her door.

Finally, semantics assumes that sentences have truth conditions—that a competent speaker knows the truth conditions of a sentence, and that sentences can be true or false. Now, semantics is traditionally about the truth conditions of sentences as type, not about whether, given facts, they are true. If we were interested in the truth assessment of tokens, then we would be interested in the way spatio-temporally located linguistic entities, that is sentences, fit the facts. Given knowledge of meaning and facts, speakers are widely presumed to know when a sentence is true and when it is false. All in all, truth assessment gives an epistemic flavor to the actual discussion, of the type that Borg, for example, calls "creeping verificationism" (2004: 238).

Travis suggests that correspondence between sentence tokens and facts is not the relevant relationship when it comes to accounting for the data. His argument shows that the same relatas accept different truth assessments: given the same facts, two tokens of the same nonindexical sentence can be assessed, respectively, as true and as false. In the debate raised by Travis, it is first assumed that the truth conditions of any sentence, except indexical ones, are identical with the truth conditions of its token, and vice-versa. It is also assumed that these are the only relevant truth conditions taken into account in truth assessment. And Travis is well known for arguing that both of these assumptions are false.

Suppose now that it is utterances rather than tokens that are truth assessed. Utterances are not linguistic entities, but rather actions performed using such entities. It is commonly assumed that the truth conditions of sentences are the only truth conditions available in the truth assessment of utterances. I wish to reject this assumption. Semantics is interested in the truth conditions of sentences, that is, in the conditions put on the world if a sentence is to be true. In this respect, semantics does not address the truth assessment of tokens and utterances. It is not interested in whether these conditions are satisfied for a token or an utterance of a sentence, or in whether these conditions are all there is to the truth assessment of tokens or utterances. It rather focuses on the truth conditions of sentences as type. As Travis correctly points out, truth assessment is a very complex and clearly underexamined topic. Given the same facts, one could argue that a token can be assessed as true, when considering certain aspects of facts, such as the painted color of the leaf, and as false, when considering different aspects of facts, namely the natural color of the leaf. The relevant aspect of facts finds no echo in the uttered token. That being said, the intuitive truth conditions of the utterances in Travis' examples remain unaccounted for.

2 A New Perspective

My proposal regarding color adjective sentences focuses on communication and is utterance-oriented, in the vein of Perry (2012). Emphasizing utterances rather than the traces they leave seems natural, since it is utterances that speakers are mostly in contact with in their daily lives. Of course, speakers are also routinely exposed to tokens, without access to their underlying utterance, as in the case of "Caution, wet floor" on a sign on the floor, or that of "Leave a message and I will call you back as soon as possible" on an answering machine, but it is utterances that are predominantly used in face to face communication.

My proposal is also multipropositionalist. In multipropositionalism, an utterance of a sentence determines many different propositions, contents, or truth conditions,[4] depending on different constraints taken into consideration. Many truth conditions are hence made available as the truth conditions of an utterance,[5] as they are all relative to different constraints on this utterance. In contrast, Travis' view depends on his taking tokens, and not utterances, as primary, and on determining one single content. In doing this, he only takes into account meaning or semantically determined constraints on truth; a point to which I will come back later on. Speakers producing utterances, however, have background assumptions and follow certain principles, like, for instance, Grice's (1975) conversational maxims: "Make your contribution as informative as is required (for the current purpose of the exchange)", "Try to make your contribution one that is true", and "Be relevant". In his approach, Travis does not investigate the

---

[4] In this picture, there is no difference between proposition, content, and truth conditions.

[5] As Perry puts it, "the concept of 'truth conditions of an utterance' is a relative concept" (Perry 2012: 93).

truth assessment of utterances, neither does he exploit background assumptions and conversational maxims; he rather emphasizes on the traces left by utterances, that is their tokens, and highlights the context bound, ad hoc nature of the truth assessment of tokens.

1   Compositionality

Most semantic frameworks endorse the Principle of Compositionality, which applies to complex expressions as type, and, according to which, "the meaning of an expression is a function of, and only of, the meaning of its parts together with the method by which those parts are combined." (Pelletier 2004: 133). Yet, the principle of compositionality remains vague: "what counts as a part? What is meaning? What kind of function is allowed?" (Pelletier 2004: 599). In addition, as is the case with most basic principles, its status is controversial. Is it a hypothesis (cf. Szabo 2012) or a methodological principle (cf. Janssen 1997: 419)? Is it a metaphysical principle, valid for any human language; yet, one that cannot be proven? Despite these shortcomings, the principle is backed by strong arguments. There is an infinite number of complex expressions in natural languages. Given now that languages are learnable and an infinite number of new complex expressions, including sentences, are to be understood within them, then all complex expressions in a language must be composed from a finite number of learnable lexical items, each having meaning organized according to the language's syntactic rules (cf. Davidson 1965). Even so, such arguments remain neutral with respect to what meaning is, and put no specific requirement on it. Also, the overall learning argument is grounded in psychology and the finite capacities of speakers. From this perspective, the notions of sentence and truth have no special role to play in defending compositionality, so Travis does not question this general argument for compositionality.

On the truth-conditional semantics paradigm, semantics must give the meaning of an infinite number of sentences as type. In this setting, to give the meaning of a sentence is to give the truth conditions of this sentence, and not those of a token or utterance of it. Following the argument for compositionality, the truth conditions of a sentence are to be given by the lexical items in that sentence only. And since semantics is expected to give the truth conditions of an infinite number of sentences, it must assume that these sentences are composed from a finite stock of lexical items. To give the meaning of an expression is thus to give its contribution to the truth conditions of the sentences in which it occurs (Dowty, Wall and Peters 1981: 7). In this respect, compositionality is primarily compositionality of types. Such an argument endorses a specific notion of meaning of lexical items as truth-conditional elements, or as determinants of truth-conditional elements. Therefore, the truth-conditional version of the principle of compositionality is methodological in nature, as it dictates a strategy to develop semantic theory (cf. Janssen, 1997, 2012), and is not offered as an empirical generalization. In light of this, Travis' counter-example targets the methodological principle and argues that the meaning of sentences does not determine their truth conditions.

According to multipropositionalism now, linguistic meaning is a property of lexical items as type and is something we can learn. Setting semantic ambiguity aside, the linguistic meaning of a lexical item is the same for different utterances of that item. In other words, the linguistic meaning of an expression as type is a rule determining the semantic, meaning-fixed contribution of that expression to the content of utterances that comprise it. Such a perspective on meaning fits the learning argument for compositionality and should be favored if an utterance of a sentence has a manifold of contents or truth conditions, since a view on meaning as a contribution to the truth conditions of sentences with monopropositionalism in mind is too constraining to explain the facts. Just to give a representative example, it cannot even account for the fact that, even though the sentence "I am hungry" has the same linguistic meaning in different utterances, it can still differ in content or truth conditions from utterance to utterance, being true if I utter it, and false if you do (cf. Perry 2012).

2   Truth Conditions and Sentences

Many different notions of truth can be found in philosophy. Sometimes truth is treated as a metalinguistic notion, with no connection to facts, as in the case of Tarski (see Burgess and Burgess 2011) who uses this notion in T sentences:

"s" in L is true if and only if p,

where s is a sentence of the object-language L, and p is a copy of s in the semantic metalanguage; with truth applying to the metalanguage of semantics, and effectively linking a sentence from the object-language with one from the metalanguage. Also, as Davidson (1967) contends, "*is true if and only if*" in this context can be replaced with "*means that*", and vice-versa. In this respect, T sentences give a theory of meaning for any language, where the sentence s in the object-language is given a structural description, and the sentence p in the metalanguage gives the truth conditions of the sentence s. In this respect, the assignment of truth conditions in T sentences is insensitive to extralinguistic intuitions and facts. Obviously, Tarski does not pay attention to indexical sentences, and offers a theory of sentences as type, so T sentences do not tell you whether a sentence is true after considering facts.

Truth conditions are also assigned in semantics to moral evaluations, like 'Killing is wrong', and aesthetic judgments, like 'Bardot is beautiful', to use Davidson's (1967) famous example. Again, it is never argued that such sentences are true or false, when confronted with facts, because contending that they determine truth conditions—realized or not—and are true or false depending on facts is a strong and controversial position, but nonetheless a side issue. All in all, the semantic notion of truth does not connect sentences as type to facts. So, Travis raises an issue concerning the truth assessment of tokens. On the other hand, multipropositionalism is utterance-oriented and gives conditions on the truth of utterances as opposed to conditions on the truth of token sentences.

3   Truth Conditions and Utterances

In the multipropositionalist framework, the meaning of a sentence as type is not a truth valuable entity. Rather, it is the contents of utterances that are—and by contents we mean the conditions put on the world for the utterance to be true. From this perspective, semantics is interested in how the linguistic meaning of expressions contributes to the different contents of utterances in which they occur and places constraints on the truth of these utterances. It first emphasizes contents determined only by meaning, or semantic constraints on the truth of utterances, and known *a priori* by competent speakers. Semantically determined contents are mechanically extracted from the lexical items of the sentence as type and faithfully echo sentences. Perry (1988) assigns such contents the role of the cognitive significance of the utterance. A semantically competent speaker understands and can accept as true the cognitive significance of an utterance without any knowledge of the world. For example, given her semantic competence only, a speaker knows that an utterance of "*Birds have wings*" is true if and only if *birds have wings*. Every utterance of that sentence has the same mechanically extracted semantic content and, *ipso facto*, the same cognitive significance.

For utterances of some sentences, like, for instance, proper name and indexical sentences, contents in the role of cognitive significance are not constant. Here, the linguistic meaning of "*I*" as type is philosophically interesting because it is known a priori and allows for a generalization concerning different utterances of "*I*"; it determines a content constituent: *the speaker of the utterance*. Such a constituent contains the utterance itself as a constituent, and gives different content constituents for different utterances. As a consequence, it introduces different identifying conditions into the semantically determined content of utterances enabling different utterances of "*I*" sentences to exhibit different cognitive significance. In this setting, semantics is interested in the way "*I*" contributes to the truth conditions of any utterance, not in its actual contribution to a specific one. Consider, for example, an utterance **u** of "*I am short*", and its semantic, context-independent contribution to content.

(1)   Given that the sentence is in English, the utterance **u** of "*I am short*" is true if and only if *the speaker of u is short*.

(1) supposes linguistic meaning only, and connects an utterance of a sentence to its semantically determined content. It thus gives semantic conditions or constraints on the truth of the utterance **u**. A different utterance of the same sentence would have different semantically determined truth conditions or constraints because it is a different utterance.

Let's now turn to an utterance of "*The leaf is green*" and consider the linguistic constraints on its truth.

(2)   Given that the sentence is in English, the utterance **u** of "*The leaf is green*" is true if and only if *the leaf is green*.

In this case, the adjective "*green*" is context-insensitive. So, all utterances of "*The leaf is green*" have the same semantically determined content that a speaker knows *a priori*, as well as the same cognitive significance. Here, what (2) makes explicit is the meaning determined conditions or constraints on the truth of any utterance of "*The leaf is green*".

Strictly speaking, semantics stops at what is known a priori by linguistically competent speakers. Extralinguistic facts do not impact semantics, the compositionality of the meaning of sentences as type, and the semantically determined content or truth conditions of utterances. Since facts are not taken into account, semantically determined content is not the content which is assessed as true. So, Travis is right in thinking that assessing the truth of a token or an utterance require going beyond linguistic meaning and the semantic contents it determines by considering facts. However, assessing a token or an utterance as true when considering facts presupposes semantics, semantically-fixed truth conditions, and compositionality, as this goes well beyond the semantic project.

4   Official Content

Let's now go back to my utterance of "*I am short*". As already mentioned, "*I*" is sensitive to features individuating the utterance. So, my utterance of "*I*" designates me as the speaker of the utterance. All in all, once facts about the utterance are taken into account, (3) seems to hold.

(3)   Given facts about the utterance, the utterance **u** of "*I am short*" is true if and only if **RV** *is short*,

where **RV** is the actual speaker of the utterance himself. These truth conditions, i.e. **RV** *is short*, result from semantically determined content and utterance individuating features, with the reflexive meaning of "*I*" automatically selecting the relevant element. Such content, however, is not utterance reflexive; on the contrary, these truth conditions are utterance independent, in that they are realized whether or not there is an utterance—in other words, I am short whether or not I produce an utterance of "*I am short*". Perry calls this the *official content* of an utterance; a content that includes constraints on the truth of utterances which are obtained after considering meaning and facts about the utterance. This official content is *what is said* in perhaps an artificial sense of "*say*": you and I do not say the same thing when uttering "*I am short*", as our utterances have different official contents.

Of course, what the linguistic meaning of "I" determines when taking into account the facts individuating the utterance is important in linguistic communication, but much less relevant from a semantic point of view. Semantics is first and foremost about the factors that determine "what is said", rather than about "what is said" per se. In this respect, the official content of utterances is a plausible candidate for the truth assessment of utterances, since it is by considering facts that my utterance can be true, and yours false. Let's say then that in assessing the truth of an utterance, what is considered is the official content of that utterance, and whether or not it fits the facts.

In this way, monopropositionalism is abandoned, yet truth conditions are preserved. Indexical utterances introduce at least two different contents that are distinguished by the factors that are taken into account when making these contents explicit. One has the role of the cognitive significance of the utterance and emphasizes what is understood by relying on linguistic meaning only; the other has the role of the official content of the utterance, and is obtained once facts about the utterance are taken into account. This picture can generalize to utterances of any sentence, including those of nonindexical sentences. Such indexical motivated arguments support the multipropositionalist view, according to which, an utterance determines a manifold of contents, rather than a unique one. From this perspective, identifying the meaning of a lexical item with its contribution to truth conditions is an oversimplification, since meaning is given by rules, not truth-conditional constituents. Moreover, different contents or truth conditions with different roles take center stage; focusing on one single content is misleading, as it ignores what is taken into account when making an utterance's contents explicit, and essentially confuses their different roles.

Let's go back to the utterance of "*The leaf is green*," and consider its official content. "*The leaf*" is a description, and descriptions are referring terms introducing objects into contents (Perry, 2012, chapter 5). Setting aside the fact that this description is incomplete,[6] the most plausible referred to object here is **THE LEAF**.

(4)   Given facts about the utterance, the utterance u of "*The leaf is green*" is true if and only if **THE LEAF** *is green*.

THE LEAF is the object referred to itself. (4) gives us what the speaker said in our artificial sense of "said". Since there are no context sensitive terms in the sentence, a different utterance of the same sentence talking about the same leaf would have the same cognitive significance, as well as the same official content. Following Travis (1997), two utterances of color sentences can differ in their truth assessment even when they share the same cognitive significance and official content. So, based on Travis' argument (1997), one could at most conclude that the content as cognitive significance as well as the official content of the utterance is the same in both cases, but that the content assessed as true differs in each utterance.

The content as cognitive significance cannot be modified without altering the meaning of an utterance since it only depends on this meaning; thus, arguing that the linguistic meaning of the two utterances differs lacks plausibility. And indeed, Travis does not deny that the tokens or the utterances have the same linguistic meaning and hence, in the present picture, the same semantically determined content. Moreover, as we have already seen, the cognitive significance of an utterance is independent of facts as well as what satisfies our intuitions on the truth of utterances of a sentence having that cognitive significance. Similarly, the official content of an utterance is also meaning dependent, constrained this time by facts about the utterance and truth assessed. Still, it can exist without the utterance. The leaf has the property of being green whether or not one utters "*The leaf is green*". In the present case, the utterance's official content, or what is said, is the same for both utterances because the facts about the utterance, and the facts *tout court*, do not differ. For an uneducated ear, in Travis' example, Pia said the same thing twice. However, *prima facie*, official content, or "*what is said*", does not capture fine-grained intuitions about the truth assessment of each utterance. In this I agree with Travis, who argues that

---

[6] Due to space restrictions, I will not address issues related to incomplete descriptions in the present paper.

> Understanding requires sensitivity. Understanding words consists, in part, in sensitivity to how they fit with the circumstances of their speaking. Part of that is sensitivity to how they need to fit in order to be true. (Travis 1996: 102).

So, the speaker, Pia, may have said the same thing twice, but, intuitively, this is not what is assessed as true or false. The meaning of a sentence and facts about the utterance do not always give all the relevant conditions or constraints needed to assess whether an utterance of that sentence is true. Yet, we want to preserve both the intuitions that (a) the two utterances have the same cognitive significance and (b) that, on both occasions, the speaker says the same thing or used a sentence that puts identical constraints on the truth of her utterances; neither the cognitive significance of the utterance nor what is said need be modified. The problem, however, remains: what Pia says is not enough to assess the truth of her utterances. So, the difference must be located elsewhere.

5   True Utterances

As Ludlow (1989) discusses, the semantically-determined truth conditions of sentences with relative gradable adjectives, such as "*tall*" or "*strong*," do not, prima facie, give the truth-assessed content of their utterances. An utterance of "*Peter is tall*" can be assessed as true when considering five years olds, while another utterance of the same sentence can be assessed as false when considering basketball players. All in all, an utterance of "*Peter is tall*" is assessed as true only after considering a potential comparison class, and, more specifically, the comparison class that the speaker had in mind when producing her utterance. So, the relevant comparison class is important as far as truth assessment is concerned.

But, in this paper, I do not want to add to the already important literature on relative adjectives. I am mentioning them, because a similar phenomenon is at work as far as the utterances of a color sentence are concerned. As Lahav notes, expressing a widely shared intuition, when writing about "*red*",

> In short, what counts for one type of thing to be red is not what counts for another. Of course, there is a feature that is common to all the things which count as (nonmetaphorically) red, namely that some part of them, or some item related to them, must appear wholly and literally reddish. But that is only a very general necessary condition, and is far from being sufficient for a given object to count as red. (Lahav 1989: 264).

According to common sense, color adjectives, like "*green*", semantically determine conditions, such as *be green*, that apply to objects. Yet, these conditions can apply to part of an object, or the whole object, and are generally very plastic in that respect. This feature does not give rise to problems for the semantically determined truth conditions of utterances: in "*the leaf is green*", "*green*" determines the condition of being green. Hence, it does not affect the compositional nature of color adjective sentences.[7] But it does raise problems for the truth assessment of color sentence utterances. Which surface or part of an object is relevant for the utterance at hand? Which surface or part of an object is the speaker talking about? With no additional specification about the relevant object, trying to assess a color sentence token or utterance as true is a failed project. All semantically competent speakers are familiar with this aspect of color adjectives: Hearing a speaker say that she is looking for a red house, you might ask which part of the house is red—Is it the bricks? The roof? The inside walls? Color adjectives are intersective like this. In this respect, "The leaf is green" is equivalent to "*There is a leaf and it is green,*" with "*green*" giving a feature of the object at hand. However, it does not give any information on the dimension or aspect of the object that it is a condition of.

Following Lahav's intuition, the utterance of "*The leaf is green*" does not qualify as true, unless specifications or additional conditions on the relevant object are added. In this, he is right. Color attribution to an object is sensitive to aspects of the object that the speaker is interested in—Is the speaker talking about part of the object? Which part? About the whole object? About a normal aspect of the object? So, when assessing the truth of a color sentence utterance, background assumptions about the speaker as well as constraints on the utterance's relevance, informativity and truth are to be taken into consideration.

Suppose now that another speaker of "*The leaf is green*" is a biologist interested in the biology of leaves. Suppose further that she is talking about the leaf Pia was talking about, in which case, her utterance has the same cognitive significance, *the leaf is green*, as well as the same official content, **THE LEAF** *is green*, as Pia's earlier utterance(s). The view that all utterances of sentences have their own truth conditions, especially conditions relevant for their truth assessment, fully semantically determined is questionable. That is why I will use the term *subsemantic constituent* relevant to the truth of the utterance, a term that underlines the fact that such constituents are not part of the truth conditions of the sentence, as they are not determined by linguistic meaning, but are still part of the conditions on the truth of the sentence's utterances. Conditions, *like being a natural color*, can be such subsemantic constituents. *Prima facie*, there is an extra, not meaning-determined but rather background-and-maxim-constrained condition put on the truth of the biologist's utterance of "*The leaf is green*;" given our background assumptions about the speaker and the sup-

---

[7] On this point, I disagree with Lahav's position of color adjectives.

position that she is following conversational maxims, her utterance is most likely about the natural color of the leaf at hand. In this respect, the official content of this utterance needs to be refocused on the basis of such subsemantic constituents so as to fit the intuitions about the truth assessment of the utterance. But this refocusing of the official content is meaning independent, *ad hoc*, and utterance specific, since it concerns truth assessment, filling the slack left by linguistic meaning between utterances and facts, whatever the latter may be. Being solely a feature of the truth assessed content of the utterance, the subsemantic constituent does not depend on the sentence, nor does it depend merely on facts. In my view, it is speaker-background relative and maxim-constrained.

With this in mind, let's go back to the biologist's utterance.

(5)   Given conversational maxims and background assumptions about the speaker of **u**, the utterance **u** of "*The leaf is green*" is true if and only if **THE LEAF** *is green and green is its natural color.*

or "if and only if **THE LEAF** *is naturally colored green.*"[8] The refocused conditions on the truth of the utterance contain a subsemantic constituent, a condition like *being its natural color*, which is provided for the specific utterance on the basis of background assumptions and maxims. In this picture, compositionality is not called into question for the uttered sentence, nor does the supplemented material impose semantically-determined conditions on the truth of the utterance. A different utterance, **u'**, given by a different speaker and in a different background, or even by the same speaker but in a different background, could be about the painted color of the leaf, with being painted green being the relevant constituent. A speaker unable to determine any subsemantic constituent for her utterance of "*The leaf is green*" would not be able to explain why her utterance is true, or even what it is that makes her utterance true. Conversely, hearers unable to identify the refocused conditions on the truth of an utterance of the aforementioned sentence would not be linguistically at fault, but rather unclear about the speaker's background assumptions.

Admittedly, this view can account for the fact that different utterances of the same token of "The leaf is green" can be respectively true and false, since each utterance's official content could depend on the contribution of different subsemantic constituents. In Pia's example that was presented at the beginning of this paper then, if both utterances were intended to have the same subsemantic constituent, being its painted color for instance, both of them would be true, but the second would be irrelevant because the

---

[8] Such a small variation is tolerable and does not affect my main point. I also disregard and put aside other aspects of the color attribution—such as "Completely green?", "Partly green?"

biologist would, obviously, be interested in the natural color of the leaf. If the second utterance is about the natural color of the leaf, however, then it is false. There is an utterance-grounded explanation for this difference in the truth assessment of "The leaf is green". Going back to the utterance by the biologist, it is the case that she did not say anything false; yet, the re-focused, speaker-dependent, official content of her utterance, which is the relevant content in the utterance's truth assessment is false: the leaf 's natural color is not green. Using her own background assumptions and following the conversational maxims, she wrongly assesses her utterance as true, but her mistake has nothing to do with the meaning of the sentence or its semantically-determined truth conditions. It just ensues from her background assumptions concerning the leaf.

3 Concluding Remarks

In this paper, I have argued that, given background assumptions and conversational principles, the official content of utterances can be refocused. The truth of an utterance now is assessed on the basis of refocused content and facts, but this assessment is made using a nonsemantic, common-sense notion of truth that connects utterances and facts. That is because linguistic communication is flexible. Semantics, on the other hand, does not need to assign to utterances linguistic meaning that connects them to fine-grained, structured conditions in order to account for intuitions about their truth.

The problem of identifying under which conditions, beyond those semantically provided, the utterance is true is a familiar one. However, it is not a semantic issue, as it has nothing to do with meaning and semantically determined truth conditions. In concluding that meaning undermine truth conditions and in drawing dramatic consequences for the semantic program, Travis talks about the semantically-determined truth conditions, or the cognitive significance, of the utterance. Yet, he is actually addressing the official content of utterances, and this view has quite different consequences. Travis' point clearly questions the view that assessing the truth of an utterance depends solely on meaning and facts. However, this view is not part of the core of semantics. If I am correct, the truth assessment of utterances may sometimes demand the addition of subsemantic truth-conditional components to the official content of an utterance, but it does not necessitate the addition of meaning-determined truth-conditional material, or the addition of material in a systematic way that justifies a generalization on sentences and utterances.

Semanticists are wrong in adopting a view according to which the meaning of a sentence as type determines truth conditions that perfectly mirror facts and always fit the truth assessment of the sentence's utterances, as in so doing, they ignore the complexity of the assessment of the truth of utterances and wrongly reject semantically innocuous alterations. By assuming that the assessment of the truth of utterances depends only on meaning and facts, Travis mislocates the impact of counterexamples for color-term sentences on semantically-determined truth conditions, with disastrous consequences for truth-conditional semantics. Ignoring meaning as a rule, he loses the focus on rules assigned to expressions as type. What is more, emphasizing tokens, he neglects utterances and supposes that the truth conditions of a sentence are always identical to the truth conditions of its utterance. Missing the distinction between cognitive significance and official content, he confuses both roles and fails to pinpoint the impact of the problems raised by the truth assessment of color adjective sentences' official content, rather than their cognitive significance, and the *ad hoc* fix available for this official content.

Often, the truth of the token left by an utterance is assessed when the utterance is no longer available. What is then considered is the utterance's official content. Official contents are sometimes stable and unresponsive to utterances, like the official content of tokens of "*Whales are mammals*," all utterances of which have the same official content and need no subsemantic constituent to be assessed as true. Sentences like this were once taken as paradigmatic in semantics. Utterances of indexical sentences, like "*I am short*", on the other hand, do not all have the same official content, but their difference can be traced back to the meaning and utterance features. Such utterances are not truth assessable unless information about the utterance is obtained. The official content of an utterance of a nonindexical sentence is also sometimes insufficient for the truth assessment of the utterance. This content though is responsive to utterances by way of background assumptions and conversational maxims, as in the case of the official content of an utterance of "*The leaf is green*". In this case, official content and truth-assessed content differ, but now the difference in the truth assessed content of the utterance is meaning independent.

All in all, when we ignore the source utterance of a token, its official content is sometimes impossible to assess as true or false. Let me change the example. You find a note in an old book, which says "*The apple is red*", and you do not know who wrote it or when it was written. Is the speaker talking about the skin or the flesh of the apple? Whether this utterance is true or false depends on background assumptions and facts. Not only are the facts out of your reach, but ignoring the speaker's background assumptions and relying on the utterance's official content alone, you cannot identify the assessed, refocused official content of this particular utterance. Suppose now that Anne's son is selecting apples for cooking, when he says *"Here is a red apple"* (Bezuidenhout 2002: 107). Is this utterance true? What is the adjective applied to, the skin or flesh of the apple? Which condition should be supplemented in this utterance's refocused content? Given his background assumptions, we surmise that his utterance is about the skin. So, if the apple has red skin, then the utterance is true. In different circumstances, with a different background, however, the utterance's official content could be about the flesh of the apple.

To sum up, my view deploys many different contents and preserves the idea that the semantically-determined contents of color sentences are not modified to fit the assessment of the truth of utterances. The only altered content, the official content, is refocused on a subsemantic condition on the basis of background assumptions and principles of conversation. In this approach, color adjectives provide no reason to question compositionality or truth-conditional semantics in a multipropositionalist framework. Some see the supplemented subsemantic constituent as semantically relevant. This is a path that semanticists need not follow.

Acknowledgements

I want to thank the audience at the Intercultural Pragmatics Conference in Malta. Eros Corazza made helpful comments on a previous version of this paper. Research for this work has been made possible thanks to the Social Sciences and Humanities Research Council of Canada.

References

Allwood, Jens, Lars-Gunnar Anderson & Osten Dahl.1977. *Logic in linguistics*. Cambridge: Cambridge University Press.

Bezuidenhout, Anne. 2002. Truth-conditional pragmatics. *Language and Mind* 16. 105–134.

Borg, Emma. 2004. *Minimal Semantics*. Oxford: Oxford University Press.

Burgess, A. G. & John P. Burgess. 2011. *Truth*. Princeton and Oxford: Princeton University Press.

Clapp, Lenny. 2012. Indexical color-predicates: Truth-conditional semantics vs. truth conditional pragmatics. *Canadian Journal of Philosophy*. 2012. 71–100.

Davidson, Donald. 1965. Theories of meaning and learnable languages. In Yehoshua Bar Hillel (ed.), *Proceeding of the 1964 International Congress for Logic, Methodology and Philosophy of Science*, 383–394. Amsterdam: North-Holland Publications.

Davidson, Donald. 1967. Truth and meaning. *Synthese* 17. 304–323.

Dowty, David, Robert E. Wall & Stanley Peters. 1981. *Introduction to Montague semantics*. Dordrecht: Reidel.

Grice, H. Paul. 1975. Logic and conversation. In Peter Cole & Jerry L. Morgan (eds.), *Syntax and semantics 3: Speech acts*, 41–58. New York: Academic Press.

Hansen, Nathaniel. 2011. Color adjectives and radical contextualism. *Linguistics and Philosophy* 34. 201–221.

Janssen, Theo M.V. 1997. Compositionality. In Johan van Benthem & Alice Ter Meulen (eds.), *Handbook of logic and language*, 417–473. Amsterdam: Elsevier.

Janssen, Theo M.V. 2012. Compositionality: Its historic context. In Markus Werning, Wolfram Hinzen & Edouard Machery (eds.), *The Oxford handbook of compositionality*, 19–46. Oxford: Oxford University Press.

Kaplan, David. 1989. Demonstratives. In Joseph Almog, John Perry & Howard Wettstein (eds.), *Themes from Kaplan*, 481–563. New York: Oxford. University Press.

Kennedy, Christopher & Louise McNally. 2010. Color, context and compositionality. *Synthese* 174. 74–98.

Korta, Kepa & John Perry. 2011. Critical pragmatics. *An inquiry into reference and communication*. Cambridge: Cambridge University Press.

Lahav, Ran. 1989. Against compositionality, the case of adjectives. *Philosophical Studies* 57. 264–279.

Ludlow, Peter. 1989. Implicit comparison classes. *Linguistics and Philosophy* 12. 519–533.

Pelletier, Francis Jeffrey. 1994. The principle of semantic compositionality. *Topoi* 13. 11–24.

Perry, John. 1988. Cognitive significance and new theories of reference. *Noûs* 22. 1–18.

Perry, John. 2012. *Reference and reflexivity*. Stanford: CSLI Publications.

Rothschild, Daniel & Gabriel Segal. Indexical predicates. Mind & Language, 24. 467–493.

Sainsbury, Mark. 2001. Two ways to smoke a cigarette. *Ratio* 14. 386–406.

Szabo, Zoltan Gendler. 2001. Adjectives in context. In Robert M. Harnish & Istvan Kenesei (eds.), *Perspectives on semantics, pragmatics, and discourse*. 119–146. Amsterdam: John Benjamins.

Szabo, Zoltan Gendler. 2012. The case for compositionality. In Markus Werning, Wolfram Hinzen & Edouard Machery (eds.), *The Oxford Handbook of Compositionality*, 64–80. Oxford: Oxford University Press.

Travis, Charles. 1994. On constraints of generality. In *Proceeding of the Aristotelian Society* 94. 165–188.

Travis, Charles. 1996. Meaning's role in truth. *Mind* 105. 451–466. Also in Travis, Charles. 2008. *Occasion-sensitivity*, 94–108. Oxford: Oxford University Press.

Travis, Charles. 1997. Pragmatics. In Bob Hale & Crispin Wright (eds.), *A Companion to the philosophy of language*, 87–107. Oxford: Blackwell. Also in

Travis, Charles. 2008. *Occasion-sensitivity*, 109–129. Oxford: Oxford University Press.

Vicente, Agustin. 2012. On Travis cases. *Linguistics and Philosophy* 35. 3–19.

Index

197